Paradoxes of Emancipation

Syracuse Studies in Geography

The series Syracuse Studies in Geography is distinguished by works in historical geography, political economy, and environmental geography but also publishes theoretically informed books across the breadth of the discipline.

Also in Syracuse Studies in Geography

Border Humanitarians: Gendered Order and Insecurity on the Thai-Burmese Frontier
Adam Saltsman

From Rice Fields to Killing Fields: Nature, Life, and Labor under the Khmer Rouge
James A. Tyner

Market Orientalism: Cultural Economy and the Arab Gulf States
Benjamin Smith

Remapping Modern Germany after National Socialism, 1945–1961
Matthew D. Mingus

Spatializing Authoritarianism
Natalie Koch, ed.

Paradoxes of Emancipation

Radical Imagination and Space in Neoliberal Greece

Dimitris Soudias

Syracuse University Press

Copyright © 2023 by Syracuse University Press
Syracuse, New York 13244-5290

All Rights Reserved

First Edition 2023

23   24   25   26   27   28   6   5   4   3   2   1

∞ The paper used in this publication meets the minimum requirements
of the American National Standard for Information Sciences—Permanence
of Paper for Printed Library Materials, ANSI Z39.48-1992.

For a listing of books published and distributed by Syracuse University Press,
visit https://press.syr.edu.

ISBN: 978-0-8156-3816-2 (hardcover)
978-0-8156-3809-4 (paperback)
978-0-8156-5691-3 (e-book)

Library of Congress Cataloging-in-Publication Data

Names: Soudias, Dimitris, author.

Title: Paradoxes of emancipation : radical imagination and space in neoliberal
Greece / Dimitris Soudias.

Description: First edition. | Syracuse : Syracuse University Press, 2023. |
Series: Syracuse studies in geography | Includes bibliographical references
and index.

Identifiers: LCCN 2023006766 (print) | LCCN 2023006767 (ebook) |
ISBN 9780815638162 (hardcover) | ISBN 9780815638094 (paperback) |
ISBN 9780815656913 (ebook)

Subjects: LCSH: Democracy—Greece—History—21st century. | Liberty—
Greece—History—21st century. | Greece—Politics and government—
History—21st century.

Classification: LCC JC574.2.G8 S68 2023 (print) | LCC JC574.2.G8 (ebook) |
DDC 320.449509/05—dc23/eng/20230508

LC record available at https://lccn.loc.gov/2023006766

LC ebook record available at https://lccn.loc.gov/2023006767

Manufactured in the United States of America

*I dedicate this book to my niece, Elina Zoe Soudia,
and my nephew Mateo Jonas Soudias.*

Contents

Acknowledgments   *ix*
Acronyms   *xiii*
Map of the 2011 Syntagma Square occupation   *xv*

Introduction
The Future Will Be Better Tomorrow   1

1. Modernizing Greece
From Barbershops to Hair Salons   37

2. "Waking Up"
Spatialized Crises and Unthought-Of Experiences   78

3. Aspiring the Utopian
The Alter-Politics of Radical Imagination   116

4. Challenging the Dystopian
The Anti-Politics of Demystification   158

5. Paradoxes of Emancipation
Between Resistance and Reproduction   196

6. Toward an Alter-Neoliberal Critique   239

Epilogue   250

Bibliography   265
Index   299

Acknowledgments

This project began as a doctoral dissertation on the Tahrir Square occupation in Egypt, and became a book on the radical imagination in Greece and beyond. I want to thank many people who have made this journey a successful one. First of all, I am indebted to all of my interlocutors, for if not for them, I would not have come to think that which I wrote. My PhD supervisors Thorsten Bonacker and Cilja Harders have offered me the right balance of guidance and independence, and they continue to support me and my work, for which I remain enormously thankful. I would like to thank all of my colleagues at the Center for Near and Middle Eastern Studies at Philipps-Universität Marburg, and particularly my colleagues at the "Research Network Re-Configurations" (which was generously funded by the German Ministry of Education and Research). I would also like to thank the Center for Middle Eastern and North African Politics at Freie Universität Berlin for supporting the early beginnings of my PhD thesis, and the DFG Collaborative Research Centre/Transregio 138 "Dynamics of Security" for kindly funding the final stretch.

I am deeply grateful for my community of inquiry—Ali Sonay, Anja Hoffmann, Francisco Mazzola, Hülya Ertas, Leila Haghighat, and Perrine Lachenal—all of whom have read my words critically and meticulously. Throughout this journey, I could always build on the intellectual support and friendship of Maike Neufend and Christoph König. Maike always managed to resolve the seemingly unresolvable with great calm and reason, and Christoph was willing to read and sharply comment on notice so short, I would consider it to be rude. Maike and Christoph have been indispensable for bringing the dissertation, upon which this book rests, to maturity. I would like to thank Michael Allan for brainstorming

x   Acknowledgments

the title of this work in a surprisingly industrial way (I did tweak it a bit though!), and Eileen Byrne for polishing the language of my first draft.

In the transition from thesis manuscript to book, I want to thank Koen Bogaert, and Michael Allan yet again, for showing me the ropes when I wrote my book prospectus. At Syracuse University Press, I am lucky to have worked with Peggy Solic, Laura Fish, and Kelly Balenske, and I am also thankful for the diligent copyediting by Jessica LeTourneur Bax and the thoughtful insights of my two anonymous reviewers.

I am grateful to my colleagues and friends at the Hellenic Observatory of the London School of Economics, particularly Areti Chatzistergou, Spyros Economides, Kevin Featherstone, Philipp Katsinas, Vassilis Monastiriotis, and Sofia Vyzantiadou. I benefited greatly from the support of the Aikaterini Laskaridis Foundation, which provided me with a fellowship at the University of Amsterdam through which I have been able to finalize my book manuscript. In the same vein, I would like to thank the Netherlands Institute for Advanced Study, especially Jan Willem Duyvendak, for their generosity, and for hosting the theme group "The Politics of (De)familiarization: The Common and the Strange in Contemporary Europe"; working with the sharp and humble Maria Boletsi and Florian Lippert has been truly wonderful.

My dearest friends who have been there for me through thick and thin include David Jacob, Josephine Troischt, Ceyda Keskin, Zine Lackner, Pauline Morley, Viktor Riad, Manolis Levedianos, Viktor Slota, Philipp Danes, Elena Lambrou, Ilka Eickhof, Faduma Abukar Mursal, Elina Georgakila, as well as my sister Maria-Christina Soudia, and my parents, Zoi Theofanidu and Efstathios Soudias.

Finally, I want to thank Filyra Vlastou-Dimopoulou, my partner, my friend, and my intellectual companion. You make me happy.

Segments of chapter 2 appeared in the following:

Soudias, Dimitris. 2020. "Spatializing Radical Political Imaginaries. Neoliberalism, Crisis, and Transformative Experience in the Syntagma Square Occupation in Greece." *Contention* 8 (1): 4–27.

Soudias, Dimitris. 2018. "On the Spatiality of Square Occupations. Lessons from Syntagma and Tahrir." In *Riots and Militant Occupations. Smashing a*

System, Building a World—A Critical Introduction, edited by Alissa Starodub and Andrew Robinson, 75–95. New York: Rowman & Littlefield.

Segments of chapter 1 and chapter 5 have appeared in the following: Soudias, Dimitris. 2021. "Subjects in Crisis: Paradoxes of Emancipation and Alter-Neoliberal Critique." *Sociological Review* 69 (5): 885–902.

I would like to thank David Jacob for the production of a map of the Syntagma Square occupation, and the cover art of this book, and for providing me with the permission to use it.

Acronyms

ANTARSYA	Front of the Greek Anti-Capitalist Left
COVID-19	Coronavirus disease 2019
DEI	Public Power Corporation
EC	European Commission
ECB	European Central Bank
EEC	European Economic Community
EMU	European Monetary Union
EPAnEK	Operational Program for Competitiveness, Innovation, and Entrepreneurship
EU	European Union
GATT	General Agreement on Tariffs and Trade
GDP	Gross domestic product
GEM	Global Entrepreneurship Monitor
HDI	Human Development Index
IMD	International Institute for Management Development
IMF	International Monetary Fund
KKE	Communist Party of Greece
KoinSEp	Social Cooperative Enterprise
LAOS	Popular Orthodox Rally
MP	Member of Parliament
ND	New Democracy
NGO	Nongovernmental organization
NPM	New Public Management
OECD	Organisation for Economic Co-operation and Development
OTE	Hellenic Telecommunications Organisation
PASOK	Panhellenic Socialist Movement
PPP	public-private partnership
SWOT	Strengths, Weaknesses, Opportunities, Threats

SYRIZA	Coalition of the Radical Left
TBSS	Time Bank of Syntagma Square
TINA	There Is No Alternative
UN	United Nations
UNDP	United Nations Development Programme
WEF	World Economic Forum

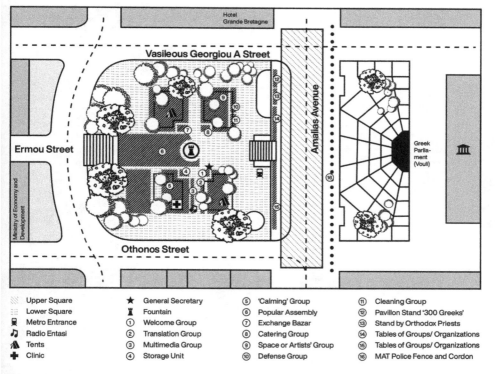

Map of the 2011 Syntagma Square occupation. Copyright © 2022 by David Jacob.

Paradoxes of Emancipation

Introduction

The Future Will Be Better Tomorrow

It was a sunny winter day when I met with Petros in a café in the picturesque neighborhood of Plaka, back in 2017. In this part of Athens, with its buzzing restaurants, bars, and shops linked by labyrinthine alleys for tourists to saunter along, one almost forgets the years of crisis Greece has been going through. The twenty-five-year-old was jovial, but visibly drained. Understandably so, considering that he was merely one exam away from graduating from university (with a degree in economics, no less). We were scheduled to talk about his experience of taking part in the occupation of Syntagma Square in the heart of Athens in 2011. Back then, Greeks of all ages and most political persuasions set up a protest encampment in the heart of the city. Lasting more than two months, the occupation contested the Greek government's policy of implementing the austerity measures set out by the troika of the European Commission, the European Central Bank, and the International Monetary Fund. Many people I talked to had highlighted the transformative character of participation and I was eager to listen to Petros's experience. But from the outset, our conversation started—seemingly—elsewhere:

> My parents lived in a Greece that still offered opportunities to work and live well. Not exactly well, but in dignity, let's say. . . . Usually, in the vision of the Western world, ideologically and politically, things get better. In the nineties, they even said there's no history, right? "Everything's great, super. We're great." But in fact, this thing changed. . . . [My] generation starts, perhaps, to clash for a future that they haven't yet seen, but from which they understand, in a way, that it won't be the best

possible. And that it will certainly be a lot worse than the future the previous generation had—a thing that historically is novel, if you will, since World War II. (Petros, personal communication, February 9, 2017)

Against the Disneyesque background of Plaka, Petros's words seemed oddly out of place. But belonging to a generation of highly educated young adults who cannot seem to find much opportunity in the Greece of austerity and crisis, Petros sees a social imaginary that he has never quite been able to experience collapsing in front of his eyes.

As capitalism unerringly steers itself from one crisis to the next, it undergoes significant transformations. In light of this, our definitions and expectations of what normatively constitutes happiness, justice, worth, or value, is also put under scrutiny: as we move through time and space, and live through different crises, we resignify experiences and profoundly reevaluate our past and present selves in ways that alter our imaginations of the future. This book is a politico-sociological attempt to lay bare how the imaginary of capitalism is changing in times of crisis, how we imagine the future with us in it, and what we ought to do to prefigure and confront it.

In an age of "permanent economic emergency" (Žižek 2010), "permanent austerity" (Laskos and Tsakalotos 2013a), "mutant neoliberalism" (Callison and Manfredi 2019), or "zombie neoliberalism" (Peck 2010b), it appears as though for Petros, the only "certain" thing is that the future will be "worse" than the present. In neoliberalism, Zygmunt Bauman observes, "uncertainty is here to stay. We are challenged with a task, which I think is unprecedented—and the task is to develop an art, to develop an art of living permanently with uncertainty" (quoted in Dziadosz 2013). Struggling with so daunting a burden, the underlying stress and precarity of uncertainty is being normalized in neoliberalism (Lorey 2015). We are to imagine the potentialities of the future not so much through opportunity, but through threat. We are to be calculative and assume risk. We are to become austere in virtue and ascetic in lifestyle, reducing what is possible to what is necessary. In this light, neoliberalism is not in crisis as much as it is crisis. Are we left in paralysis before the totality of neoliberalism then?

"What do you do?" I ask Petros. "Because now you're still studying. And as soon as you finish, you'll get into that panicky phase?"

PETROS: No, I personally try to constitute a different . . . reality. And of course not around myself. So my reality, and if you will, perception of things and so on, is to communicate to people through various practices. . . . You understand, that's a political conception?

DIMITRIS: Where did that come from though?

PETROS: This probably arose from all the experiences I had. . . . From December[1] to the Squares, to the student association I was in. My participation in the occupations we staged. These various things . . . solidarity, for example, these emanate through a continuation. They aren't waypoints. They're lanes. You know. They're, more or less [pauses], how should I tell you? It's your answer and attempt to change an everyday life that doesn't benefit you and that doesn't lead you anywhere. (Petros, personal communication, February 9, 2017)

Instead of the gloominess of resignation, Petros imagines ways of tackling the uncertainties of the future differently. Jacques Rancière (2011b, 13) reminds us that "the framing of a future happens in the wake of political invention rather than being its condition of possibility." Touching on his previous experience with demonstrations and protest camps, Petros's imagination of the future is not so much rendered by defeat, but by the struggle that things could indeed be better. "A lot of people in Greece . . . tried to view things a little differently," Petros continues. This changing imagination, he assures me, was "born in the squares" (personal communication, February 9, 2017).

1. Petros is referring to the December 2008 riots in response to the murder of fifteen-year-old Alexandros Grigoropoulos by a policeman in the Exarcheia neighborhood of Athens. In the words of Rania Astrinaki (2009, 101), "What occurred during the six days after Alexis's murder was beyond any anarchist's fantasies, any politician's nightmares, any leftist's predictions, and any social scientist's perceptiveness. Wrath propelled thousands of high school students (whom we had deemed apolitical) and university students and other youths, as well as parents, teachers, and others. . . . But many of us who participated in the demonstrations observed, felt, and lived something that exceeded our capacities for understanding, as might be the case in all such moments of political effervescence."

4   Paradoxes of Emancipation

Like the majority of my interlocutors, Petros points to the transformative character of participating in the Syntagma Square occupation, especially with regard to political subjectivation. He told me how the square "fueled" him into "being politically active in a collective," how it "reanimated political values," started to "change the individual," and generally "drove a lot of people to think a little differently about how they can situate themselves in society" (personal communication, February 9, 2017). In this light, the guiding questions of this book are: Why do participants in the Syntagma Square occupation emphasize the transformative character of their experience? What do participants aspire to and what do they demarcate their selves from against the backdrop of crisis, austerity, and neoliberalization? And what remains of their participation experience with regard to subjectivity years onward?

A central claim throughout this book is that the transformative quality of the Syntagma Square occupation lies in its spatiality, which signifies a demarcation from, and a radical alternative to, the capitalist imaginary. I will show that it is in light of this that participants are careful to demarcate their current selves from their selves prior to the participation experience. As such, I argue that the subject is not the foundation of political practices. Rather, the formation of subjectivity ought to be traced in these practices. But because neoliberalism has succeeded in incorporating critical activity in its mode of functioning, participants of the Syntagma Square occupation, paradoxically, also reproduce some of the values and rationalities they challenge and intend to overcome. In order to investigate these claims, I suggest conceiving of social relations—particularly subjectivities and spatialities—as both structuring and structured (in a Bourdieusian sense). With the exception of Karaliotas (2017) and Kaika and Karaliotas (2017), the relationship between spatiality, subjectivity, and experience in Syntagma Square remains underexamined. Further, subjectivity and spatiality are, however tacitly, treated as products. Little attention is given to the underlying practices of their mutually constitutive formation. This book seeks to address this gap by making sense of transformative experience through the dialectics of subjectivity and spatiality.

Studying processes of subject formation through the spatiality of the Syntagma Square occupation is a gateway for following the ways in which

Introduction   5

participants imagine and anticipate uncertainty and the future. This is primarily because square occupations are spatially manifested challenges to the normative orderings of the status quo (Schumann and Soudias 2013; Soudias 2018). As I will show, they are sites where unthought-of discourses and practices can emerge that "'prefigure' or set the stage for *new subjectivities and by extension* ideally a new society" (Haiven 2014, 75; emphasis added). Analytically, therefore, the Syntagma Square occupation can be viewed as a microcosmic heuristic device to critically engage with broader theoretical and political issues: the crumbling promises of the capitalist imaginary, subject transformation in times of crisis, the envisioning of alternative futures, but also the limits of emancipatory practice in neoliberalism and how we, at times, reproduce the very values and rationalities we oppose.

To address these issues, my analysis builds on a number of conceptual dimensions. These include the radical imagination, the square, social dialectics, subjectivity, intersectional experience, and critique. I suggest conceiving of them as conceptual figures of thought (Harders 2015) that lurk in each chapter in different ways and sensitize and ground my study. In introducing them here, I seek to provide the grounds for their further development throughout this book.

The Radical Imagination

> My confidence was satisfied that things could be different. . . . A confidence . . . that we need to resist somehow finally wasn't only mine but was also that of many other people who found themselves in the same place as I did at the same time as I did. And we discussed together how we could do something around diverting the memorandum[2] in Greece in 2011. And this surely changes you. Because you see it also with others. (Petros, personal communication, February 9, 2017)

2. Petros is referring to the First Economic Adjustment Programme for Greece, a memorandum of understanding on financial assistance between the troika of the European Commission, the European Central Bank, and the International Monetary Fund, and the Hellenic Republic in order to cope with the Greek government debt crisis.

6 Paradoxes of Emancipation

At a time when the zeitgeist of political elites is guided by a neoliberal governmental rationality that seeks to render everything private that is (or was) public—from common goods and services, to social relations, emotions, and the regulation of the self—occupations of squares make a bold claim to commoning responsibility and wealth (Stavrides 2016). Against the backdrop of totalizing self-responsibility and increasing competition, occupations of squares are an expression of commonality in the search for solidarity. As an out-of-the-ordinary act, the practice of occupation also means to radically imagine otherwise. Imagination, then, is inherent to practices. For political philosopher Cornelius Castoriadis (1998, 87), "To do something . . . is projecting oneself into a future situation which is opened up on all sides to the unknown, which, therefore, one cannot possess beforehand in thought, but which one must necessarily assume to be defined in its aspects relevant to present decisions." As the future is unknown, and the world is not encapsulated in determined causal relations, practices allow for the generation of processes of change, which, by definition, create the future and different social realities. This is what various scholars have referred to as the radical imagination (Castoriadis 1998; Hage 2015; Haiven and Khasnabish 2014; Lefort 1986). As a figure of thought, the radical imagination can be viewed as an aspirational term that signifies a response to the "crises of imagination" (Haiven 2014) that one may well read into Petros's first statement. The radical imagination, at least in part, negates experience.[3]

Without the radical imagination, we accept status quo phenomena as normal and reasonable—that there is in fact "no alternative," that austerity is a "rational" response to those who lived "beyond their means," that the ultimate pursuit of lasting happiness is found in, say, "consuming life" (Bauman 2007) or positive thinking (Ehrenreich 2010). To the extent that we lack the radical imagination, we internalize or at least accept such paradigms. Petros's introductory statement is a case in point:

---

3. The negation of experience can be read alongside Walter Benjamin's (1999, 734) concept of "poverty of experience," where people "long to free themselves from experience; they long for a world in which they can make such pure and decided use of their poverty . . . that it will lead to something respectable."

referring to Francis Fukuyama's (1992) idea that history largely came to an end with the victory of liberal democracy over communism ("they even said there's no history"), Petros caricatures the promises and virtues of modern capitalism ("things get better"). Indeed, our tacit knowledge and understanding of such (acceleratory) ideas as opportunity, prosperity, fairness, growth, improvement, well-being or wealth render capitalism as a social imaginary which, in the words of Castoriadis (1998, 145), can be conceived of as a "singular manner of living, of seeing and of conducting its own existence . . . the source of that which presents itself in every instance as an indisputable and undisputed meaning." In Greece, Petros suggests, the capitalist imaginary was a social reality as much as elsewhere. In the 1980s, then-prime minister Andreas Papandreou promised that everybody would be able to ascend to the middle class. Especially in the ensuing period, known as "modernization" from 1996 onward—the heyday of Greece's neoliberalization and economic boom, peaking with the 2004 Summer Olympics—consumer and lifestyle culture proliferated rapidly as the country's GDP converged with, and at times outstripped, the European Union average. Because everyday life is firmly entrenched in the status quo of capitalist social relations—steeped in what Pierre Bourdieu (2013) famously refers to as *illusio*—our normative expectations of the world around us are deeply affected by these relations. As a structuring force, the capitalist imaginary succeeded in accounting for the constitution of tradition and modernity, how we define needs and desires, and, ultimately, our imagination of what is worth striving for. As Ingerid Straume (2011, 30) remarks, through the "Fata Morgana of perpetual growth and unlimited expansion, capitalism holds a promise of surplus, overabundance, in which we all can take part, when our turn eventually comes. In this respect, capitalism is a beautiful dream." If only we seize the opportunities in front of us—the promise goes—if only we are "proactive," work hard and "invest in our future," we will one day be able to "make it." Surely, one would assume, Petros's degree in economics will have positive effects to that end.

In times of crisis, however, social imaginaries can unravel. For Marxist geographer David Harvey (2014, 4), crises are "moments of transformation in which capital typically reinvents itself and morphs into something else. And the 'something else' may be better or," as Petros initially suggests, "worse for the people." In this light, the cogency of the capitalist imaginary can be put into doubt. This is because crises are situations in which our ordinary conduct is in turmoil, as normative expectations do not match everyday realities. With the consequences of the 2008 financial crisis unfolding in Greece it appears—for Petros anyway—that capitalism broke its promise. Suddenly, competing for middle-class belonging is no longer a gateway to riches. Instead, the rhetoric of opportunity seeks to camouflage its self-betrayal, as it now merely offers a temporal escape from economic uncertainty.

The promise of capitalism started crumbling long before the 2008 financial crisis. With the breakthrough of neoliberalism in the 1970s following the crisis of Keynesian Fordism, certainty and economic security started to fade as governments slowly dismantled their welfare systems. The capitalist imaginary began to change, as now a "violent threat" (Davies 2014) haunted political leaders in an awkward Darwinian twist: maximize competitive advantage over other countries or perish. The genius of neoliberal thought was to conceive of a model of governmental rationality where uncertainty, if carefully cultivated, can drive people into competition (Hayek 1992). For us to conceive of the world as increasingly economically uncertain, competitive and antagonistic, previously state-held responsibilities needed to be devolved down to us. Structural reforms of, say, labor deregulation and welfare privatization, do just that. As a governmental technique (in a Foucaultian sense), such reforms task us to become "resilient," ready for anything, "incentivizing"[4] us to compete against each other, in the "cruel optimism" (Berlant 2011) that if we subject ourselves to this logic, we will one day be able to free ourselves from it. In neoliberalism, state-market-subject relations are reconfigured in ways that treat and evaluate everything "as if" it is a market (Davies 2014). The market is mobilized discursively so that we reimagine everything as questions of

---

4. As Dardot and Laval (2017, 170) anticipate in their meticulous study on neoliberalism as a normative logic: "Apparatuses of rewards and sanctions, and systems of incentives and 'disincentives,' will ultimately replace market sanctions in guiding individual choices and conduct where market or quasi-market situations are not wholly feasible."

economics, with the ultimate goal of maximizing utility in an increasingly competitive and (economically) uncertain world.

Political sociologist Justin Paulson (2010, 33) refers to this state as the "*un*radical" imagination, as it never goes beyond what has been experienced; whatever is imagined is only imagined within the confines of the status quo. Envisioning ourselves as rich and wealthy in the hope of escaping uncertainty signifies an unradical imagination precisely because it rests on the structuring logics of capitalist reproduction. This is not to say we are incapable of critiquing or thinking critically. But, as I will show throughout this book, the evaluations and judgments we perform in our quotidian are often immanent to neoliberalism and its rationalities: self-optimization, best practices, or efficiency maximization—to name just a few techniques of evaluation that neoliberals claim allow for managing uncertainty—include the possibility of critique and comparison, but only so as to brace us for further uncertainty.

The radical imagination, then, aspires to depart from the capitalist imaginary and is less a question of ethical judgment (although it can be), as much as a description of a politico-sociological process (Haiven and Khasnabish 2014, 6). As I will show, the emergence of the radical imagination is characterized by a certain balance between anti-politics and alter-politics (Hage 2015, 58). Anti-politics here is not defined as depoliticization or as being apolitical. Rather, it signifies a reaction against, or rejection of, the practices and discourses associated with the politics of power. As the radical imagination stems from experience, and our experiences of the world are different (different intersectional experiences of, for example, gender, sexuality, race, age, class, ethnicity, physical ability), on a phenomenological level it emerges from variation: from conflicts over how values and norms are negotiated and envisioned in practice (Paulson 2010). Anti-politics requires the act of distancing and demarcating oneself from the existing order; against and in confrontation with the practices of government, of power, of normative orders, of ordinary conventions. In a nutshell, it is a form of critique that demystifies the politics of power to its actualities of domination and subordination (e.g., Abrams 1988).

On the other hand, alter-politics aims at providing alternatives to that order. As the feminist psychologist Lynne Segal (2017, 55–56) tells us in this regard, "It is only when people's distress can be turned into solidarity with others who are vulnerable, with anger directed at the injurious practices of those dictating the conditions that make our lives more precarious, that politicizing depression might connect us with any collective practices of resistance or utopian dreaming." The alter-political quality of the radical imagination lies precisely in that it is ontologically and epistemologically so fundamentally different from the experience of the status quo. Indeed, the Greek word for *radical—rizospastiko—*translates literally as "root-breaking" and projects a mode of the future that is marked by what Bourdieu (2000, 68) refers to as denaturalization and defatalization. The radical imagination begins with acknowledgment—that it is only possible with and within what one is against—so as then to exercise abductive discovery, a willingness to add another meta-level, a quest for rattling the ontological foundations of the social worlds we inhabit. Even if the radical imagination signifies a process of reform, it must be one which questions and shakes the very ground on which the status quo rests. As Haiven (2014, 225–26) adds in this regard, it "should never reach the level of providing a schematic or a plan for what the future ought to look like, because any such plan would already be poisoned from steeping in our own time and place. Thus we would use the tainted tools of our own current oppression to build a dystopian future in the name of utopia."

The Syntagma Square occupation is a spatiality that brings together and prefigures the alter-political and antipolitical qualities of the radical imagination. As significations, alter-politics and anti-politics are not always easily distinguishable: an antiauthoritarian ethic, for example, is alter-political precisely because it is against authority. Here, "the point is not," as Judith Butler remarks, "to find the right typology, but to understand where typological thinking falls apart" (Butler and Athanasiou 2013, 35). With regard to the ethical character of the radical imagination, this has to do with the fact that there are multiple and incommensurable moral spheres available to us through which we seek to justify our practices and criticize those of others. For now, it suffices to understand that linking anti-politics and alter-politics illuminates how the radical imagination in Syntagma Square "works."

The Square

> Syntagma . . . changed established things of protest. It overturned the established order. (Panagiotis, personal communication, October 6, 2014)

A further central claim of this book is that the Syntagma Square occupation was an extraordinary spatiality that conditions the possibility for the emergence of the radical imagination. First, this is because the extraordinary practice of occupying is an act against the orderings of the status quo. Second, the orders within the occupation of the square offered a radical alternative to the status quo. Indeed, in many places around the world, the years that followed the global financial crisis of 2008 saw some new movement in the previously gloomy landscape of street politics. Observers have pointed out that the seditious emergence of the Arab Uprisings, Occupy Wall Street, and the "movement of the squares" brought forth mass manifestations of wrath and hope that revitalized the use of public space for resistance (Dhaliwal 2012; Feigenbaum et al. 2013; Halvorsen 2015; Kavoulakos 2013; Marom 2013; Soudias 2015, 2018) and democratized and politicized authoritarian polities or technocratic decision-making and crisis management beyond conventional forms of contestation (Hager 2011; Hatem 2012; Hoskyns 2014; Stavrides 2012; Wilson and Swyngedouw 2015; Zevnik 2014).

The Syntagma Square occupation needs to be seen within this wave of protests, departing from "ordinary"[5] modes of discontent and radically envisioning new ones. With the costs of the crisis being socialized downward, through wage cuts and tax hikes, and institutional spaces for the expression of political disagreement virtually shut down, Greece was hit by a wave of protests evolving from February 2010 onward. Although

---

5. In Greece, these more "ordinary" practices of contestation include labor union demonstrations, the hanging of protest banners on symbolic infrastructure (ministries, even the Acropolis) by communist labor union activists, sit-ins and the squatting of buildings by antiauthoritarian demonstrators, the refusal to pay for public services such as transportation or highway tolls (Psimitis 2011, 196).

12   Paradoxes of Emancipation

mostly organized by such groups as communist labor union organizers, the antiauthoritarian and anarchist milieu, and members of the radical Left (Kousis 2015; Psimitis 2011), people who had so far been barely or not at all exposed to street politics started to join these mobilizations against austerity. Among them were my interlocutors. Inscribed in a wider "movement of the piazzas" (Leontidou 2012) that unfolded in over thirty-eight central squares in cities all over Greece, the Syntagma Square occupation lay at the heart of the movement. Starting on May 25 and lasting until the end of July (Souliotis 2013, 246), Syntagma represented the convergence of a socioeconomically and ideologically heterogeneous "multitude" animated by those directly hit by the economic crisis (Kaika and Karaliotas 2017; Katsambekis 2014; Sotirakopoulos and Sotiropoulos 2013), but linked with previously existing groups of anarchist and radical leftist activists.[6] Referred to as Aganaktismenoi[7] (Indignants), protesters in Syntagma drew on direct action practices by the Greek anarchist movement, and the strategies and tactics used by the Spanish Indignados who had started their protests in Puerta del Sol in Madrid only ten days earlier (Giovanopoulos 2011; Roos and Oikonomakis 2014).

Reducing the Syntagma Square occupation to its most essential qualities, it signifies a liminal, spatially manifested expression of contestation against the status quo, and for something entirely different. In this sense, the Syntagma Square occupation served as a radical public pedagogy—that is, a site of informal, collective, and transformative modes of learning and knowing (Giroux 2004b). This became possible because the longue

---

6. Roy Panagiotopoulou (2013, 445) tries to capture the demographics of those occupying the square with survey data as follows: gender, 45.7 percent female; age, 15–24 years (13.6 percent), 25–34 years (25.3 percent), 35–39 years (27.4 percent), 50+ years (33.2 percent); party support, Panhellenic Socialist Movement (22.7 percent), New Democracy (14.2 percent), Communist Party of Greece (9.6 percent), Coalition of the Radical Left (12.0 percent), Popular Orthodox Rally (2.6 percent), other/no vote (31.6 percent). Although this data certainly does not depict a full representation of Syntagma, it does indicate the heterogeneity of participants, which many of my interlocutors referred to.

7. Although much disdained by many participants, who preferred to frame their participation within the "movement of piazzas," Greek broadcast media continued to refer to protesters as Aganaktismenoi, a word meaning "indignant people." (Papapavlou 2015, 91).

durée of an occupation differs from the ephemerality of other political events, such as protest marches, referendums, or elections, thus allowing for the emergence of transformative experiences.

Although protesters were all being affected in various ways by the austerity measures, they nevertheless differed in their social situations, coping strategies, and narratives of blame (Theodossopoulos 2014). Indeed, crisis, austerity, and neoliberalization had an intersectionally uneven impact. Migrants and women suffered disproportionately by rising unemployment, precariousness, and impoverishment (Kouki and Chatzidakis 2021; Daskalaki et al. 2020; Tsimouris 2014) as well as an increase in everyday forms of violence (Vaiou 2014). These realities influenced the makeup of Syntagma Square, thus "creating a plural embodied space of discontent" (Athanasiou 2014, 3).

Early on, Syntagma Square witnessed a profound demarcation regarding its territoriality. This spatially manifested cleavage was expressed by participants' talk of the demarcation between the "upper" and the "lower" parts of the square. The upper part has been associated with nationalist discourses and ones that could even be categorized as fascist (Bakola 2017; Goutsos and Polymenas 2014). Accompanied by Greek flags and other nationalist symbols, discourses in this part of the square evolved around betrayal and theft by the Greek political elite, as protesters faced, chanted at, and yelled at the Voulē—the Greek parliament. The lower part of the square, on the other hand, has been claimed by its occupants to have been a space of political vision, organization, and assembly. It was mainly here that occupational infrastructure was established and maintained in the face of repeated police violence. The division of labor, organization, and decision-making processes was well developed. The more than two dozen different groups in the Syntagma Square occupation can be broadly separated into organizational and thematic groups. The organizational ones took responsibility for running the occupation. They consisted of a welcome group, where new arrivals could get an overview and enlist in one of the other groups. These included the general secretariat; the technical support group; the multimedia group; the translation group; the medical clinic; the defense group; the "calming" group, which resolved conflicts and tensions nonviolently; the food and catering group; or the cleaning group,

14 Paradoxes of Emancipation

among many others. The thematic groups were those presenting creative performances and alternative visions of politics. These included the time bank (similar to Pierre-Joseph Proudhon's notion of the exchange bank), the artists' group, the group of work and unemployment, the direct democracy group, the group on eco-communities and alternative currencies, the group on the economy, the education group, and many others. Decisions on political propositions or organizational issues were taken in the popular assembly—the heart of the occupation—where everybody could directly take part, discuss, and vote on a proposal. It is in this lower part of the square that participants talk of having had transformative experiences.

The lower part of Syntagma Square in particular was a radical envisioning of an answer to the question of how to build noncoercive, nonoppressive, nonhierarchical, and nonexploitative relationships and institutions today that are worthy examples of the world to be created.[8] As such, experiencing the spatial manifestation of the radical imagination in Syntagma Square has consequences for subjectivity.

Social Dialectics

> And this is the value of Syntagma Square. That there, this *butterfly effect* of inspiring one another, changing our way of life, began. (Katerina, personal communication, October 19, 2014; emphasis added)

A central conceptual figure of thought throughout this book is the study of social processes as dialectical relationships. Bringing together Bourdieusian (2013) dialectics with Foucaultian (2008) biopolitics, I presume a reconciliation between structure and agency through structured structures (*structures structurées*) that are predisposed to act as structuring structures

---

8. This approach to "doing" practices is essentially prefigurative and will be elaborated on in chapter 3. In the words of the eminent social movement scholar Alberto Melucci (1985, 801), prefiguration signifies "a goal in itself. Since the action is focused on cultural codes, the *form* of the movement is a message, a symbolic challenge to the dominant patterns. . . . As prophets without enchantment, contemporary movements practice in the present the change they are struggling for: they redefine the meaning of social action for the whole society."

(*structures structurantes*). On the one hand, subjects are the result of social structures, more precisely governmentality. On the other hand, subjects also structure practices and spaces as products of situated normative expectations and orders. For illustrative purposes, we can assume that crises structure spatialities and are structured by spatialities, spatialities structure subjectivities and are structured by subjectivities. And subjectivities therefore structure crises and are structured by crises. Structures act as norms and rules that condition habits of thought and conduct. In this regard, Giovanopoulos (2011, 51) describes how in Syntagma there was a "feeling that the very square or each group changed as you changed, the dialectic of this interaction between the total and the personal, was extraordinarily intense."

While there is some discrepancy between Bourdieu's relatively circular conception of reproduction and his recognition that social structures are constantly in process and subject to change, Nick Crossley (2003, 44) rightly points out that Bourdieu recognizes a degree of conflict, struggle, and change as normal features of processes of reproduction. Here, inventive actions "can both modify existing structures and generate new ones, breaking the 'circle' of reproduction." This is to say that subjectivation is a dialectical process, structuring and structured by the particularities of crisis and space that my interlocutors experience and practice. The subject is always "within" a situation, a part of the world and of the conditions of this world. The ways in which dialectics find their expression, however, are open and unpredictable. It is this radical contingency that allows transformative, even emancipatory, processes to unfold (Rebughini 2014).

The Subject

> Every human is different. I too have the DNA of my parents. But the DNA does not remain the same. We can change our DNA. Or transform it. (Katerina, personal communication, February 7, 2016)

> What I want to say is that I see through myself, from [Syntagma] to now, a continuous education in many things I had no idea about before. (Katerina, personal communication, March 23, 2017)

Against the backdrop of the many protest camps and occupations of squares from 2011 onward, scholars have pointed to the emergence of a "new political subjectivity" (Hanafi 2012), "insurgent subjectivity" (Juris 2013), or "radical subjectivity" (Rossdale 2014), to name just a few. In different ways, these conceptualizations seek to investigate the relationship between contestation and participant experience, in an effort to make sense of lasting consequences as to subject formation. Going beyond the latently functionalist assumptions of individual participation and biographical "impact" in social movement studies (Giugni 2004; McAdam 1999; Vestergren et al. 2016), these theorizations view the experience of participation and subjectivity not through the lenses of psychologized individual behavior, but rather as the product of (intersectionally unequal) social relations. As opposed to the internalized and durable habitus (Bourdieu 2013), conceptually the focus of these case studies on subjectivity allows the relative alterability and changeability of the self to be sensitized (Arthur 2012).

With regard to the Syntagma Square occupation in particular, research has focused on the relationship between politicized subjectivity and democracy (Bakola 2017; Gerbaudo 2017; Karaliotas 2017; Prentoulis and Thomassen 2014; 2012; Roussos 2014; Tsianos 2016). Drawing on radical political theory, these studies assume a politicization of protesters' subjectivity through their participation in the square. However, these case studies rarely theorize the processes of these "new" subject formations and, relatedly, there is little systematic empirical research on what remains of these experiences as to subjectivity years later. This is especially curious in view of the fact that, Petros explains, "Everything is a continuation of things" (personal communication, February 9, 2017). In order to understand change, we ought to look at the temporal characteristics of what was prior to and after transformative situations as perceived by the subject. As mentioned earlier, in the case of the Syntagma Square occupation, participants are careful to demarcate their current selves from their selves prior to their experience of taking part in the protest. This book attempts to shed light on why that is. In so doing, I address the absence of processes of subject formation in times of crisis in Greece by theorizing beyond single empirical instances.

That humans are to be understood as subjects is a product of modernity (Illouz 2012). This is reflected not least in Michel Foucault's processual conception of subjectivity—a constant state of becoming, in which the past is working itself out in the present through the materiality of power. Methodologically, he casts light on the idea of the subject through a genealogy, or historical ontology, of subjectivation practices. Here, Foucault's (1982, 777) interest is to "create a history of the different modes by which, in our culture, human beings are made subjects" through various means of objectification. Drawing on Foucault, Judith Butler's (1997) term *psychic life* conveys the formation of subjectivities in and through power. Based on the concept of "subjection," which "signifies the process of becoming subordinated by power as well as the process of becoming a subject" (2), Butler's notion lends itself to the ways in which subjectivities self-constitute in and through practice (Scharff 2015, 5).

As Burkhard Liebsch (2016) rightly observes, Foucaultian approaches to subjectivity are often negativistic, in the sense that they presume subjectivation practices to be biased towards the reproduction of the status quo, with little leeway for a self that strives for "remaking" herself in a more emancipatory fashion. Liebsch sees the reason for this in the fact that "being a subject means to be subjectivated in terms of a life that does not allow one to *be oneself in order to become another*" (76). To Foucault, this essentially means not being free, as becoming free—much as in the Berlinian (1969) notion of negative liberty—means standing against any form of imposed subjectivation. In a word, Foucault is skeptical of the emancipatory capacities of subjectivation precisely because it rests on our submission to ourselves for others.

Perhaps due to the rather paralyzing outlook of this conceptualization, Foucault expanded the purview of his analysis to the government of the self. From the early 1980s onward, Foucault shifted his focus further toward resistive acts, as his later work on the subject and critique essentially addresses how not to be governed (Foucault 1997a; 1997b). It is therefore analytically fruitful to distinguish between two modes of the "making of" subjects: subjectification (*assujettissement*), or the ways in which the self is objectified as a subject through the exercise of power/knowledge by others; and subjectivation (*subjectivation*), or the ways in which individuals govern and fashion themselves into subjects based on what they believe to be worth striving for (Milchman and Rosenberg 2009). In this line of thinking, just because the subject is an immanent effect of practices does not mean that it is fixed and unalterable, entirely produced by the status quo of power and knowledge, governmental rationalities and disciplinary techniques.

While the potentiality for (political) subjectivation may indeed be universal, it remains inaccessible to those who fully identify with their selves. Subjectivation, therefore, requires an antipolitical quality. In this light, more contemporary theorizations on subjectivity emphasize its formation through the (normative) negativity of experience (Kurik 2016; Lehmann 2016; Liebsch 2016; Rancière 1999; Soudias 2021b)—that is, the formation of the subject against and in confrontation with the discourses and practices of government. Indeed, the notion of "being against" renders the subject inherently political. Subjectivation, therefore, requires the experience of disidentifying from the self and the world around us (Prozorev 2014). From the viewpoint of the self, subjectivation signifies the requalification of ordinary experience (Rancière 1999, 35–36) with the ensuing perceived need or desire to change the practice that led to that experience. Here, the "ethico-political task is exactly to seek to improve our capacities of self- transformation . . . against subjection" (Cremonesi et al. 2016, 8).

In that sense, the subject is not the foundation of political (or other) practices. Rather, the formation of subjectivity ought to be traced in these practices (Prozorev 2014). Much of what I do in this book is inquire into the ways in which the (politicized) subject is constituted in practice against and in confrontation with the practices of power. In pragmatist terms, tracing subjectivity in practices means to understand the subject as "consequences-in-practice" (Tavory and Timmermans 2014). Such an understanding of subjectivity expands assumptions that subjects are primarily constructed through discourse (see Laclau and Mouffe 2001). From a cultural studies approach to practice theory (Bourdieu 2013; Crossley 2003; Reckwitz 2002, 2003), a subject is the sequence of their practices of, say, (self-)reflecting, feeling, remembering, planning, contesting, destroying, building, etc. The "doing" of practices in its temporality and contextuality is prone to changes. Marked by heterogeneity, nonalignment, and, sometimes, incommensurability, subjects have the potential to render their actions and patterns of understanding unpredictable, thus allowing for changes and transformations. This "hardheadedness" (*Eigensinnigkeit*), as Andreas Reckwitz (2003, 296) calls it, is not the result of some type of prestructured autonomy, or the subject's individuality. Rather, it is the consequence of the practical necessity to deal with different and diverse routinized forms of conduct and heterogeneous meanings. So sure, maybe in Europe and North America "we are really liberal subjects in various states of imperfection, constantly trying to better ourselves" (Stephens and Papadopoulos 2006, 4). But the notions of neoliberal subjectivity structured around, say, a Protestant work ethic, liberal self-improvement, and Benthamite efficiency maximization are not the result of our capacity for self-reflection as much as they are shaped according to social requirements—as products of historically, locally, and culturally specific complexes of practices (of the self) and governmental rationalities. Subjects are therefore best "understood through the ways in which people produce or turn over places and spaces for their own uses" (Pile 2008, 210). This is why this book is interested in investigating the dialectics between subjectivity and spatiality, and particularly how processes of subject formation can be spatialized.

By narrating their (changing) understandings of experiences, interlocutors perform meaning-making practices that orient their selves toward particular discourses. According to Nikolas Rose (1999, xxii; emphasis added), these orientations reveal self-understandings of subjectivity along the following dimensions:

> *Ontological* (as spirit, as soul, as consciousness, as creatures of pleasure, of habits, of emotions, of will, of unconscious desire, as individualised or collectivised in various ways); *epistemological* (as knowable through observation, through testing, through confession . . .); *ethical* (the kinds of selves they should seek to be, virtuous, wise, moderate, fulfilled, autonomous, civilized); *technical* (what they must do to themselves, the practices, regimens, by which they should act upon themselves to reform or improve themselves, in order to become autonomous, free, fulfilled).

20 Paradoxes of Emancipation

In talking about, say, solidarity, self-organization, self-governance, but also police violence, capitalism, or self-improvement, the very reiterative enunciations of identifying or disidentifying with these discourses signify a practice of subjectivity. This means my analysis traces the contours of my interlocutors' subjectivities while providing insights into how they are constituted in conversation.

Intersectional Experience

> DIMITRIS: So what was going on in Syntagma that was so different [from everyday life]? [Was it] that things happened spontaneously?
> ANDREAS: Yes. For this thing to function, there needed to be this process, for it to succeed.
> DIMITRIS: But couldn't we say the same thing for society in general?
> ANDREAS: Yes. Certainly.
> DIMITRIS: So what's the difference?
> ANDREAS: The difference is that others have not yet gotten into that spirit. They haven't *experienced and lived* Syntagma. (Andreas, personal communication, February 11, 2016; emphasis added)

Experience is a key signifier in the ways in which my interlocutors refer to their participation in the Syntagma Square occupation. Rather than assuming a behavioral psychological understanding of experience (see Bradley 2005; van Stekelenburg et al. 2011), this book follows approaches that render experience as intersectionally constructed. The word *experience* here is used to refer to a narrative (re-)construction of social realities "so that afterward we can find words to talk about what happened" (Abrahams 1986, 50). Experience embodies both meanings and feelings and is illustrative of what individual subjects do. This is to say that experience reveals practices—the conventional patterns of culturally learned and interpreted habits of thought and action that make them understandable to others (Abrahams 1986; Morris 1970). A transformative experience, then, is one that challenges these conventional patterns. Viktor Turner (1986, 36) remarks that "it is structurally unimportant whether the past is 'real' or 'mythical,' 'moral' or 'amoral.' The point is whether meaningful guidelines emerge from the existential encounter within a subjectivity of what we have derived from previous structures or units of experience in living relation with the new experience." This is to say that the way we make sense of our subjectivity needs to be checked against what we think we know from the past in relation to what we confront in the present and, by extension, what we hope to encounter and are scared of tackling in our imagination of the future.

What this highlights is that experiences, and how they are represented, are far from hardwired. As subjects move through time and space, they reframe and resignify experiences. In this sense, regimes of representation are constitutive processes of meaning-making, rather than reflexive, after-the-event narrations. In the words of Bauman (2008, 8), "The stories told of lives interfere with the lives lived before the lives have been lived to be told." For Foucaultian thought, this has to do with the paradoxes of experience. "Experience is conceived of as dominant structure and transformative force, as existing background of practices and transcending event, as the object of theoretical inquiry and the objective of moving beyond historical limits" (Lemke 2011, 27). Therefore, the ways in which this book conceives of experience is much in line with Joan Scott (1991). In her words, "Experience is not the origin of our explanation, not the authoritative (because seen or felt) evidence that grounds what is known, but rather that which we seek to explain, that about which knowledge is produced" (779–80).

Critique

> Whatever changed, individually or more collectively, did so because people were weaned off what they'd grown up with. Also, it's because they acquired the understanding of critical thinking. In order to get to this place, you need to pass through the state of self-criticism. And this takes years of self-flagellation. And it doesn't ever end. Because we don't live under free societal conditions. (Lukas, personal communication, February 23, 2016)

Changes of subjectivity lie in our ability to reflect critically upon our experiences and, ultimately, our selves. Critique, therefore, can be regarded as

22   Paradoxes of Emancipation

a force that allows us to be self-reflexive and to distance ourselves from experience ("Were weaned off what they'd grown up with," as Lukas mentions). It is what makes us constantly renegotiate the validity of imaginaries, established norms, orders, values, and conventions. For Foucault (1997b, 32), critique signifies "the movement by which the subject gives himself the right to question truth on its effects of power and question power on its discourses of truth." In this sense, studying critique is studying how it is practiced and performed.

The study of critique lies at the heart of Boltanskian (2011) "pragmatic sociology." Grounded in the "uncertainty that permeates social life" (80), subjects

> are not content to act or react to the actions of others. They review their own actions or those of others in order to make judgements on them, often hinging on the issue of good and evil—that is, *moral judgements*. This reflexive capacity means that they also react to the representations given of their properties or actions, including when the latter derive from sociology or critical theories. (Boltanski 2011, 3)

In this view, "moral activity is a predominantly critical activity" (Boltanski 2011, 4). Boltanski distinguishes between two different modes of critique that he refers to as "registers." The "practical register" is "marked in particular by a low level of reflexivity and a certain tolerance for differences" (83). This register is illustrated when, for example, we become aware of societal pains but find ways of coping and getting by for as long as these pains are not unbearably excruciating. On the other hand, there is the "metapragmatic register," where reflexivity is deepened in ways that shift our attention away from tolerating what is happening "to the question of how it is appropriate to *characterize* what is happening" (67). When my interlocutors point to their unthought-of experiences with police repression, or show dissatisfaction with the position that political parties took toward the occupation, they perform ethical judgments on state-institutional arrangements in disidentifying ways. These critiques are therefore metapragmatic. Their meaning must be seen against both the egalitarian character of the Syntagma Square occupation as well as the subordinating nature of state-institutional arrangements.

This is because, ontologically, critique "only exists in relation to something other than itself: it is an instrument, a means for a future . . . it oversees a domain it would want to police and is unable to regulate" (Foucault 1997b, 25). Critique, therefore, requires imagination in that it anticipates that things should not be as they are. Functionally, however, critique is often treated as subordinate to positively constituted knowledge(s). This is why, in Foucault's thinking, the activity of critique is often informed by a "juridico-discursive" habit of thought and action, focusing on "judging and condemning, negating and rejecting. According to this model, critique necessitates the determination of rational standards of evaluation and the application of those standards to social reality" (Lemke 2011, 29). In this vein, by drawing on "rational" standards and evaluations, my interlocutors' practices at times also unwittingly reproduce the orderings of the status quo: critiquing neoliberalism by drawing on neoliberal discourses and techniques challenges neoliberalism only at the cost of its (partial) reproduction.

Journeys of Emancipation

The six chapters in this book narrate and theorize from my interlocutors' processes of subject (re-)formation before, during, and after the Syntagma Square occupation. Chapter 1, "Modernizing Greece: From Barbershops to Hair Salons," investigates how my interlocutors narrate their selves prior to their participation in the Syntagma Square occupation—in the period of what was dubbed "modernization," under then-prime minister Costas Simitis. Curiously, despite the fact that my interlocutors were financially considerably better-off than after the beginning of the financial crisis, they narrate their selves almost exclusively in negative terms. I argue this has to do with the ways in which they have resignified the experiences they had during the Syntagma Square occupation. This is based on the assumption that my interlocutors' narrations of their experiences tell us a lot more about how they view themselves in the moment of speaking than about how things "really" were "back then." I show how the period of modernization was in fact used to signify neoliberalization. In many ways similar to President Bill Clinton's and Prime Minister Tony Blair's Third Way, "modernization" signifies the attempt to introduce a neoliberal governmentality (in a Foucaultian sense) throughout the Greek state. The second part of chapter 1 delves into how my interlocutors experienced the modernization period. The policy reforms of privatization, labor market flexibilization, and financial liberalization constructed conditions of uncertainty by devolving onto the individual previously state-held responsibilities, so as to contribute to the molding of an individualist, self-interested, and latently competitive subjectivity. Effectively, modernization reordered (rather than "deregulated") norms of economic activities, social relations, and subjectivities in an effort to increase competitiveness in a utilitarian fashion. As such, neoliberal modernization in Greece is a culturalist project of economizing what was previously deemed political, social, and cultural, aspiring to treating everything as if it is a market.

Chapter 2, "'Waking Up': Spatialized Crises and Unthought-Of Experiences," is about how my interlocutors signify and confront the uncertainties of the future in light of changing normative expectations in times of crisis. Departing from my interlocutors' much-used metaphor of "waking up," this chapter seeks to theorize the conditions of possibility for the spatialized emergence of the radical imagination of the Syntagma Square occupation. Because the subject is always situated within a socio-spatial dialectic, what is argued here is that the structural logics enabling and constituting the spatial production of the Syntagma Square occupation cannot be seen separately from how my interlocutors signify crisis. At the heart of this assumption lies the liminal character of crisis. The structuring quality of crisis produces the Syntagma Square occupation as a spatiality that is marked precisely by crisis' antistructural capacity. As such, a spatial approach to the Syntagma Square occupation allows understanding Syntagma as both a (structural) consequence of and an (antistructural) answer to the crisis in Greece. To approach the condition for the possibility of "waking up," the chapter first theorizes on crisis and its significations, before elaborating on their spatial manifestation within the Syntagma Square occupation. I describe how the "upper" part of the square was marked by a "regressive" signification of crisis—where participants' imagination of the future is reduced from what is possible to what is necessary. The "lower part," on the other hand, is marked by a "progressive" signification of crisis. Here, doxic assumptions are raised to the level of discourse, where they can be radically reimagined. As normative expectations "slip out of alignment" (Crossley 2003, 47) with the actualities of space, individuals are shocked out of their habitual acceptance of taken-for-granted norms and into a more critical attitude. These processes enable what I refer to as the *unthought-of*: an experience that transcends normative expectations and allows the previously doxic and tacitly internalized to be reevaluated.

Chapters 3 and 4 focus on the situation (Clarke 2005) of the Syntagma Square occupation. Chapter 3, "Aspiring the Utopian: The Alter-Politics of Radical Imagination," investigates the alter-political practices and affectivities of the occupation in relation to the status quo. It is claimed in this chapter that inquiring how my interlocutors "do" practices reveals the underlying guiding (ethical and moral) principles of their undertaking. The empirical argument of chapter 3 is that the radical imagination of the Syntagma Square occupation is characterized by principles of an egalitarian and antiauthoritarian ethic that stands in stark contrast to the neoliberal principles and individualizing subject positions outlined in chapter 1. These principles consist of collectivity, equality and mutual respect, self-governance and autonomy, self-organization, and solidarity. Because the subject is constituted in practice, the transformative character of participation in the Syntagma Square occupation that my interlocutors describe lies precisely in the prefigurative and collective layout of how these principles are practiced. This contributes to shifting normative expectations and conventions "in" these spaces and between subjects.

If chapter 3 is about the imagination of radical alternatives, chapter 4, "Challenging the Dystopian: The Anti-Politics of Demystification," is about disagreement, conflict, confrontation, and violence. In this sense, this chapter investigates the antipolitical practices and affectivities of the radical imagination. It does so by investigating the relationship between my interlocutors' negative experiences with the state during the occupation, and the political quality of subjectivation. It sheds light on how the

Syntagma Square occupation was an experience of what my interlocutors refer to as "political maturation." This is true for both groups of interlocutors: those self-described "apolitical" ones and those with a "firm political identity" prior their participation in the Syntagma Square occupation. It is argued here that my interlocutors effectively demystify state-institutional arrangements, particularly executive government and parliamentary representation, to the actualities of domination and subordination. They do so precisely because of the repressive ways in which the state presented itself to them during the occupation. In doing so, my interlocutors also repoliticize debates and democratize narratives of crisis management: they challenge the depoliticized notions of both the technocratic ideal of neoliberal governance and the anti-crisis discourse of There Is No Alternative (TINA). These processes become all the more pertinent and intelligible against the backdrop of my interlocutors' experience with, and practice of, the alter-political capacities of the Syntagma Square occupation (chapter 3). The experience of state repression constructs an almost Manichean juxtaposition between the aspiring equality and self-governance of the Syntagma Square occupation, and the domination and subordination the Greek state attempted to enforce there. By bringing violence to the square, the state tried to impose its own game upon the occupation. This led to internal conflict among the occupiers, with a split along the lines of retaining the radical imagination on the one hand, or countering violence by justifying and resignifying their own modes of violence, on the other. I show that, as practices, the critiques that my interlocutors' experiences with the state gave rise to congeal into the emergence of meaningful guidelines as (politicized) subjectivity. Based on my interlocutors' narrative accounts, chapter 4 theorizes the ways in which this process comes about. I argue that the formation of political subjectivity lies in anti-politics. Political subjectivation requires that the normative negativity of experience as to the livability of a common life results in being against and in confrontation with the (governmental) practices that render the livability of a common life precarious. But this subjectivation also requires an eager openness to alternative political practices and imaginaries. That is to say, the political quality of subjectivation materializes in the ways in which the political is (re-)conceived in practice.

Chapter 5, "Paradoxes of Emancipation: Between Resistance and Reproduction," broadly speaking, scrutinizes what remains of the Syntagma Square occupation experience years onward. In terms of my abductive research strategy, this chapter scrutinizes the consequences-in-action that my interlocutors narrate. In short, it delves into how my interlocutors today demarcate their current subjectivity from how they view themselves, and their experiences, to have been during and before the Syntagma Square occupation. In so doing, chapter 5 pays particular attention to the kinds of subjectivities and spatialities that emerged as a consequence of (the practices of) the occupation. Regarding subjectivities, it is argued here that my interlocutors orient their selves toward the radical imagination of the Syntagma Square occupation. Or to put it differently, the guiding principles of the radical imagination (alter-politics, chapter 3) and the demystifying critiques of state-institutional arrangements (anti-politics, chapter 4), serve as meaningful guidelines for my interlocutors' subjectivity: collectivity, solidarity, self-organization, mutual respect, autonomy, and self-government all form the egalitarian and antiauthoritarian precepts that my interlocutors aspire to in their everyday lives. Regarding spatialities, chapter 5 argues that the extraordinary spatiality of Syntagma Square has been transferred into my interlocutors' quotidian activities in the solidarity movements and social economy organizations that mushroomed in Greece after the Syntagma Square occupation, and their activities in the refugee solidarity movement that have intensified following the 2015 border closing. These spatialities, it is further argued, serve the critical function of "public pedagogies" (Giroux 2004a, 2004b), which offer concrete, everyday alternatives to the status quo of neoliberal reproduction. The second part of chapter 5 looks closely not only at the ways in which these subjectivities and spatialities (functionally) undermine the status quo of neoliberal (governmental) rationality but also at the ways in which they reproduce it. In the *New Spirit of Capitalism*, Luc Boltanski and Ève Chiapello (2017) convincingly argue that political and economic elites "from above," as much as ordinary people "from below," are allowed and even expected to mobilize the empowering resources inherent in their critical, reflexive, and productive capacities. Against this backdrop, I shed light on the paradoxical relationship between those emerging subjectivities and spatialities on the one hand, and neoliberal governmental rationality on the other. Specifically, I investigate how, at times, the latently entrepreneurial character of these emergent subjectivities and spatialities, as well as the increasingly psychologized self-management of the subject, unwittingly feed into neoliberal imaginaries of statehood and subjectivity.

Departing from Theodor Adorno's tenet that "there is no right life in the wrong one", chapter 6, "Toward an Alter-Neoliberal Critique," seeks to find a way out of the seeming totality of neoliberal rationalities. By theorizing from the five previous chapters, this chapter seeks to tackle the following question: how, and according to which principles, is it possible to distinguish between emancipatory processes of transformation and immanent critiques that reproduce and foster the domination of neoliberal rationalities? The radical imagination of the Syntagma Square occupation, and its spatialized public pedagogy, provides an ontological foundation upon which these questions can be answered. By challenging managerialism and utilitarian forms of organization and (everyday) evaluation, entrepreneurialism, economized practice, and the increasing psychologization of the self amongst others, chapter 6 formulates an initial theorization for an alter-neoliberal critique.

Research Approach

My interest in investigating emancipatory, transformative experiences in Syntagma Square emanated from my participation in another encampment at the time: Tahrir Square in Cairo in 2011. Like many other participants I talked to during and after this occupation, I found it difficult to fully put the euphoria and hope associated with this experience into words, and I wanted to better understand why that is (Schumann and Soudias 2013). With Tahrir Square in mind, when I began fieldwork in Athens in 2014, one of the first questions I asked participants of the 2011 Syntagma Square occupation was "What was it like being in Syntagma?" "You cannot understand if you were not there," was one of the more frequent, yet opaque, answers I received. Many interlocutors drew from the arcane and metaphorical for their answers, describing their experience of participating in the 2011 occupation as "magical," not least because of the square's "aura" or "spirit" as the occupation continued. Interlocutors tend to describe their experience in Syntagma as inherently transformative, as one that "changed" them, caused them to "wake up," or made them "politically mature."

What these observations require is engaging with the methodological question of how I can systematically observe and theorize from my interlocutors' self-narrated transformative experiences as to subjectivity in ways that do justice precisely to the quasi-epiphanic quality of transformation. I argue what is required is an abductive analysis (Tavory and Timmermans 2014) of the meaning-making practices of participants of the Syntagma Square occupation. Abduction assumes discovering something new, like an idea, and involves "making an inference from puzzling facts to hypotheses that might well explain them" (Haig 2008, 7). The case for such an approach lies in the fact that it allows a meta-level to be added to my interlocutors' discoveries. Epistemologically, this approach accommodates how my interlocutors make sense of their novel discoveries, precisely because when they narrate transformative, unthought-of experiences that clash with their normative expectations (chapter 2), my interlocutors are essentially describing processes of abductive discovery.

Discovering the constructed nature of previously held doxic assumptions is a key aspect of transformative experience. To discover something already assumes particular epistemological and ontological positions. This is why this book builds on early American pragmatist thought, especially that of Charles S. Peirce, because of its antifoundationalist and anti-essentialist epistemological assumptions. Peirce (1931) stressed "that in order to learn you must desire to learn, and in so desiring not be satisfied with what you already incline to think." The imperative that follows for him then is, "Do not block the road of inquiry." There are, of course, many ways to block this road. But unlike logical positivists, who limit inquiries through their overly aggressive demand for foundations modeled after the hard sciences (de Waal 2013, 105), Peirce and other pragmatists reject the notion that a scientific claim to truth reflects an independent external reality. In this way of thinking, events and objects have no essence, no ultimate or final nature. What pragmatism therefore shares with, for example, constructivism, is the axiomatic: Both are unprovable in their most basic presuppositions. They draw their justifications solely through the stringency of their explanatory power and the rigor of their arguments (Strübing 2008, 37). In this view, the world "out there" can only be reached by experiencing and acting "in" it. For pragmatists, there is no ahistorical, acultural, essential, deterministic, foundational, or transcendent knowledge in the sense that it can "guide us to some heavenly methodological redemption from messes, ambiguities, contingencies, materialities, multiplicities, embodiments, and even contradictions" (Clarke 2005, 18). There is no meaningful "voice from nowhere" (Haraway 1991).

This means that whatever knowledge I produce is situated: temporary, relational, intersectionally positioned, and nonrepresentational (Clarke 2005; Haraway 1991; Thrift 2008). Indeed, the ways in which the story of this book is told, is colored by my very own intersectionally positioned experiences as a white, heterosexual, male who grew up in Germany as a son of Greek immigrants. How my interlocutors view me, and how I view them, the power relations playing out between us in conversations, how I select empirical materials, and how I connect them to theoretical considerations, is very much influenced by my positionality. First, this points to this book's "insider-outsider" perspective (Dwyer and Buckle 2009). Second, this highlights how I too hold doxic assumptions that I cannot always question and contest, and that I too am struggling to fully resist the very logics of neoliberal rationality I critique in my interlocutors' conduct. And third, the situatedness of knowledge takes into account how positionality and experience change over time. Indeed, this book reads, and acts, differently in 2022, at a time when economists predict yet another global recession, than when I began drafting it as a doctoral dissertation in 2017 when Donald Trump became president of the United States, modified it into a book manuscript in 2019 while conservative Kyriakos Mitsotakis took the prime minister's office in Greece from left-wing Alexis Tsipras, and revised it after peer review during a global pandemic in 2021.

In light of these positionings, this book attempts to tell a nonrepresentational story about my interlocutors' experience before, during, and after the Syntagma Square occupation. To do so, I investigated the meaning-making practices of twenty-nine participants of the 2011 Syntagma Square occupation between 2014 and 2018, by way of multiple rounds of semi-structured interviews, informal conversations, ethnographic walks over Syntagma Square, and participant observation of my interlocutors' activities in solidarity initiatives and events. My analysis builds on memo writing and constructivist-grounded theory coding, where I coded interviews and field notes in an initial coding round and a focused coding round (Charmaz 2006), as well as multiple rounds of situational mapping (Clarke 2005) to delineate the relations between codes. Coding was based on words that reflect practices (e.g., "being spontaneous"), rather than concepts (e.g., "spontaneity"). Initial coding served an abductive and exploratory purpose. Focused coding, then, means "using the most significant and/or frequent earlier codes" (Charmaz 2006, 57), to categorize data and route my analytical direction. These codes had a prefigurative function for the structure of the book and its respective chapters. On this basis, following the tenets of abductive analysis, I carved out variation: theorizing from the similarities and differences of practices within, for example, an interview with an interlocutor, over time in light of what they narrate as "before" and "after," and across different situations. Moving back and forth between empirical data and theoretical observations allowed me to familiarize, defamiliarize, and revisit my observations so as to guard against my "favorite" theorizations and facilitate alternative inferences.

I approached most of my interlocutors in my first fieldwork phase in 2014 through snowballing via common friends and acquaintances as well as by approaching participants, speakers, and facilitators at the 2014 Festival of Solidarity and Cooperative Economy in Athens. I kept in touch and followed up with almost all of my interlocutors in the following multi-month fieldwork phases in each year between 2014 and 2018. My interlocutors had been between twenty-two and fifty-eight years old during the 2011 occupation. Although it is difficult to assess, my sense of the socio-economic background of my interlocutors and how they situate themselves is that they broadly belong to the middle class (Wright 1989), or what Ehrenreich and Ehrenreich (2013) have referred to more adequately as the "professional managerial class."[9] All but Kyriaki, Stamatis, and

---

9. Ehrenreich and Ehrenreich suggest the use of the term *professional managerial class* to highlight that the middle strata of workers are subject to capitalism and at the

32   Paradoxes of Emancipation

Aggelos have tertiary education, but owing to the financial crisis, all but three work odd jobs, including freelance architecture, journalism, graphic design, private tutoring, waitressing jobs, gardening, and brochure distribution. The two individuals with relatively stable employment are fifty-six-year-old Kyriaki, a private nursery school teacher, and thirty-two-year-old Zoe, a private school teacher; both have fixed-term contracts of less than a year, which so far have been repeatedly extended.[10] And then there is Vasilis, a fifty-two-year-old journalist who has a permanent position with a large private television station in Greece. The younger interlocutors, such as twenty-five-year-old economics student Petros, thirty-three-year-old unemployed architect Sotiris, or thirty-two-year-old struggling freelance journalist Thodoris, receive financial support from their parents or live with them. All of my interlocutors had been obliged to change their habits toward needs and desires radically as the financial crisis in Greece had made their lives more precarious.

Many of my interlocutors say they had no previous experience of protests—or "the movements," as they call it—often describing themselves as "apolitical" or "inexperienced" prior to the Syntagma Square occupation. Among these are Stamatis, a seasonal waiter in his mid-forties who has become increasingly interested in solidarity economies since his participation in the Syntagma Square occupation. Then there is Maria, a financially struggling freelance graphic designer in her early forties who has a wealthy family background but fell into depression and financial hardship once the crisis hit Greece. After the Syntagma Square occupation, she became active in collective solidarity kitchens and an artists' cooperative. Then there is thirty-nine-year-old Katerina, a business and advertising graduate from a working-class background, who states:

---

same time invested with power to manage and discipline others in society and in the workplace.

10. Kyriaki's and Zoe's work contracts last for one academic year. Over the summer months, they are formally unemployed (as their contracts end and they are let go) and are incentivized to apply for unemployment benefits. With the end of summer, they are formally rehired for another academic year. This practice has become increasingly common among employers in Greece since the financial crisis.

Before Syntagma Square I didn't really go to protests very often, I didn't take part in demonstrations, I wasn't in the movements before. . . . I would say that I was someone who had an interest in issues, but who wasn't involved in parties or politics. (Katerina, personal communication, October 19, 2014)

As I will show in more detail in chapter 5, Katerina is participating in a half dozen solidarity initiatives today.

As opposed to the self-described "apolitical" interlocutors, there are those who have described themselves as having been heavily involved in protests (e.g., the 2006–7 student movement, the 2008 Athens riots) or as having been active in political groups and collectives (including political parties or squats) prior to the Syntagma Square occupation. These include Lukas, an eloquent manager-turned-anarchist with a political science background, in his mid-fifties, who has been part of anarchist collectives since the 1990s. Then there is Sotiris, who says he was politicized in the 2006–7 student movement during the occupation of the Polytechneio—the National and Technical University of Athens. Among the younger interlocutors is Petros, who was seventeen in 2008 when police officers murdered fifteen-year old Alexandros Grigoropoulos. Petros was politicized during the subsequent three-week long riots in Athens, not least because he could relate to the generation of the murdered Alexandros.

It is difficult to give a general account of my interlocutors' politics, as they were very diverse. Thanos and Andreas, for example, sympathized with social democracy (pre–Third Way). Others—such as Kostas, Lukas, and Panagiotis—identified with the anarchist and antiauthoritarian movement in Greece. Thodoris and sixty-two-year-old shopkeeper Marili support the extra-parliamentary parties of the Far Left, such as the Front of the Greek Anti-Capitalist Left (ANTARSYA), and the Coalition of the Radical Left (SYRIZA), prior to its accession to power. Katerina and Maria had even voted for Nea Dimokratia, the Conservative Party, prior to the Syntagma Square occupation. One of the many things I learnt from my interlocutors is how generally frustrated they were over Greek party politics during the Syntagma Square occupation. This shows in how they all say they were unequivocally opposed to what they perceived to be an infiltration of the occupation by SYRIZA members (chapter 4). These accounts date back to 2014, long before SYRIZA's accession to government in 2016.

The intensity with which my interlocutors participated in the Syntagma Square occupation varied in time spent and activity. Some of them, such as Katerina, veteran activist Penelope, environmentalist Viktoria, or Eleftheria—who had been active in the refugee movement long before the 2015 migration crisis—were there from the very beginning and spent (almost) every day in the square. Likewise, Lukas stresses rather emphatically, "I went every day. Almost. I mean, I was absent very few days. I could not [sighs], I could not live without this" (personal communication, February 23, 2016). Half of my interlocutors told me they went to Syntagma Square every day (and night) or almost every day, and many of them were very active in the various groups in the square. Stamatis remarks that "the hard core were 50–100 people" (personal communication, March 2, 2016) who basically participated every day and "ran" the occupation. Others— such as Kyriaki, Thodoris, or Panagiotis—came less frequently. Kyriaki could only come after work. And Panagiotis and Thodoris were, as I will show in chapters 3 and 4, respectively, critical of what they saw as the lack of a political agenda for the Syntagma Square occupation.

Except for Thodoris and Panagiotis, all of my interlocutors were organized—although with varying intensities—in some form of political group or solidarity initiative until my study came to an end in 2018, be it the Alternative Festival of Solidarity and Collaborative Economy, the now-defunct squat at the City Plaza Hotel that had been turned into a collective refugee accommodation, or the social and solidarity economy organization Athens Integral Cooperative (chapter 5). Quiet interestingly, those who were the least politically active in the years that followed the occupation were also those who participated the least in the Syntagma Square occupation.

Some of my interlocutors, such as Vasilis or Aggelos—the latter a former dance-club owner and current co-initiator of an eco-community, in his late forties—preferred the setting of a more formal interview situation. Most of the others favored more casual, informal conversations in cafés or parks. Other than conversations, ethnographic walks over Syntagma Square were a fruitful way of getting a grasp of my interlocutors' experiences in the square. The first walk I did was with Viktoria, who was the second interlocutor I met. We have become friends ever since and she has been a critical reader of my early draft chapters. Now in her early forties, Viktoria studied conflict studies in Belgrade as the Yugoslav Wars began and subsequently moved to the United Kingdom for a postgraduate degree in the same subject. Her experiences of witnessing violent conflict influenced her almost pacifist stance toward the violent episodes in Syntagma Square (chapter 4). I remember my first walk with Viktoria very vividly. She showed me around the square, and shared with me anecdotes that left us both in tears. Ethnographic walking therefore, by way of evoking the imagination, provokes a sensory experience that allows observations to be shaped and revisited.

As a critical study of processes of subject formation against the backdrop of neoliberalization, my research approach needs to be susceptible to the fact that it is structured within and by the social imaginary of capitalism (Castoriadis 1998) Further, my analysis must be aware of "neoliberal ways of thinking, measuring, evaluating, criticizing, judging and knowing" (Davies 2014, 12), so as to minimize their reproduction. As opposed to Marxist approaches that tend to understand neoliberalism as the liberation of capital from political interference, this book's approach views neoliberalism as an epistemological agenda, "a grand integrative narrative" (Mirowski 2011, 7). Neoliberal ways of thinking, building on positivist and utilitarian-inflected sciences in particular, seek to replace critique with technique, and judgment with measurement. In other words, neoliberalism seeks to disenchant (Davies 2014) or deny (Schlaudt 2018) political, social, cultural, etc., spheres through economics. In this sense, neoliberalism demands that everything be treated and evaluated "as if" it were a market situation. In order to do this, and to study the ways in which my interlocutors seek to radically envision alternatives to the status quo, the political aspiration of my research approach draws from a line of reasoning analogous to Philip Abrams's (1988) study of the state. That is, my approach needs to recognize the relative cogency and affective appeal of neoliberal rationalities, and to treat them as a compelling object of analysis as well as an illuminating heuristic device. To do this, however, I must avoid making concessions to the logics of neoliberal rationalities. I leave it to the reader to judge how well I manage to achieve this.

1

Modernizing Greece

From Barbershops to Hair Salons

Months before Greece joined the European Monetary Union in 2001, then–prime minister Costas Simitis turned to the press and announced jubilantly, "We're modernizing, we're becoming European. The barbershops (*Koureia*) will become hair salons (*Kommōtēria*) and the coffee houses (*Kafeneia*) coffee shops (*Kafeteries*)" (quoted in Makridakis 2015). Perhaps Simitis was so elated because his legacy project of modernization (*Eksygchronismos*, which translates as "becoming contemporary") finally gained a foothold as Greece's joining the single European currency was about to be secured. After taking over leadership of the social democratic party Panhellenic Socialist Movement (PASOK) from the widely popular Andreas Papandreou in 1996, Simitis and the party's wing of "modernizers"[1] were on course to transform the country dramatically.

> LUKAS: It was the era of pure lifestyle, glossy magazines, cosmopolitan advice. Like a fast-forward Americanization. Actually an empty life.
>
> DIMITRIS: Why do you say that?
>
> LUKAS: Empty life? Because it was a life without real values. The value was money.
>
> DIMITRIS: And how were you living back then?

---

1. Modernizers were prominent especially within PASOK under Simitis, when they also made their mark in rivaling conservative Nea Demokratia, as their policies converged considerably with those of the conservatives after Simitis took office (Calotychos 2013; Featherstone 2008).

LUKAS: I was a part of it. I was doing okay, more or less. You know. More or less means more with money and less without it [laughing]. . . . I was good in what was asked of me as a middle-management person. But it wasn't me. I was good at it, but it wasn't me. As much as I feel bad about accepting it as a fact, but I was more part of the system than I am now. In a way I was fully integrated. Because I was using the company car to go fishing, for example. And my salary I put into the capitalist circuit. . . . I was still consuming. So I was still in need of a more permanent job. . . . The regular job. What a title. Two bad words in one sentence. . . . And now, even if I wanted to return—which I don't—my age group [early fifties] is an outcast for the productive system. I'm glad! Even if I wanted to, I cannot go back [laughing]. So in a way, the system provides me with a permanent consciousness that I will never go back [laughing]. (Lukas, personal communication, February 6, 2017)

In many of the conversations with my interlocutors about their experiences during the period of modernization, there was a strange narrative rhythm between belittling their former selves—reminiscent of how adults talk about the naïveté of adolescence (but without the rebellion)—and disparaging the societal everyday as "empty," "without spirit," or even "rotten." Certainly, the Syntagma Square occupation was transformative for my interlocutors, and comparing most things against this ineffable experience appears destined to be overshadowed. But considering that, materially at least, all of my interlocutors were much better off in their previous lives than they are in today's seemingly permanent state of crisis in Greece, some puzzling questions arise: What was it about that "era" before the occupation that made it so utterly undesirable as an experience? Why do my interlocutors seem so very comfortable with self-distancing, even disidentifying ("I wasn't myself") from their former selves during that period? And what does this tell us about experience and subjectivation?

This chapter is about how my interlocutors perceive themselves to have been before they took part in the Syntagma Square occupation. This is because, as Thodoris points out:

You have these major events in recent Greek history—and Syntagma is one of those—but there is a continuity. You know, you can't talk about Syntagma without talking about what happened before. Before and after. (Thodoris, personal communication, October 17, 2014)

These questions lead to the period of "modernization" in Greece—a large-scale reform agenda initiated in 1996 by the social democratic prime minister Costas Simitis, which substantially reshaped the structural relations between the individual, the market, and the state. As both Giorgio Agamben (1998) and Michel Foucault (2008) have argued in different ways, the state in modernity is constituted and reproduced through the inclusion of its subjects into the mechanisms and calculations of power. This chapter claims, then, that the agenda of modernization is best viewed as neoliberalization, signifying an attempt of introducing a neoliberal governmental rationality, or "governmentality," onto the Greek state. By "acting at a distance" (Rose 1999), modernization seeks to neoliberalize the state. What this implies will be discussed in much detail throughout this chapter. For now, neoliberalization means that market-based principles and techniques of evaluation are raised to the level of state-endorsed norms (Davies 2013, 37). This involves the transformation of subjectivities. In a nutshell, neoliberal modernization seeks to create quasi-market conditions that devolve risk onto individuals (Ferguson and Gupta 2002, 989) in order to nudge them toward a more individualist, self-responsible, consumerist, and competitive subjectivity. This is because from the viewpoint of neoliberal thought, as Pierre Dardot and Christian Laval (2017, 107) observe, it is not "by 'nature'" that people know how to conduct themselves, but rather "it is thanks to the market, which constitutes a process of education. It is by invariably placing individuals in a market situation that they will be able to learn to behave rationally." In this sense, privatization and, say, labor market flexibilization, are not forms of deregulation as much as they signify a reordering of norms governing economic activities, social relations, and the self. In order to inquire into the ways in which modernization affected my interlocutors' lives and their embeddedness in more structural settings prior to taking part in the Syntagma Square occupation, references to

40   Paradoxes of Emancipation

"the Simitis period," "modernization," or "before Syntagma" serve as key empirical hints in their narrative accounts.

> Modernization, as a vision, was a new card. "Let's become different, let's become European"—very important. And now this is being played. It is being played very harshly. It's not just modernization . . . that we are Europeans and that we are Europeans at any cost that may have, is being played right now. (Panagiotis, personal communication, October 6, 2014)

It is important to point out that when interlocutors narrate how they perceive themselves to have been before the Syntagma Square occupation, this tells us a lot more about how they view themselves in the moment of speaking than about how things "really" were "back then." Instead, as Joan Scott (1991, 779–80) remarks:

> We need to attend to the historical processes that, through discourse, position subjects and produce their experiences. It is not individuals who have experience, but subjects who are constituted through experience. Experience in this definition then becomes not the origin of our explanation, not the authoritative (because seen or felt) evidence that grounds what is known, but rather that which we seek to explain, that about which knowledge is produced.

This means that experience is not hardwired, but rather constituted in conversation and resignified as the subject moves through time and space. As anthropologist Viktor Turner (1986, 36) remarks, it "is structurally unimportant whether the past is 'real' or 'mythical,' 'moral' or 'amoral.'" Rather, the point is whether meaningful guidelines emerge as subjectivity in its demarcation from that perceived past.

To investigate my claims, this chapter is divided into two parts. The first reflects on the structuring capacities of neoliberal modernization by shedding light on how it serves the purpose of introducing a new type of governmentality onto the Greek state. In this vein, it will also look at the epistemological precepts upon which neoliberal modernization rests. The second part delves into how my interlocutors claim they experienced the modernization period. On the one hand, this points to the ways in which measures of privatization and deregulation created conditions of uncertainty that were conducive to the formation of individualizing subjectivities. On the other hand, my interlocutors' accounts about the period of modernization point to how, today, they demarcate themselves from this subject position.

Modernization and Competitiveness

While PASOK never made the exact contents of the modernization project explicit (Ioannides 2012, 49), what was clear from the outset was that modernization signified neoliberal modernization: an agenda of large-scale economic and social reforms seeking to qualify Greece for the third stage of the European Monetary Union. This, PASOK hoped, would establish a more orderly, open, and integrated capitalism that would place the country at the core of the European Union by increasing national competitiveness. The reform mix of privatization, deregulation, and (to a lesser extent) fiscal discipline suggests that the main political-economic problem in Greece was inflation rather than unemployment. It assumes that the state has a tendency to strangle private initiative, and that the welfare state weakens the incentives influencing workers in the labor market. Modernization has often been viewed as a combination of neoliberal policies with institutional and educational initiatives aimed at providing a social side to economic neoliberalization (see Featherstone and Papadimitriou 2008). In fact, it much more accurately can be said to have represented the state's near abandonment of its welfare functions (Douzinas 2013, 35). While Greece under Andreas Papandreou had taken a more social-democratic direction in the 1980s, Simitis's shift in the direction of neoliberalism came much later than it did elsewhere in Europe, as Lukas remarks:

> It was the change of eras through the same dinosaur [referring to PASOK] . . . which actually was not only a dinosaur. It was also a

42   Paradoxes of Emancipation

chameleon.[2] Let's say it was like [Tony] Blair [referring to Third Way politics], with the common, let's say, "delay" with which things happen in the Balkans. (Lukas, personal communication, February 6, 2017)

With this self-orientalizing "delay," which Lukas reproduces in his account, and with prior reform attempts having been short-lived,[3] Simitis stressed the urgent need for modernization.

Meanwhile, in EU circles, there was likewise a sense of imminent change. From 1990 onward, social democracy was undergoing a redefinition in the wake of the collapse of authoritarian communism in Europe, the diminishing relevance of Keynesianism, and an increasing convergence of left-wing parties with conservative positions through Third Way politics (Gamble and Wright 1999). Influenced by the creeping rise of the Chicago School of Economics and Law, New Public Management, Virginia School Public Choice, and the "national competitiveness" paradigm in Europe, political leaders were persuaded to increasingly view politics through the lens of (neoclassical) economics. States were to behave "as if" they were market actors, "like a big corporation competing in the global marketplace," as President Bill Clinton said at the time (quoted in Krugman 1994, 29). Competitiveness ascended to become the key paradigm for measuring a nation's success, fusing the entrepreneurial, strategic decision-making of business leaders with the executive decision-making of political leaders. Through what I call the "logic of numbers,"[4] a nation's competitiveness is perpetually evaluated and compared in so-called competitiveness rankings, by aggregating complex social relations into a single figure that is checked not only against competitors but also against an idealized

---

2. Lukas's sentiment very much resonates with Tsakalotos's (2008, 25) assessment that PASOK "replaced a third-worldist populism, in which everything from abroad was suspect, with a third-worldist modernization, in which nothing rooted in society is worth building on."

3. Laskos and Tsakalotos (2013a, 22) speak of two "incomplete attempts" at neoliberal modernization under PASOK in the period 1985–87 and under Konstantinos Mitsotakis's New Democracy government in 1991–93.

4. Also of interest in this regard is Schlaudt's (2018) conception of "political numbers."

benchmark constructed by competitiveness experts. If one is to believe competitiveness experts such as Michael Porter or Stéphane Garelli (and judging by the authority attributed to their views, it seems many leaders do), nation-states faced a common existential fate, "which is to define the communities they lead against a presupposed backdrop of ever increasing global competition" (Davies 2014, 129). Such a fear-driven view of an uncertain world is what William Davies termed the "violent threat." So with a sense of urgency, and as a result of the launch of the European Single Market, a number of policy commissions were established by the European Commission in 1990 to gauge what it would take to improve competitiveness. In times of "several macro-economic uncertainties . . . competition is becoming ever more global and more intense both on the world and on the Community markets . . . competitiveness in the Community will increasingly be determined by the ability to confront major global challenges, in particular competition from major world partners" (European Commission 1990, 1–3). The rather palpable Schmittian view in which the European Commission frames the world, and the language it chooses to use—uncertainty, competitiveness, and markets—shows how deeply engrained neoliberal principles have become in policymaking.

This short excursus into the European Union's rationalities is important for understanding the context in which modernization in Greece is embedded. Because, as Panagiotis hinted at earlier and as Kevin Featherstone and Dimitris Papadimitriou (2008, 14) point out, modernization has "little meaning without reference to the need to adapt to the EU." In that sense, modernization refers to a deepening interdependence with the European Union and a greater internalization of its (policy) norms, which, as indicated earlier, were increasingly centered on competitiveness.[5] In a nutshell, competitiveness is to be improved by shifting away from state regulation, relatively high levels of taxation, and welfare provision. John

---

5. In 1993 former EC president Jacques Delors made the pursuit of this objective public in a council meeting by stating that growth and unemployment could only be managed by increasing the European Communities' competitiveness (European Council 1993).

44   Paradoxes of Emancipation

Koliopoulos and Thanos Veremis (2010), as "modernizing intellectuals" (Roudometof 2012, 244), summarize rather favorably in this regard:

> Once in the much coveted eurozone, Greece would no longer be able to export her troubles by devaluing the currency (she would no longer have one). She would not be able to raise her deficit at will to pay herself money that she had not earned. What she would have to do would be to keep improving the real economy by cutting labor costs, freeing the labor market of its shackles, limiting the role of the state, and increasing the competitiveness and wealth-creation ability of the private sector. It would not just be low inflation that Greeks would have to get used to. It was also a new economic environment in which success would come with a price tag that read: determination, risk taking, perseverance, self-discipline, and consistency. (Koliopoulos and Veremis 2010, 194)

The modernizers' endgame is to impose such conditions on Greece for the sake of competitiveness. To achieve this, modernizers draw on the usual suspects of the universalist neoliberal playbook: privatization of state assets, labor market "liberalization," financial deregulation, pension cuts, and the "rationalization" of the administration.

Indeed, as the reforms were materializing, Greece was doing better—statistically speaking. If one is to accept the metrics set by neoclassical economics, the Simitis years and those that followed were a success story of "catching up." After having been "the most divergent" (Featherstone and Papadimitriou 2008, 14) from the Maastricht convergence criteria in the 1990s, Greece became a model student of neoliberal reform, with growth consistently above the EU average from 1995 to 2008 (Laskos and Tsakolotos 2013b, 38). Greek GDP per capita converged (more or less) with that of the European Union as a whole, and the country's rating on the United Nations' Human Development Index was on the rise from 1990 onward (United Nations Development Programme 2022).

In 2004, "with the Olympics, this whole thing peaked," Thodoris observed with hindsight (personal communication, August 28, 2016). For modernizers, the Olympics were an opportunity to show the world how far Greece had come by reinventing and rebranding the country's capital. Strategies of "selective investment" were to turn Athens into a competitive and entrepreneurial city (Souliotis et al. 2014) of the likes of London or Paris. Massive infrastructure developments, ever larger shopping malls, remodeled museums, iconic buildings by celebrity architects, urban condos, fancy cafés, business-incubator projects, and galleries for "the creatives"—all were to market Athens as "a world-class destination" by fetishizing its antiquity in more modern terms (Chatzidakis 2014, 33). For Koliopoulos and Veremis (2010, 162), Greece's success story appears to be one of emancipation.

> As it moved up in the world, modern Greece has been mostly governed by western-oriented elites that drew their inspiration more from the values of the Enlightenment, emphasizing individual effort and favoring the competitiveness inherent in the function of free markets and less from the notion of a paternalistic state extending protection over those feeling "non-privileged" and resenting it.

In this narrative, the efforts of Simitis and his modernizers were a much-needed attempt to free Greece from the shackles of its "traditional" "underdog culture" (Diamandouros 1994), which was marked by clientelism in politics, inward-looking development, and an overblown, inefficient state. But modernization was far from consensual (Stathakis 2001). Teachers' union strikes lasting weeks, in response to worsening work conditions, student rallies and university occupations against (failed) attempts to privatize parts of Greek higher education (the privatization of education was prohibited under the 1975 Constitution), and widely observed general strikes against pension cuts and an increase to the total working age were a few prominent examples of how the agenda was anything but a smooth process.[6] Nonetheless, all these developments provide a glimpse

---

6. It is beyond the scope of this book to cover the full range of resistance acts against neoliberal modernization, but it is appropriate to mention that some of my interlocutors had been involved in resistance. Stamatis, Sotiris, and Thodoris, for example, were closely involved in the student movement of 2005–6 against the privatization of universities. Andreas was engaged in the environmental movement from 2004, and participated in the protests against the government's handling of the massive forest fires of 2007. And Lukas had been flirting with anarchist ideas and protests since the 1990s. All of them took

46   Paradoxes of Emancipation

of what modernizing and "becoming European" came to signify from the 1990s onward.

Several years into the sovereign, financial, and social crisis in Greece, Simitis's words leave but a bitter aftertaste for many people. "We wanted to become Europeans," Petros told me with a strange mix of righteousness and sober disillusionment, "and now we are paying the price" (personal communication, March 2, 2016).[7] After relative gains in the late 1990s (World Economic Forum 2000), Greece made heavy losses in national competitiveness rankings year after year, sliding from thirty-sixth place in 2000 to sixty-seventh place in 2008 (Petrakis 2012, 53). This was part of a more general trend in which the northern European countries climbed up the ranks, with ever increasing competitiveness, while the peripheral countries of the European south were being outpaced. When the global financial crisis of 2008 led to worldwide recession, the Greek economy started to falter. By that time, Simitis had been succeeded as prime minister by Kostas Karamanlis, leader of the rival New Democracy conservatives. When Karamanlis decided to bail out the collapsing Greek banks, public debt started to rise dramatically. The flow of cheap credit stopped abruptly, and Greece's GDP shrank by almost 3 percent in 2009 as unemployment rose to almost 9 percent. As we now know, the deficit figures were rigged: Simitis and then-governor of the Bank of Greece Lukas Papademos (who would become a technocrat-caretaker prime minister in 2011) oversaw the payment of a fee of $300 million to Goldman Sachs for shifting billions of euros of debt off the public accounts. Revised Eurostat figures would show a 2009 deficit of 15.4 percent of GDP, and public debt at 127 percent of GDP (Kouvelakis 2011, 21–22). Facing strikes and

---

part in the 2008 riots in protest at the murder of fifteen-year-old Alexandros Grigoropoulos by a police officer.

7. I heard variations of this self-orientalizing phrase from many of my interlocutors. Peculiarly, for my interlocutors today, Simitis's agenda induces what Sadiq Jalal al-'Azm (1981) referred to as "orientalism in reverse." By building on Edward Said's seminal work on Orientalism, al-'Azm theorizes how the Orientalized accept the Orientalist view that they are essentially different from "the West," but then turn this into an argument for cultural protectionism, involving resisting "foreign" influence.

a wave of riots after a police officer murdered fifteen-year-old Alexandros Grigoropoulos in Athens in December 2008, Karamanlis fought shy of imposing the austerity program that European leaders were now impatiently demanding. It was his successor, Georgios Papandreou of PASOK (son of former prime minister Andreas), who put the country under "the measures," as they are infamously known in Greece, legitimizing the implementation of the International Monetary Fund–European Union–European Central Bank program via a fear-driven narrative of "There Is No Alternative": either avoid default or face complete economic disaster (Souliotis 2013). In effect, these measures are a more extreme version of the modernization agenda: even stricter privatization and deregulation of the economy (especially labor), severe cuts in public expenditure (especially in the welfare sector), and disproportionate tax hikes, all of which signify a state of "permanent austerity" (Laskos and Tsakalotos 2013b). For adherents of the modernization project, the crisis was proof that Simitis's reforms had not gone far enough. Spelling out what many in the modernizers' camp must have thought, one prominent observer brought the culturalist agenda of modernization to the fore. In this view, the crisis is essentially one of "behaviors, values, attitudes, perceptions," attributed to the "eastern culture of conduct," only to be overcome by the desperate need to fix "behavioral deficits" (Ioakimidis 2011). In this narrative, it was Greece's underdog culture that once again obstructed the country in its aspiration to ascend into the ranks of Western nations.

Modernization as Culturalism

The temptation to blame failures in processes of modernization on cultural and behavioral traits is an integral part of the underlying epistemological presumptions of "modernizing," or of "becoming contemporary." This is because the notion of adopting standardized precepts that are universally "good" for a capitalist understanding of development is inherent to modernization theory (Lerner 1958; McClelland 1961; Rostow 1990; for Greece, see McNeill 1968). In its crudest form, this strand of literature assumes a positivist, universal, and unilinear process of transition from traditional to modern societies (much like in the Weberian distinction).

The latter are, by definition, predominantly the advanced industrialized countries of Western Europe and North America. Only by assimilating to the "superior" moral and organizational principles of their Western counterparts can traditional societies ascend into their ranks. In this sense, modernization theorists are concerned with analyzing and getting rid of the obstacles to arriving at the Western ideal. It is exactly on this basis that they have argued that economic development goes hand in hand with cultural changes, and particularly with the adoption of individualist values (Inglehart and Baker 2000). The heyday of modernization theory was in the mid-twentieth century; there are numerous postcolonial critiques that, by way of postmodern and constructivist arguments, convincingly and rigorously demolished many of its precepts (Bhabha 2004; Lockman 2010; Mitchell 2002; Said 2003). Yet its epistemological and metaphysical presumptions have survived these critiques: they are creating material realities today. And my interlocutors, too, reproduce the self-orientalizing notions of modernization theory in their narratives.

In Greece, "one could go so far as to say that [modernization] has become the dominant ideology from more or less the beginning of the republic in the first half of the nineteenth century" (Laskos and Tsakalotos 2013a, 13). Simitis's take on modernization indicates how this paradigm is far from archaic. In his own words, "Participation in the [EU] integration process was the strongest lever for our exit from a reality of developmental deficits and social *backwardness*" (quoted in Featherstone 2008, 177; emphasis added). For students of Orientalism, talk of "backwardness" in particular is one of the more obvious markers of essentialization (Lockman 2010, 135), while "developmental deficits" only acquires meaning in relation to a (European) ideal. Euclid Tsakalotos (2008, 25) points out that modernization was about "importing techniques, policies and institutions from the more advanced capitalist societies. History, and the particular characteristics of a society, play little role in such a conceptualization, representing merely the 'old.'" Costas Douzinas (2013, 35) on the other hand, argues that the promoters of modernization were "liberal academics and technocrats, educated in the West, with strong links in Brussels and Washington." In a self-orientalizing fashion, he claims that they "despised the 'oriental' and 'religious' aspects of Greek culture."

Discourses in Greek academia only perpetuated such views, even if academics were fully aware of their underlying Eurocentric presumptions (see Mouzelis 1996). At the heart of the modernization discussion from the late 1970s onward is political scientist Nikiforos Diamandouros's influential work on Greece's "cultural dualism." Influenced by the modernization zeitgeist, he presumed a polarity in Greece between a modern liberal culture (influenced by Greek antiquity) and a more "static" Byzantine-Ottoman culture. Here, the former is a culture of "distinct preference for reform . . . rationalisation of state and societal structures along liberal, democratic, and capitalist lines, and respect for the rule of law" (Diamandouros 2012, 14). On the other hand, there is "a powerful underdog culture," made up of the "extensive, traditional, more introverted, and least competitive strata and sectors of Greek society." This culture is marked by, among other things, "low productivity, low competitiveness . . . the aversion to reform" (20–21). As Anastassios Anastassiadis critically remarks, Diamandouros essentially argues that "when the culture of Antiquity prevails, modernization progresses; conversely, when the Byzantine-Ottoman culture gains the upper hand, modernization fails. Imposed on Greek political history, this framework identifies "modernizing heroes" who introduce the Greeks to Western enlightenment, only to be resisted and defeated by the obscurantist forces of the 'orientalizing' masses" (quoted in Delalande 2012). In such a narrative, the dominated, exploited, and marginalized groups are the "object of study, but never the subject of change" (Tsakalotos 2008, 10). Roughly speaking, Diamandouros was to Simitis what Anthony Giddens was to Tony Blair, in that he contributed to endowing Simitis's agenda with political authority by legitimating the virtues of modern rationality (in a classically Weberian sense).[8] It was an attempt to garner support for modernization in an effort to create the conditions of uncertainty which would ultimately, it was implied, make those "least competitive strata" more productive and competitive.

---

8. Diamandouros has been acknowledged as being in the camp of modernizers (Calotychos 2013, 18) and he recognized Simitis's importance for introducing reforms long before his election as prime minister (Diamandouros 1994, 51). Diamandouros later even served as the country's first ombudsman in the Simitis administration.

50 Paradoxes of Emancipation

The polity upon which and through which any reforms were to be implemented was the Greek state. Skeptical of collective actors who might be capable of blocking what he perceived to be much-needed structural reforms, Simitis had sought to put an end to clientelist politics by "getting things in order" through "restoring meritocracy" and technocratic rationalization (quoted in Ioannides 2012, 49). Certainly, practices of inflated pay rolls in the public sector, turning a blind eye to tax evasion, and the privileged treatment of certain clienteles were just a few symptoms of a malaise at the level of the state that needed to be tackled.[9] Yet the ways in which modernizers sought to frame the need for reform was by orientalizing Greek state-institutional arrangements. Sociologist Nicos Mouzelis, for example, seeks to define a modern worldview in stark contrast to the traditional state. He does so by bemoaning the state's "grotesque size" and describing it as a "persistently patrimonial" entity "controlled by clientelistic parties" that is "unable to react intelligently to a rapidly changing international environment" (Mouzelis 1996, 222). Ironically, however, this critique was never about the state's actualities of domination of subordination (chapter 4). Instead, this narrative seeks to construct opposition to modernization as inferior. Opponents are viewed as inherently populist due to the ways in which they block reforms, or they are ridiculed outright. For Diamandouros (1994, 20), viewing the state as the "protector of the weak" is a "view of modernization common among late developing societies, which reflects this culture's ambivalence towards the liberal, Western model of socioeconomic change and which historically manifests itself in the willingness to search for, and experiment with, 'alternative' routes to modernity." As I will show in more detail in the next chapter, the fact that the very search for alternatives is viewed negatively indicates modernizers' unrelenting approach to any critique of their project. However, by failing to take into account the anxieties and fears of those who were opposing modernization and searching for alternatives, the critique of populism

---

9. Laskos and Tsakalotos (2013a, 24) remark that Greece's clientelist system was one "that was as inefficient as it was unjust, but one that had traditionally contributed to keeping a lid on social pressures: directly by vertically integrating sections of society, and indirectly by undercutting horizontal and class organizations which could challenge the power of elites."

that PASOK modernizers so often imposed became simultaneously a critique of solidarity and equality, all in the name of meritocracy and competitiveness. This critique is grounded in a view of the state that implies it must, in modernizing, acquire those Western-oriented "higher" functions of reason that are necessary to exercise "control and regulation against the irrationality, passions, and uncontrollable appetites of the lower regions of society" (Ferguson and Gupta 2002, 982), or else perish in light of global threats. In short, for Greece to be modern—to be productive and competitive—"the overpoliticized . . . orientations of the Greek state" (Mouzelis 1996, 222) needed to be reformed toward EU norms. The state has to be transformed and needs to pass responsibility to the individual. In this sense, "it is no longer capital that is to be molded into the (territorially integrated) geography of state space, but state space that is to be molded into the (territorially differentiated) geography of capital" (Brenner 2004, 16).

Modernization as Neoliberalism

The values, norms, and beliefs around which the rationality of the modernization project was to transform and restructure state and society were neoliberal in "spirit."[10] Neoliberalism, in short, seeks to establish that market-based principles and techniques of evaluation are raised to the level of state-endorsed norms (Davies 2013, 37). This involves the transformation of subjectivities through changes in relationships among individuals, the market, and the state, the precise definitions of which are themselves topics of considerable controversy and debate (Davies 2014; Peck 2010a; Polanyi 2001). In that sense, neoliberalism is an ideological project with totalizing aspirations. But it is also a process with limitations—often set by its own (hermeneutic) contradictions and what Mirowski (2014) dubs "double truths"—rather than a *fait accompli*[11] (Kingfisher and Maskovsky

---

10. Neoliberal "spirit" refers to William Davies's (2014, 60) usage. Building on Max Weber's *Spirit of Capitalism*, it is understood as a set of ethical motivations—a "philosophical idea that justifies practical engagement on a moral and psychological level."

11. In this regard, economic geographer Jamie Peck (2010a, 41–42) acknowledges that the "essence of neoliberalism was not extracted, like pure mountain spring water, by Hayek and his fellow pilgrims at Mont Pèlerin, only later to be blended, cut, and adulterated

52   Paradoxes of Emancipation

2008, 115). Neoliberalism is not, as is often assumed, something that evolved "spontaneously" over time and is everybody's fault (hence no one's fault). Such a narrative only contributes to neoliberalism's claim to a natural, ontological givenness of its own rationalities. Instead, as modernization shows, neoliberalism is an inherently constructivist endeavor (Brown 2005, 40–44), guided by an ideologically driven, more or less systematic effort by identifiable actors to restructure not only the economy but also the state and social relations in more market-friendly terms—as if they were in a market situation (Brown 2015; Dardot and Laval 2017; Davies 2014; Harvey 2007; Mirowski 2014; Mirowski and Plehwe 2009; Peck 2010a). If the role of the state under the ordoliberal political-economic orders of Keynesian and Fordist capitalism was to supervise the rules of competition, the neoliberal principles of modernization seek to elevate economic efficiency and competition to the level of state norm.

Competition, then, lies at the core of neoliberalism. Early neoliberal thinkers such as Friedrich Hayek (2005), and later on Milton Friedman (1982), were suspicious of any sort of state planning, as they feared it would only increase the risk that totalitarian regimes the likes of Nazi Germany or Stalin's Soviet Union might reemerge. For Hayek in particular, competition as an inherent function of the market was certain to prevent state planning due to the uncertainty of its outcome.[12] Therefore, competition is to be employed as a formal principle of the state in order to reconstitute social and political institutions. As Foucault remarks (2008, 147), the "society regulated by reference to the market that the neo-liberals are thinking about is a society in which the regulatory principle should not be so much the exchange of commodities as the mechanisms of competition." For Hayek and other Austrian neoliberals, competition was regarded as a process of discovering relevant information "on the part of the subject, who

---

by less-principled governmental distributions; it was a volatile cocktail from the beginning. . . . It did not rest on a set of immutable laws, but a matrix of overlapping convictions, orientations, and aversions, draped in the unifying rhetoric of market liberalism."

12. Neoliberals regard "competition as superior not only because in most circumstances it is the most efficient method known but because it is the only method which does not require the coercive or arbitrary intervention of authority" (Hayek 2005, 45).

seeks to outstrip and precede others in discovering new opportunities for profit" (Dardot and Laval 2017, 103). Neoliberalism therefore radicalizes a number of ideas about classical liberal subjectivities (the desire to improve one's lot, to do better than others) and recenters them on competition in terms of antagonism and rivalry. Contrary to classical liberalism, neoliberalism admits that competition will not occur naturally. As I will show in the second part of this chapter, the triumph of neoliberalism comes about as the conditions for its success are constructed in concerted effort.[13]

The genius of neoliberal thought lies in its conceiving of competition in an almost symbiotic relationship with uncertainty. Uncertainty is the effect of competition as well as the very condition for individuals to assume competition in that it imposes upon them stress and precarity. So, the various components of labor market reform, privatization, financial deregulation, and so on that make up Simitis's modernization need to be seen in this relationality. Neoliberals have cherished this "competitive uncertainty," as Will Davies (2014) dubs it, because they claim to have the tools and measures necessary to render it periodically empirical, intelligible and manageable. For neoliberals such as Gary Becker (1962), "investing" in one's "human capital" lies at the core of managing uncertainty. To navigate through uncertainty, individuals must be molded (subjectification) into self-regulating (subjectivation), "flexible" subjects with "a large degree of resilience" to "manage themselves in uncertainty" (Garelli 2006, 235).

If politics is the pursuit of certainty via planning, neoliberalism can broadly be viewed as the *"pursuit of the disenchantment of politics by economics"* (Davies 2014, 4). This disenchantment has concrete ontological and epistemological consequences for questions pertaining to "the political." By disenchanting politics through economics, neoliberalism reduces

---

13. "To create conditions in which competition will be as effective as possible . . . these tasks provide a wide and unquestioned field for state activity. . . . Planning and competition can be combined only by planning for competition, not by planning against competition" (Hayek 2005, 46). In this regard, Foucault (2008, 279) remarks, "For there to be certainty of collective benefit . . . it is absolutely necessary that each actor be blind with regard to its totality. Everyone must be uncertain with regard to the collective outcome if this positive collective outcome is really to be expected. Being in the dark and blindness of all the economic agents is absolutely necessary."

political metaphysics to political physics. In effect, and this will be shown in more detail in chapter 4, what this does is to empty out the ethical and performative components of politics to the point where they are depoliticized: politics is rendered merely technical and administrative (Hui 2011, 12), as modernization is presented as an ethically and politically "neutral" project (Tsakalotos 2008). In a rather Benthamite fashion, only the positive, measurable, and empirical has value. Anything that is "tacit, invisible or deontological" is considered to be a form of "metaphysical nonsense" (Davies 2014, 83). Neoliberalism is therefore inevitably a positivist endeavor.[14]

As an economized rationality that no longer values the metaphysical, neoliberalism requires its own mode of enquiry. Positivist science—especially neoclassical and behavioral economics, neurosciences, and cognitive behavioral and positive psychology—offer just that, furnishing neoliberal discourses through "solid academic backing" (Dardot and Laval 2017, 102). As argued earlier, the logic of numbers—that is, the quantification of social relations to aggregate metrics—allows critique and judgment to be replaced by technique and measurement. The most complex social, political, economic, and even cultural relations can be represented in a single figure. In this regard, competitiveness evaluations include plenty of "noneconomic" data in their assessment of a nation's overall competitiveness. This simplification allows these figures to be rendered competitive, as complex relations can now be compared and ranked. Even moral values, such as "work ethic," are evaluated in how they contribute to competitiveness (see Levinson and Peng 2007). The GDP, the United Nation's Human Development Index, and privately owned (and often even patented) methodologies of measuring "national competitiveness"[15] by such

14. This is case in point for why I claim in chapter 6, that any critique of neoliberalism must be anti-positivist in its ontological layout so as to minimize the reproduction of neoliberalism.

15. For Greece, Konsolas's doctoral dissertation (1999) offers an illustrative example of how analyses of competitiveness are performed, using Michael Porter's patented "Diamond Framework." Here, four sets of determinants (factor conditions, demand conditions, related and supporting industries, and firm strategy, structure, and rivalry) are conceived and applied in order to evaluate how they "promote or hinder the creation and sustainability of competitive advantage for industries within a nation" (15).

organizations as the World Economic Forum, the International Institute for Management Development, or the Organisation for Economic Cooperation and Development are but a few examples. In effect, the reach of neoclassical economics in particular stretched far beyond its primary domain of individual choice in markets and became pivotal to the (un-) critical audit of public authorities, bureaucracy, and decision-making (Foucault 2008, 246f.).[16] In a world characterized by competition and uncertainty, the logic of numbers has its own authority, aesthetics, and affective appeal (Porter 1995). Acts of formalistic simplification[17] are a route out of the "hermeneutic pluralism and associated dangers of politics" (Davies 2014, 3). They constrain ambiguity and reduce uncertainty, but only for the purpose of bracing actors to resume competition and face further uncertainty. Yet what they also constrain, and it is no coincidence—as I will show in chapter 2 in particular—is the creative and imaginative capacity of politics. Numbers depoliticize.[18]

Having gained a reputation for being a technocrat, and having been nicknamed "The Accountant," Simitis's managerial leadership style was

16. Foucault (2008, 246) remarks, "The economic grid will or should make it possible to test governmental action, gauge its validity, and to object to activities of the public authorities on the grounds of their abuses, excesses, futility, and wasteful expenditure . . . It involves scrutinizing every action of the public authorities in terms of . . . efficiency with regard to the particular elements of this game, and in terms of the cost of intervention by public authorities in the field of the market. In short, it involves criticism of the governmentality actually exercised."

17. A prime example for such simplification is the work of renowned competitiveness scholar Michael Porter (1998) on "competitive advantage." Treating competitiveness and profitability (like that of a firm) as key to decision-making, Porter successfully managed to provide templates to political leaders through which they were to develop quasi-business strategies for nations, regions or cities. In this respect, Davies (2014) remarks that unlike neoclassical economics, which rests on presumptions as to individual rational choice, business strategy lacks any generally agreed-on methodology. Porter therefore, like many others in his field, was left to his own devices to construct a methodology through which he could measure "competitive advantage" (which he too constructed). That is how neoliberalism's positivism is socially constructed.

18. In this sense, it is worth considering whether neoliberalism disenchants politics (by economics), or denies it altogether (Schlaudt 2018).

56 Paradoxes of Emancipation

paradigmatic of this depoliticization by way of disenchanting politics through economics. Modernization signifies an uncritical and unimaginative implementation and administration of neoliberal principles, more so than politics, which can be disputed, creative, and imaginative. This corresponds to a Weberian view of modernity in which the world is disenchanted (*entzaubert*) by positivist science and bureaucratic systems, where qualities are reduced to quantities, and the likelihood of outcomes can be modeled and calculated in a causalistic way (Carroll 1999). The fact that Simitis's modernization tried to rationalize public policy and administration through the adoption of New Public Management[19] techniques and instruments with an increased involvement of "experts" (Ladi 2005) is testimony to this. Similarly, Seraphim Seferiades (2003, 189) observes how the implementation of the European Employment Strategy in Greece was one that tended to "'depoliticize' the issue of employment, fashioning its discourse in an apparently technical language." In even crasser terms, Christos Laskos and Euclid Tsakalotos (2013a, 23) point out that modernization "did not incorporate any vision, let alone intervention . . . the details of, say, monetary union, or European employment policy, were merely seen as the way that 'proper' economies sought to modernize and integrate." This indicates not only the neoliberal character of Simitis's project but also its firm situatedness in the universalist presumptions of modernization theory more generally.

In summary, neoliberal modernization is not just a bundle of economic policies toward some type of "market extremism" (see Trouillot 2003). Neither is it Victorian laissez-faire[20] (see Foucault 2008, 132). Instead of

---

19. New Public Management (NPM) basically reinvents the public sector along private sector managerial lines with a claim to universality and political neutrality. NPM's core principles include the slowing-down or reversal of public spending and shifts toward privatization, public-private partnerships (PPP), and organizing public sector agencies as if they were private enterprises (Hood 1991).

20. "It is important not to confuse opposition against the latter kind of planning with a dogmatic laissez-faire attitude. The liberal argument does not advocate leaving things just as they are; it favours making the best possible use of the forces of competition as a means of coordinating human efforts" (Hayek 2005, 45).

extending the reach of the market, neoliberalism is more about how social relations are remade in the name of the market (Bruff and Starnes 2019). Neoliberalism attempts to take measures (such as competitiveness rankings) and principles (such as uncertainty and competition) from the market in order to perform judgments (about competitiveness and efficiency) across social and political spheres (including the state itself), treating them as if they were markets. It does so by creating a distinctive governmental rationality as a necessary condition.

Modernization as Governmentality

To get to this point, for neoliberalism to exist at all, a "rationality of government" (Gordon 1987, 1991), or "governmentality"[21] in accordance with neoliberal principles needs to be introduced through "permanent vigilance, activity, and intervention," as Foucault so presciently pointed out (Foucault 2008, 132). Here, government is conceived of as a form of conduct in which rulers aim to regulate subjects, in a more or less calculated way, according to particular norms and conventions. For Foucault, "to govern is to structure the potential field of action for others" (quoted in Dardot and Laval 2017, 169). He includes the potentiality of human action as intrinsic to government's approach to disciplining subjects. Rationality refers to the fact that government obtains and bases its legitimacy on the absence of arbitrariness, as is common in despotism (Schlaudt 2018, 167). In synthesis, then, the rationality of government is the "conduct of conduct," the conditions of the forms of thought guiding conduct (Dean 1994, 25).

21. Mitchell Dean (1994) claims Foucault's neologism may also stand for "mentality of government." I see analytical value in both and therefore suggest using them depending on the analytical focus. Rationality is analytically fruitful if rationality refers to governing through the absence of arbitrariness in a classically Weberian sense, guided by the aspiration of efficiency maximization. Mentality I find illuminating as a cognitive metaphor referring to governing in relation to the increasing psychologization and behavioralization of the subject and human conduct in neoliberalism more generally (chapter 5). This latter trend looms especially large since the aftermath of the 2008 financial crisis (Davies 2014, 2015a; Mirowski 2014).

58   Paradoxes of Emancipation

Modernization is an attempt to introduce a neoliberal governmentality upon the Greek state, in that it seeks to induce the prime neoliberal principle of competition by constructing conditions of uncertainty. Recognizing the disciplinary dimension of modernization and referring to the phenomena of "career logic and the individualist lifestyle," Lukas remarks, "the Simitis era was the nuclear physics of neoliberalism, [when] these phenomena *were somehow forced upon the people* as the 'new development of economy'" (personal communication, February 6, 2017; emphasis added). Lukas hints at the constructivist character of the modernization agenda, where reform interventions penetrate subjectivity. For Wendy Brown (2005, 43), policy intervention in particular is key to neoliberal governmentality:

> Because neoliberalism casts rational action as a norm rather than an ontology, social policy is the means by which the state produces subjects whose compass is set entirely by their rational assessment of the costs and benefits of certain acts, whether those acts pertain to teen pregnancy, tax fraud, or retirement planning.

This is indicative of neoliberalism seeking to construct docile subjects through (policy) interventions that organize docility in a self-regulating fashion. Thodoris offers a similar clue in this respect. For him, Simitis's agenda "was a 'more polite' narrative of the [Margaret] Thatcher era, but twenty years after. So even in this sense we are undeveloped" (personal communication, August 28, 2016). I am not sure whether Thodoris said it in awareness of Margaret Thatcher's infamous dystopia that "economics are the method. The object is to change the soul" (quoted in Butt 1981). In any case, on the one hand, this furthers the claim that modernization affects processes of subject formation in that it signifies the implementation of a new governmentality. On the other, his reference to "underdeveloped" points out how these processes tacitly internalize the culturalist precepts of modernization.

Conceiving the relationship between governmentality and subjectivity in their dialectics as structuring and structured structures is a helpful analytical figure of thought for understanding how they are linked.

Foucault (1991) draws attention to the ways in which human behavior is governed: by others; through various state and nonstate institutions and agencies, discourses, and norms (subjectification); and by selves through techniques of disciplining and self-regulating in terms of "taking care of the self" (subjectivation). As Nikolas Rose (1999) shows, liberal representative democracies have at their disposal—relative to more authoritarian or totalitarian polities—only limited direct, coercive interventions into individuals' lives. Governmentality is a means of acting "upon the choices, wishes, values and conduct of the individual in an indirect manner" (10). The subject "is not to be dominated in the interests of power, but to be educated and solicited into a kind of alliance between personal objective and ambitions and institutionally or socially prized goals or activities" (10). It is to be molded and made docile not solely through discipline and punishment (Foucault 1995)[22] but also through persuasion and anxieties roused by the norms of government: subject yourself to constraints, so one day you'll be free. Governmentality in its relation to subjectivity, therefore, signifies a set of incentivizing impetuses that are to stimulate subjects into regulating themselves in particular ways.

In the next part of this chapter, I will scrutinize these impetuses more closely—that is, the ways in which the modernization agenda affected my interlocutors' processes of subject formation. I claim labor market reforms, financial deregulation, and privatization in particular introduced a neoliberal governmentality with a view to molding self-regulating, individualist subjectivities. They affected my interlocutors in the ways in which they regulated themselves, especially with regard to work and consumption, encouraging them to behave as if they were in a market situation.

Uncertainty and Self-Responsibility

As mentioned earlier, the guiding ideas of modernization were as expected as they were unimaginative, consisting of the privatization of state assets

---

22. Foucault's (1995) work in particular takes up on Jeremy Bentham's infamous concept of the panopticon. Here, neoliberalism as governmentality follows Bentham in his causal formula: "The more strictly we are watched, the better we behave."

60   Paradoxes of Emancipation

and the deregulation of the economy. In Greece, as elsewhere, financial and labor deregulation were at the forefront of reform efforts. Reforming the welfare state and the pension system were equally important, but as my interlocutors did not hint at them, which may well have been to do with the fact that they were either in jobs at the time or enrolled in universities and supported by their parents—I will not delve into them. As this is not a book on the details of the reforms themselves, and as others offer thorough accounts elsewhere (Featherstone 2005; Featherstone and Papadimitriou 2008; Ioannides 2012; Laskos and Tsakalotos 2013a; Pagoulatos 2003; Papadimitriou 2005; Seferiades 2003; Sotiropoulos 2004; Stathakis 2001), in this second part of the chapter I will focus on what privatization and deregulation do in relation to subjectivity. From the viewpoint of neoliberal thought, private actors always have greater knowledge[23] of business conditions than the state, and hence setting them "free" is more economically efficient (in a Benthamite sense) than public regulation and intervention. Hence, privatization and deregulation redefine what is within the competence of the state and what is not, as the state passes responsibility to private actors, such as firms and individuals. Featherstone and Papadimitriou (2008, 156) remark that "by the 1990s the stress was undoubtedly on deregulation and the abandonment of state aids distorting competition." Yet apart from the neoliberal ideological commitments of Greece's modernizers, the drive to privatize and deregulate was also associated with the conceived and perceived international pressures of competitiveness and uncertainty.

A spiral of competitive financial deregulation originated after Bretton Woods in 1974 and carried through into the 1990s, when the United States unilaterally lifted capital controls, and was followed in this by a range of European economies, including the Netherlands, Germany, and the United Kingdom.[24] In this new international environment of highly vola-

23. With regard to this Hayekian doctrine, Mirowski (2009, 435) remarks that "'the market' is posited to be an information processor more powerful than any human brain, but essentially patterned on brain/computation metaphors."

24. The United States exercised similar pressure throughout the 1980s and 1990s (and in many ways still does) on countries of the Global South to liberalize trade and

tile interest and exchange rates, the ability of national monetary authorities to control currency fluctuations was curtailed substantially. Greece was no exception to these pressures, as reforms in the country began in 1982, bolstered by the European Union's single financial market program and the country's later aspiration to join the European Monetary Union (Pagoulatos 2000). However, with financial deregulation depriving Greece of the ability to influence real interest rates, the cost of servicing public debt rose considerably. And with the European Union's monetarist Stability and Growth Pact strictly regulating government limits on deficits, political leaders were stimulated to offset their debt by generating primary budget surpluses. Because tax hikes are rarely a popular way of generating a surplus, the privatization of state assets seemed an easy fix. As a matter of fact, Greece's convergence with the Maastricht criteria was not due to the reduction of public expenditure, as much as to increased revenues via privatization. At the same time, Greece and other countries of the European periphery were encouraged to improve competitiveness by applying pressure on their workers, because monetary policy had been set by the European Central Bank and fiscal policy has been constrained by the Stability and Growth Pact (Lapavitsas et al. 2010). All this is to say that while neoliberal thought certainly was persuasive to modernizers in Greece, the violent threat of competition nudged them into more fully submitting to neoliberal principles. With regard to the European Union, one could go so far as to say it functions as a type of supranational governmentality which subjectifies member states (via their political leaders) to the neoliberal zeitgeist[25] not merely by virtue of argumentative rigor, but more importantly by creating conditions of uncertainty through a strict adherence to competitiveness. In this sense, the pressures created by monetarism and financial deregulation function as an international disciplinary apparatus.

---

capital via institutions such as the International Monetary Fund, the World Bank, the General Agreement on Tariffs and Trade, and the Bank for International Settlements (Harvey 2007).

25. In this regard, Pagoulatos (2003, 104) remarks that "domestic financial deregulation can be viewed as an integral part of a wider EC momentum of marketization, liberalization, and privatization policies converging toward a lesser or redefined state role."

These pressures yielded considerable results. Greek state revenues increased, with privatizations contributing up to 2.5 percent of GDP annually between 1996 and 2002 (Ioannides 2012, 11, 182). Simitis's government oversaw the privatization of such major state assets as Hellenic Petroleum, it listed the national telecom company OTE on the Athens Stock Exchange, and liberalized the telecommunications market. Simitis's successor, Kostas Karamanlis of New Democracy, persisted with this policy, and a total of fifty-two state enterprises were privatized, under the two administrations, in 1996–2008 (Laskos and Tsakalotos 2013b, 37). As New Democracy continued with the modernization strategy, PASOK did not organize significant opposition to the conservative party's reforms in the labor market, nor to the privatization of state assets, nor in any other policy area for that matter (Tsakalotos 2008, 24). As for finance, modernizers claimed that credit interventionism by the state had failed to increase "banking efficiency and channeling resources toward productive investment" (Pagoulatos 2003, 107). Finance was key to both PASOK's and New Democracy's economic strategies, as bankers and financial analysts, such as Lucas Papademos (technocrat-caretaker prime minister in 2012) or Yannis Stournaras (finance minister under Samaras after the outbreak of the crisis, and now governor of the Bank of Greece) played an ever increasing role in political decision-making. As a result, modernizers in Greece created the conditions for banking competition by deregulating interest rates, phasing out direct lending controls and investment requirements, and encouraging the creation of new financial instruments. Concerning labor, modernizers acknowledged the country's competitive advantages of low labor costs, but criticized the fact that Greece had the EU's second highest rate of unemployment and a "poor productivity record," with labor productivity per hour at a "disappointing 69.2% of the EU average," with only Portugal having a lower rate (Papadimitriou 2005, 384). In this regard, the 1998 and 2000 labor market reforms were important milestones in the modernization project. As with the other reforms, labor market flexibilization was rendered technical so as to reduce the ambiguities of political discourse. Although this meager attempt at depoliticizing employment policy did little to deter union resistance—which ultimately led to a watering-down of many of the measures—even the "lighter" reforms changed employment conditions considerably. A momentous move toward more flexibility in hiring and firing was made when temporary employment agencies and fixed-term contracts were first introduced. As a result, many forms of casual and precarious labor found their way into both the private and public sector (Karamessini 2008). Work became all the more "unfriendly" to employees (Featherstone and Papadimitriou 2008) as privatizations expanded and employment conditions were deregulated during modernization.

This trend is in evidence not just in the diminishing job security but also in the ways in which private enterprises structure the organization of work and forms of employment. As higher norms of profitability intensified through privatization (e.g., through the objective of creating shareholder value), wage earners have been increasingly subjected to systems of sanctions and incentives. As Pagoulatos (2005, 361) remarks, "Privatisation was expected to induce greater competition. . . . Privatisation, and the public listing of firms in the capital market, generated a disciplinary framework of efficiency-improving corporate governance." Driven by profitability, companies were (re)structured along targets, goals, and other benchmarks of productivity and efficiency. Thirty-eight-year old Katerina had experienced this firsthand. After returning from her studies in marketing and advertising in the United Kingdom in the mid-2000s, she found a job in sales with a major Greek mobile phone provider, which was established as a result of the privatization of the telecommunication sector.

> The entire work—the tasks, the way they were structured—was entirely capitalist. *"You are responsible* for this. You need to sell this much. Your targets are these. Ohh, you missed your targets? Why did you miss them?" Bawling, bad mood, *pressure, stress* and so on. And all that for little money. (Katerina, personal communication, February 11, 2017; emphasis added)

Discourses around productivity and increased efficiency served to disguise the transfer of risk onto the individual. Once transferred, shouldering such responsibility becomes "so daunting a task [that it] casts the actors into a state of permanent and incurable uncertainty" (Bauman 2007, 91). By

64 Paradoxes of Emancipation

passing responsibility to the individual, this process of individualization is to shape entrepreneurial, calculating, self-interested subjects. Techniques of accounting, evaluation, and audit seek to internalize norms of self-responsibility of wage earners to increase profitability, efficiency, and personal performance. Simultaneously, setting such benchmarks serves to limit wage earners' critical and imaginative capacities.[26] Certainly, the deregulation of hiring and firing practices, fear, and the possibility of unemployment add to the "negative" levers for conditioning subjects into docility. What is more, the individualization of performance (through various measures of benchmarking) furthered the principle of competition even between wage earners, in an endless process of "best practice" and optimal performance.

> At work sometimes there was competition of the likes of "who's the best salesperson?" and "who hits the targets?" and so on. . . . A few salespeople were born to tell lies and born to sell. There were two to three people who, as they say, can sell you whatever they want. They are made to tell lies. . . . You know, like brokers who don't care what they sell. They don't give a shit about the ethical part. Such people were there. These are the appropriate people for such jobs. The rest was unhappy. (Katerina, personal communication, February 11, 2017)

With numerical audit stripping judgment off its ethical and political components—because performance is measured along efficiency, growth, or profitability—the occurrence of lying may not be necessarily dubbed morally "wrong." On the contrary, lying or cheating may even be somehow considered justified, if it is motivated by a desire to win. Being competitive is to ignore how a game should be played and to focus on how one's skills can be employed against those of opponents (Massumi 2002, 77). Under the

---

26. "I tried doing it well. I did trainings, I used the tools and things I learned in my (marketing and business) studies a lot. But it was an environment that didn't care so much about doing things differently or in another way. The motive was very particular (referring to profit), and we needed to follow that. Like in every job. You had to say particular things to costumers. You had targets that you needed to fulfill. And every time you have to say a lot of bullshit, because the products were not all good" (Katerina, personal communication, February 11, 2017).

disguise of meritocracy, which Franco Berardi (2015, 168–69) aptly refers to as a "euphemistic expression to describe a jungle in which workers wage daily wars against each other, obliged to fight for a salary dependent on productivity and economic results," solidarity and community among wage earners are broken as a result of individualization by competition. Under such conditions, "every worker is alone, facing the blackmail of merit, the humiliation of failure, the threat of being made redundant" (170), increasingly producing a work environment of envy and distrust. This supports my initial claim that privatization and labor market flexibilization are not forms of deregulation as much as they signify a reordering of norms of economic activities, social relations, conduct, and subjectivities.

This is true also for financial deregulation, which most significantly impacted subjectivities through the removal of restrictions on consumer credit. Until 2003, there was a ten thousand euro limit on consumer credit per person in Greece. Officially, the limit was to protect borrowers from taking on too much debt (Placas 2008). That the limit was completely abolished by 2003 is paradigmatic for how responsibility has been transferred to the individual. This trend was furthered as advertisements encouraged individuals to pay attention to the interest rates they were paying on their debt. Disguised as "financial literacy" (Arthur 2012; Clarke 2015), advertisers encouraged individuals to get their finances "in order"[27] through consolidation loans and offers of cards (Placas 2008, 102). In effect, what this does is to nudge individuals into reinforcing their calculative capacity by learning how to manipulate their balance sheets. In more market-related terms, assuming credit is the embrace of risk[28] in order to transform the self into a more market-friendly direction and to make it more competitive, be it through mortgage debt, student debt, or more exotic arrangements,

27. En Taxei, which translates as "in order," was literally the name of one product by Eurobank for this purpose.

28. "The truth is that my parents fell for it [taking out a loan]. My father was a driver on the public buses. He worked difficult hours. And he had a plan in his life. He knew that when he would get his pension, he would get a decent one and he would get a bonus. But that time coincided with the crisis, which means that the bonus was lost and the pension is lower. [His] plan collapsed, you understand?" (Katerina, personal communication, February 11, 2017).

such as the infamous vacation loans.[29] Lukas, who describes himself as having been a "workaholic" in a middle-management position during the modernization period, remarks rather agitatedly:

> Oh! It was the banks' party! "Take out a loan to buy a car!" "Take out a loan to buy a house!" "Take out a loan to go on holiday!" I mean, this was the whole trick—compromising your future income in present time. (Lukas, personal communication, February 5, 2017)

This relates to the notion of "mortgaged lives." Here, geographer Maria Kaika (2016) argues that PASOK's promise to make everybody in Greece a member of the middle class by giving people access to "easy credit"[30] ultimately led to the commodification of their indebtedness (see also García-Lamarca and Kaika 2016). This contributes to the constitution of entrepreneurial, self-responsible, risk-embracing subjects. It does so not least because consumer credit allows one the freedom to spend autonomously without recourse to partner or parent, challenging the ideals of the household and family unity. This, in turn, contributes to processes of individualization with self-interest at its core.

It is true that the new variety of loans did not introduce credit as a new phenomenon. As consumer credit became more readily available, however, the amount of goods obtainable to buy increased as well. As department stores, supermarkets, and malls started to accept credit cards, a more profligate style of consumption was encouraged in Greece (Arvanitaki and Stratigaki 1994). This, in turn, propagated the phenomenon of taking out loans in order to consume. As Lukas points out, "There was a craving for consumption—not for accumulation or production. . . . If you don't have

---

29. "[My parents] took out some loans for my studies and the studies of my sisters. They never took out a loan to go on vacation, or to have a good time or to buy a car. They took out loans they considered important. But those, at least some of them, still exist. They exist as debt. Fortunately not in a tragic manner. I mean, we haven't reached poverty—let me put it that way" (Penelope, personal communication, March 25, 2016).

30. "I had this colleague who had a dozen credit cards on him. During that time, Alpha Bank . . . advertised credit cards. They started calling me. And I got two of them. I fell into that trap. I also took out a loan, it was so easy" (Panagiotis, personal communication, May 18, 2017).

the money to consume, you get a loan (personal communication, February 5, 2017).

Consumerism did not arrive in Greece under Simitis; it can be traced back to the political and economic opening after the fall of the Junta in 1974 and the country's accession to the European Economic Community in 1981. Yet when Simitis announced that "barbershops will become hair salons" (quoted in Makridakis 2015), he indicated the linkage between modernization and consumer culture. For Douzinas (2013, 36), the changing subject formation from citizen toward citizen-consumer is a result of privatization. The "freedom to choose" and their sense of purchasing power made consumers strong proponents of the modernization project. Consumerism, Zygmunt Bauman (2007, 28) remarks:

> Is a type of social arrangement that results from recycling mundane, permanent and so to speak "regime-neutral" human wants, desires and longings into the *principal propelling and operating force of society,* a force that coordinates systemic reproduction, social integration, social stratification and the formation of human individuals, as well as playing a major role in the processes of individual and group self-identification and in the selection and pursuit of individual life policies. "Consumerism" arrives when consumption takes over that linchpin role which was played by work in the society of producers.

Consumerism, then, is about choice, although consumerism as such does not appear to be a choice.[31] It is a lifestyle rather than an existential necessity (Bauman 1999). In Greece, the liberalization of consumer credit, the deregulation of interest rates, the abolition of all price controls (other than medicine), and expanded shopping hours have been claimed to have contributed to "a metamorphosis towards a consumer society where

31. If we take Bauman's claim further, the consumer-subject is free to consume, even encouraged to do so, wisely and reflexively, in order to benefit themselves and others. But they are barred from changing the relations of production, thus limiting the choices they have. In this view, individual liberal freedom is not universal—not positive or negative (like in Isaiah Berlin's conception)—but immanent within the wider context of capitalist accumulation, precisely because it is contingent upon the requirements necessary for utility maximization.

68 Paradoxes of Emancipation

materialism became more valued" (Lysonski et al. 2004, 8–9). In a similar vein, Stylianos Hadjiyannis (2016, 155) argues that "it was mostly imported gadgets Greeks were craving for, following the exposure to nationwide television, foreign films, returnees from abroad, and tourism inflows." This self-orientalizing view of consumerism as a "foreign" cultural phenomenon was widely shared and reproduced among my interlocutors,[32] as the "traditionally" restrained ethic of accumulation has allegedly given way to a more "hedonistic morality of consumption, spending and enjoyment based partly on credit" (Economou 2014, 15).[33] Lukas remarks:

> It took Greece to another level. . . . Intense nightlife, growth of the restaurant sector, five-star hotels, spas. . . . [It was] like a Los Angeles, California-way of thinking. But in a Balkan state, ok?. . . . I consume, therefore I am. Yes, it was so fast. You cannot imagine how fast it was. . . . The advertising industry bloomed.[34] It was the most appreciated job in the market. (Lukas, personal communication, February 5, 2017)

My interlocutors refer to these years as those when "everybody had three mobile phones" (Eleftheria, personal communication, October 6, 2014), where the desire for luxury, distinction, and individuality was emphasized by the experientiality of consumption; by a focus on the design and style of goods and the self. On the one hand, the neoliberalization of subjectivity is defined precisely by the "transformation of consumers into commodities"

32. "So with 1996 [the election of Simitis] we had the excess of consumerism. And the idea of being European meant, more or less, being 'modern consumers' in some sense" (Thodoris, personal communication, August 28, 2016).

33. Related to this, Calotychos (2013, 206) remarks that people in Greece, a country "traditionally boasting a low level of indebtedness and with little or no access to affordable loans well into the 1990s, were suddenly besieged by unprecedented loan offers from banks. Willingly, the Greeks walked through the trapdoor of debt-driven consumerism and borrowed to their heart's content, thereby finally quenching the existential thirst to buy high-quality German consumer goods at lower costs."

34. In fact, two of my interlocutors had to do with the industry. In the 2000s, Katerina studied business, marketing, and advertising in Athens and London. Andreas "was for many years in advertising. Twenty years. From 2000 onwards I was almost entirely in advertising" (personal communication, February 11, 2016).

Modernizing Greece 69

(Bauman 2007, 12), and of replacing "the time-honored ambition to 'know yourself' with the exhortation to 'express yourself'" (Mirowski 2014, 92). On the other hand, my interlocutors' narratives hint at the ways in which they at times internalize, and partly reproduce, the moralizing and stereotyping discourses of guilt in the crisis years (Boletsi 2016); as having indeed consumed to lavishly and lived "beyond their means," thus creating (and now having to pay for) the crisis. Maria, an underemployed freelance graphic designer in her early forties, underlines this, but also points to the alienation she says she felt at the time:

> There was this rottenness in society. There was a community around me with no spirit. But it was such people that I associated with: "What car does he have? What motorbike does she have?" You know. . . . The discussions were about boyfriends, cars, and Vasilis Karas.[35] (Maria, personal communication, February 10, 2016)

Maria's observation of the lack of "spirit" is endemic, for neoliberalism praises and promotes ignorance (Mirowski 2014). In Greece at the time, the ability to want, to desire, to long for became a central aspect of existence. Work served the purpose of satisfying these norms.

> Something wasn't going right. Those around me did odd jobs and spent their money in bouzouki clubs . . . or you went to buy beautiful clothes. It was as if the aim was to have a table at the bouzouki clubs. You know, you were "somebody". . . . Their goal was to work like animals to go for five days or less to Mykonos and to Santorini and to party. (Maria, personal communication, Maria, February 10, 2016)

In neoliberalism, ethos becomes something relative, rather than fixed. Increasingly, it is conceived along the lines of status, which is an index that must be seen in relation to the ability to compete and consume lavishly. Advertising and private television[36] served the purpose of disseminating

35. Vasilis Karas is a Greek folk singer who very much embodies the mainstream bouzouki club culture of excess consumerism at the time.

36. "It was a big product, private television. New standards, new idols. . . . Americanized television, or even worse, Italianized television. . . . It was like a small Hollywood

prefabricated lifestyles; the new private television stations in particular sought to bridge the intrinsic contradiction between "a seductive but alienating possessive individualism on the one hand and the desire for a meaningful collective life on the other" (Harvey 2007, 69).[37] According to my interlocutors, happiness in Greece at the time was signified in hedonistic terms, as the immediate experience of "individual and inward" pleasure (Segal 2017, 30) vis-à-vis possessing and consuming certain objects and practicing certain lifestyles.

> A part of Greek society lived like this. They gave us the wrong role models: Tatiana Stefanidou and Eleni Menegaki[38] and the like. Every idiot was our role model. The models were role models, the pimps and those who were in television. . . . The women copied this lifestyle. We had changed, man. How should I explain? Wrong role models. . . . We lived in houses with a mortgage. We lived with fake money. Others got vacation loans. [It was] crazy! (Penelope, personal communication, March 25, 2016)

It is doubtful that individuals would voluntarily or "spontaneously," as Hayek would suggest, subject themselves to consumerist market principles solely as a result of being exposed to advertising and persuasion, or even exclusively due to the attractions of individual enrichment and "winning." Instead, turning individuals into subjects who were at once calculating and productive could only happen if the necessary conditions were in place. Labor needed to be rendered precarious in order to create uncertainty.

---

without the capital of Hollywood. I mean, it was worse than Hollywood. . . . You can be against consumption, but *the system can be so delicate in injecting new needs into you that you don't even realize that.* If you have the television on, even if you don't look at it, there is a subconscious there" (Lukas, personal communication, February 6, 2017; emphasis added).

37. Relatedly, Rahtz's work on Germany post reunification (Rahtz 2017, 112) shows the degenerative effects of mass culture, where "television represented an endpoint of the anthropological and depth-psychological drive to minimize drudgery and maximize easy pleasures."

38. Both are personalities on private television in Greece, and known for hosting tabloid talk shows.

Finance needed to be deregulated and advertised, and loans needed to be easily obtainable. For some, especially those considered to have less human capital (see Becker 1962), loans needed to be taken out in order to consume, so as to feel a sense of belonging via status. "You either had to do labor in the [informal economy], the dubious kind. Or you needed sponsors. This was the system. Or you lived on money you basically did not have, that is, plastic money" (Maria, personal communication, February 10, 2016). Others, like Lukas, needed to be ever more productive in order to continue to consume under worsening conditions of labor.

> Considering the fact that in order to be in all these places and do all these things you have to work a lot of hours, and considering also that the human measuring of time is 24 hours, when you work twelve hours there's not much time left. Not to mention there's not much brain left. So you're producing in order to consume. And you were producing less to consume more, with no end in sight. (Lukas, personal communication, February 6, 2017)

In short, privatization and deregulation facilitated the spread of consumerist lifestyles in Greece. The resulting constitution of subjects as citizen-consumers contributed to processes of individualization. When I asked Lukas why he thinks this logic of producing and consuming is so bad, he pointed to the repercussions this had for solidarity in society, by emphasizing, in a culturalist fashion, the "foreign" nature of consumerism. It happened in

> a Balkan country, where it didn't completely apply. You had individualism. Take the etymology of idiot, for example. *Idiot* means "jerk." But it also means "private owner." You couldn't care less about what was happening around you. The homeless were still there. The junkies were there—although not as many as now. But they were there. . . . Yet you stop caring. . . . You stop caring about your fellow beings, because there is a new brand of trousers, or ties, or shoes . . . or this club, or that event, or that gallery, or that social gathering, or this must-be-present-at trendy place. Or that kind of woman that I should be with, or that kind of man I should be with. Or that kind of bar I should go to. (Lukas, personal communication, February 6, 2017)

72 Paradoxes of Emancipation

Lukas shows how individualization can be parasitical on, and destructive of, solidarity. Making a self-orientalizing argument (al-'Azm 1981), he views individualism and consumerism as alien to "a Balkan country." What he also shows is that through consumerism and the embrace of individualization and lifestyle cultures, modernization can be reduced to its pleasant, self-satisfying aspects, while simultaneously serving the function of a distraction from those other reforms on the modernization agenda that create precariousness and uncertainty. This very much resonates with Bauman's (1999) reading of consumer society, in which the "freedoms" that are passed down to individuals simultaneously depoliticize and disempower. They depoliticize, because they reduce practices to acts of consumption, and consumption to preferences and choices (from given sets of goods and services). They disempower, because they leave individuals to their own devices and close down what Bauman (1999) refers to as the "agora."[39] As mentioned earlier, in its neoliberal ideal, the consumer society dedicated to utility-maximizing rationality in (quasi-)market situations ends up praising and promoting ignorance. Based on this ignorance, the subject in neoliberalism is "less a social citizen with powers and obligations deriving from membership of a collective body, than an individual whose citizenship is to be manifested through the free exercise of personal choice among a variety of marketed options" (Rose 1999, 230). This self-concerned individual was the preferred subject of Greek modernizers.

The Modernized Greek Self

Subjectivity is made up of emotions and desires, passions and feelings, beliefs and attitudes. Subjectivity is therefore not the foundation of practices but is instead formed through these practices (Prozorev 2014).

---

39. For Bauman (1999, 3), the agora is "the space neither private nor public, but more exactly private and public at the same time. The space where private problems meet in a meaningful way—that is, not just to draw narcissistic pleasures or in search of some therapy through public display, but to seek collectively managed levers powerful enough to lift individuals from their privately suffered misery; the space where such ideas may be born and take shape as the 'public good,' the 'just society' or 'shared values.'"

Modernization has sought to create conditions that bend individuals so they subject themselves to market logics. This, so modernizers hope, serves to increase Greece's competitiveness. But because neoliberal modernization is a process fraught with contradictions and failures despite its totalizing aspirations, what we witnessed in Greece under Simitis was not some sort of ideal type of neoliberal subjectivities (the *homo economicus* Ludwig von Mises so gleefully espoused), but approximations—or rather, what we witnessed was approximations nonetheless. The modernized self in Greece (as elsewhere in neoliberalizing societies) is constructed through governmental discourses and practices of neoliberalism. Modernization produces the conditions that render the subject individualized, "free," autonomous, self-responsible, self-interested, and entrepreneurial in the sense that they generate their own human capital (just as much as they are human capital—a commodity in themselves) in a rational fashion. As a subject they will now be "calculating rather than rule abiding, a Benthamite rather than a Hobbesian" (Brown 2005, 43). In the neoliberal ideal, individuals are reduced to bundles of personal "investments" (Mirowski 2014, 59).

The privatization and deregulation of state operations—and the repercussions these reforms have on the organization of the workplace as well as consumerism[40]—contribute to processes of individualization. This is because responsibilities previously assumed by the state, or institutions such as class or the family, are devolved downward to individuals. Tacitly hinting at the ethics and values of neoliberal modernization in their relation to subjectivity, former dance club owner Aggelos remarks:

> To be raised in this particular value system in principle brings out a lot of "ego." You want to be right. You "know." And when somebody else tells you that you are not right, you get defensive. This creates problems

---

40. As Foucault (2008, 144) remarks, this "involves an individualization of social policy and individualization through social policy, instead of collectivization and socialization by and in social policy. In short, it does not involve providing individuals with a social cover for risks, but according everyone a sort of economic space within which they can take on and confront risks."

74 Paradoxes of Emancipation

for the collective consciousness. (Aggelos, personal communication, January 27, 2016)

This underlines the shift from a "collectivist" to an "individualist" society in Greece, which has been proclaimed, especially in the field of behavioral psychology (Georgas 1989; Pouliasi and Verkuyten 2011). Secondly, Aggelos hints at the notion of the competitive individual, one who needs to "win" an argument. Thanos, an underemployed medical engineer in his mid-forties, offers another example in this regard:

I didn't find people who accepted the opposite opinion. Or they were very few. It's just that people usually got angry when they saw that you had another opinion. Or they tried to convince you at whatever cost, although this is not what matters. What matters for me is that you say what you think as an opinion; that the others understand it, that they think about it. That you also think about what they will say, and not that one subordinates the other and they feel "Ok, I won!. . . . Hence my opinion is better and I am better." (Thanos, personal communication, February 3, 2016)

Curiously, thinking of arguments as intellectual combat is something neoliberals have always valorized.[41] This is a recurrent theme among many of my interlocutors as they speak about what bothered them about society at the time, and is an attitude that stands in stark contrast to the antiauthoritarian and egalitarian ethic of the Syntagma Square occupation.

Individualization also created a lack of belonging and social connections among my interlocutors. Vasilis, a veteran television journalist in his early fifties, remarks:

I mean, in Athens everybody is lonely. You may have one or two friends, and that's rare. Most don't have anyone. Ok, maybe your family—although

---

41. Chicago School of Economics and Law thinkers such as Aaron Director or Ronald Coase were ever ready to seek holes in opponents' arguments and engage in rhetorical demolition. Davies (2014, 81) remarks: "An argument or idea could only survive in this climate if it could withstand a combination of rationalist attack and audit by common sense."

the family during this period of crisis in particular, isn't in a very good situation. (Vasilis, personal communication, October 24, 2014)

As a result of increasing individualization, neoliberalism fosters loneliness (Davies 2011; Monbiot 2016). It does so by eliminating anything that is not economically efficient, "which does not produce a return-on-investment" (Coville 2018).[42] As neoliberal policies seek to overcome collective institutions—be it youth clubs, libraries, unions, or social associations—they dissolve precisely the kind of projects that protect individuals from loneliness.[43] Lukas, who was in management in a stressful and demanding work environment, explained to me how he went about tackling his lack of social relations:

> I went out because . . . otherwise I wouldn't have the sense of living. So I replaced the gift of life by imitating life. . . . After twelve hours [of work], you have no brains to understand what is really happening around you. Your friends are not friends. They are bar mates. Women are not companions, they are sex objects. You don't have time to flirt. It has to be fast because you have to go back home, wake up, go to work and repeat the whole process again. (Lukas, personal communication, February 6, 2017)

It is as if life itself is turned into a commodity to be consumed efficiently, in order to minimize the feeling of loneliness. Companionship is merely a resource, "socially prescribed" by the self and medical experts (see Kilgarriff-Foster and O'Cathain 2015). Happiness is reduced to instant gratification, fully controlled by the rational mind (chapter 5).

42. "As career patterns, housing patterns, mortality patterns, and social policies follow the lead of global capitalism, much of the world seems determined to adopt a lifestyle that will compound and reinforce the chronic sense of isolation that millions of individuals already feel, even when they are surrounded by well-meaning friends and family. The contradiction is that we have radically changed our environment, and yet our physiology remains the same . . . beneath the surface we are still the same vulnerable creatures who huddled together against the terrors of thunderstorm sixty thousand years ago" (Cacioppo and Patrick 2008, 53).

43. In the United Kingdom, for example, the Conservative government instituted the Loneliness Minister to tackle these self-made trends.

76   Paradoxes of Emancipation

In sum, what my interlocutors have in common when they talk about their lives and experiences before the Syntagma Square occupation is that their narrations are in mostly negative terms. As I will show in the next chapter, this perceived negativity of experience needs to be seen against the backdrop of crisis. Though living conditions have worsened for every single one of my interlocutors since the Syntagma Square occupation, albeit to different extents, not a single one mentioned their lives before the occupation in positive ways. This indicates a clear demarcation of today's subjectivity from their perception of past subjectivities. In the context of crisis for many of my interlocutors, the Syntagma Square occupation was a moment of "waking up": the emergence of the alter-political qualities of the radical imagination (chapter 3) and antipolitical subjectivation processes that resulted from "demystifying" critiques of the status quo, particularly the state (chapter 4). In this sense, waking up signifies a form of conversion, in which interlocutors' lives took a different turn: allowing them to reconsider their experiences in the period of modernization, and construct a narrative of their precrisis selves. For Maria, this "has to do with the change in people, from the crisis onwards" (personal communication, February 10, 2016).

Refusing Neoliberal Selfhood

This chapter attended to the relationship between neoliberal modernization and subject formation in Greece prior to the financial crisis. Initiated by Costas Simitis in the early 1990s, modernization signifies a concentrated effort by political leaders in PASOK and New Democracy to implement a large-scale, neoliberal, reform agenda toward a more orderly, open, and integrated capitalism. The goal of this effort is to increase national competitiveness. Having been described as a "mechanistic importation of Western models without consideration of anthropological differences" (Douzinas 2013, 36), modernization is an inherently culturalist project. Yet, by viewing modernization as not applicable to "a Balkan country" and how it means for Greece "to become different," my interlocutors' accounts have traits of what al-'Azm (1981) refers to as "orientalism in reverse." This points to the fact that they partly reproduce the culturalist values of modernization.

Modernization affected my interlocutors' subject formation in a variety of ways. Neoliberal in spirit, modernization sought to transform the constitution of persons and the relationships among individuals. In many ways it succeeded in doing so, as modernization managed to create conditions of uncertainty that led individuals to regulate and discipline themselves as if they were in a market situation. For my interlocutors, this contributed to a wider individualization of subjectivities that was marked by consumerism, self-interest, and latent competition. Curiously, the ways in which they narrate the period of modernization and their personal experiences are marked by a sense of unease and negativity. When they share with me their sense of society being "rotten" and having "no spirit" (Maria), their feeling of being "lonely" (Thodoris), their "unhappiness" with all the "lies" in their jobs (Katerina), or their sense of guilt[44] about "reproducing the system" by "being part of the system" (Lukas), they demarcate how they perceive they are now from how they perceive they were "back then." They do so regardless of how submissively they were following the parameters set by neoliberal modernization. Through this demarcation, my interlocutors allude to changes in their subjectivities that point to a tacit refusal to subject themselves to the neoliberal norms of personhood, despite the fact that they were much better-off materially then than they are today. The ways in which my interlocutors narrate their selves to have been during the period of modernization is a partial result of the collective transformative experience of the Syntagma Square occupation. This is because the relationality between the spatiality of the Syntagma Square occupation and my interlocutors' significations of crisis—that is, the occupation as a structuring and structured consequence of, and answer to, crisis—is key for making sense of this self-attributed transformation.

44. "I was very critical and even more inhibited than I am now. I had the 'guilt complex.' I was feeling guilty all the time" (Lukas, personal communication, February 6, 2017).

2

"Waking Up"

Spatialized Crises and Unthought-Of Experiences

The fact that the future is in the making, that it is yet to be determined, is what provokes our imagination. Uncertainty, in this sense, compels us to imagine the future of society differently; worse, but possibly also better than the present. The function of uncertainty in the neoliberal imagination was referred to in the previous chapter. It imposes stress and precarity upon individuals so as to drive them into competition. For Max Haiven and Alex Khasnabish (2014, 115–16), the imagination of being able to compete for middle-class belonging has been key for the pertinence of the capitalist imaginary, for that belonging signified "a refuge from perpetual insecurity." Before Greece was hit by the 2008 financial crisis, middle-class belonging for many of my interlocutors was a refuge indeed. Maria, whose father was a banker and mother a psychotherapist, was better-off than most.

> We didn't have economic problems as a family. Not that we were rich, but my parents were educated and had very good jobs. I was not worried about bills, or about whether I could get the things I wanted. These things didn't cross my mind. (Maria, personal communication, February 10, 2016)

Others, like Katerina, whose mother worked as a cleaner and whose father worked as a bus driver, were not as financially well-off as Maria's family. But through much effort and hard work, they eventually reached a level of certainty and economic security.

> My parents from scratch, through very hard work, managed to buy a house when I was 18 years old. They didn't have connections or support. They didn't even have the education to work in a profession that is a bit more relaxed and where there was more money. They made money, but they worked very hard for it. (Katerina, personal communication, February 7, 2016)

In everyday life, habitual practices guide our conduct in a self-regulating manner, rendering uncertainties manageable and the future somewhat expectable. In the previous chapter, I established that as a result of neoliberal modernization, practices have aligned toward more individualist modes of conduct in order to tackle uncertainties.

With the beginning of the crisis in Greece and the downward socialization of its costs, the ways in which uncertainties were tackled changed dramatically. The slashing of wages and pensions, tax hikes, worsening employment conditions, and an overall increase in unemployment all had concrete material repercussions for my interlocutors. "There's nobody who wasn't hit by it," Petros remarks (personal communication, February 10, 2017). As the material consequences of the crisis started to show, normative expectations about the future changed.

> The people . . . started to feel the crisis in all its dimensions. I mean, its values and such: "I built a house and I'm okay," let's say. Everything started to crumble. . . . I speak generally and personally. I am in the same situation, in the same cauldron with the people. Few things, I have few things. Back then there were a lot of fears over what the crisis is. "What are we to expect here?" (Kostas, personal communication, February 17, 2016)

The normative expectations regarding the capitalist imaginary of being able to compete for middle-class belonging started to collapse. As the crisis hit my interlocutors' wallets, the uncertainties about the future were nothing to look forward to. Fifty-four-year-old nursery school teacher Kyriaki anxiously remarks:

> I don't know what will happen. I believe, however, that we need to take the issue more seriously. Because Greece is very behind. . . . At this

80   Paradoxes of Emancipation

moment in time we are in great uncertainty. I mean, we don't know what tomorrow will be like. Sure, we may have property . . . from our parents. But taxes [are] 10 times higher. We can't pay these taxes. Because the wages—if there are wages, because many are unemployed—they are too low! [People] took out loans, they became unemployed, they can't pay them back. You cannot cope with everyday costs! (Kyriaki, personal communication, October 19, 2014)

Reproducing the culturalist narrative of neoliberal modernization ("Greece is very behind"), Kyriaki implies that one needs to work and compete with ever stronger efforts in order to overcome the crisis. Similarly, Maria, who was accustomed to a comfortable "way of life," suddenly found herself in a situation that was unraveling.

I was in my last year at university. I got my degree. I did an internship. And then this ordeal started: I couldn't find work. Things were very difficult for me. I had gotten used to living a different way of life,. . . . And all of a sudden I lost my security. My father . . . didn't get paid. He was demoted. They didn't pay him. My father fell into depression. My mother . . . too had issues. My aunt had "red loans." We got into a situation that was very different from before—the entire family. I was forced to leave my house. I moved into a house that was like a storage room without windows. There were days where I didn't even have a single euro on me. It was difficult for me. I learnt things differently. All of a sudden, my entire life changed. (Maria, personal communication, February 10, 2016)

In times of crisis, our ordinary conduct is in turmoil. As there is a mismatch between how things should be and how they actually are, the fit between objective realities and subjective expectations falls out of alignment. The apparent givenness of social reality is unraveling. Crises, therefore, are inherently liminal situations that do not align with the structures we have grown accustomed to. In Greek, the word *crisis* (*Krisē*) refers to judgment or thinking, and forces ordinary habits of thought and action to be reconsidered. The aforementioned examples assume that crisis has a threatening character, yet the ways in which we reconsider our practices in order to tackle the realities of crisis often depend upon how we signify crisis in relation to how political decision-makers and experts present it to us.

This chapter focuses on how my interlocutors signify crisis in order to make sense of the emergence of the Syntagma Square occupation. I argue that the structural logics enabling and constituting the spatial production of the Syntagma Square occupation cannot be seen separately from how my interlocutors signify crisis. At the heart of this assumption lies the liminal character of crisis. Drawing on social dialectics, I claim that the structuring quality of crisis produces the Syntagma Square occupation as a spatiality that is marked precisely by crisis' anti-structural capacity. That is to say that the occupation is produced in practice as a liminal spatiality that is both a (structural) consequence of, and an (anti-structural) answer to, the crisis in Greece. This theorization allows us to think more carefully about the conditions of possibility for what my interlocutors refer to as "waking up": the emergence of the alter-political qualities of the radical imagination (chapter 3), and the antipolitical quality of subjectivation following on from demystifying critiques of the status quo, particularly the state (chapter 4). The ways in which my interlocutors experienced both in practice allows us to trace their self-attributed changes in subjectivity (chapter 5).

In order to theorize the condition of possibility for "waking up," this chapter is divided into three parts. The first elaborates on crisis and its significations. I argue that those decision-makers and experts managing and evaluating the Greek crisis have effectively framed it as an anti-crisis: a Schmittian state of exception that is radically extraordinary, but does not allow for alternative judgments and critiques. Influenced by this framing, it is further argued that the crisis in Greece came to be signified in two ways. The first I refer to as "regressive" signification, which shuts down the imagination regarding what is possible, restricting it to what is necessary, and is guided by the violent threat of uncertainty, rather than opportunity. The second I refer to as a "progressive" signification of crisis, which puts doxic assumptions under scrutiny and elevates them to the level of discourse, where they can be radically contested.

The second part of this chapter theorizes the precise processes of the spatial production of the Syntagma Square occupation. Here, I will look

82   Paradoxes of Emancipation

into those constitutive components that construct the Syntagma Square occupation as a liminal spatiality. As Henri Lefebvre (2007, 36) puts it, "If space is a product, our knowledge of it must be expected to reproduce and expound the process of production." Because occupations of squares are marked by stasis—that is, a prolonged temporality of presence that enables *longue durée* social processes—they allow alternative sets of practices to be originated and become routine. These practices reproduce spatiality and leave their traces on the very subjects who are performing them in ways that render these practices as meaningful guidelines for subjectivity.

The third part of this chapter is an attempt to bring together the conceptual considerations regarding crisis significations and the social production of space, in an effort to theorize the conditions of possibility for what my interlocutors refer to as "waking up." The conceptual claim made in this section is if subjects produce spaces in ways that are influenced by the liminal realities of crisis, the spaces to be produced are marked precisely by the turmoil of conduct that subjects are struggling with. The liminal nature of crisis in and of itself, however, is not a sufficient condition for the emergence of the radical imagination. This becomes evident in how significations of crisis came to be spatially manifested within the Syntagma Square occupation. Specifically, the upper part of the square was marked by a regressive signification of crisis, whereas the lower part— where all my interlocutors participated—is marked by the progressive signification of crisis.

Anti-Crisis and Crisis

By the time the global financial crisis brought Greek banks tumbling down, and especially after the crisis hit Greece in all its severity in 2010, a peculiar framework of critiques started to come apart. In line with the neoliberal and inherently culturalist presumptions of modernization outlined in the previous chapter, political and media discourses painted a picture in which a productive, efficient, and competitive European north had to bail out a lazy, excessive, and leisurely south. Fueling this narrative, German chancellor Angela Merkel stated that "too many uncompetitive members of the eurozone have lived beyond their means" (quoted in

Deutscher Bundestag 2010, 4128). For modernizers, this was proof that Greek "underdog culture" (Diamandouros 1994), with its excesses and inefficiencies, had catapulted the country further into the past. When elites single out member states and disparage their efforts toward increased competitiveness as insufficient, what they are doing in effect is elevating the neoliberal dogma of self-responsibility to the level of nations. As debt is being socialized and responsibility individualized, the mantra of the dominant crisis discourses became that no one is to be blamed for the Greek crisis but Greece itself.

Using the term *Greek exceptionalism*, this often blatantly culturalist analysis is reproduced in the (mostly neoclassical and behavioralist) neoliberal academic critiques of the crisis (e.g., Arghyrou and Tsoukalas 2011; Mitsopoulos and Pelagidis 2011; Petrakis 2012). In this line of critique, the country's failure to improve its competitiveness is decoupled from the competitive advantages of its northern counterparts: if the other countries are doing better, that means Greece is not making enough of an effort. Even in the neoliberal's own terms, this line of argument should mention— but does not—that since the single currency was launched all the other countries that had adopted the euro lost competitiveness against Germany (Lynn 2011). Nor is it thought relevant to mention that the restrictive wage policies stipulated by the German government's Agenda 2010 made it impossible for the peripheral states of the south to compete (Lapavitsas et al. 2010). Nor does it seem to be important that surplus generation of demand in the north benefited greatly from the demand generated in the rest of the European Union (Laskos and Tsakalotos 2013a), or that by virtue of the Euro's architecture, Greece was unable to recover competitively through devaluation (Anderson 2012). Instead, neoliberal critiques claim that the modernization agenda did not go far enough, due to the "lack of commitment" (Arghyrou and Tsoukalas 2011, 173) or "inability" (Mitsopoulos and Pelagidis 2011, 4) to champion reforms more seriously.

Perhaps in self-defense or desperation, Costas Simitis (2014) felt called upon to defend his neoliberal legacy from neoliberal critiques. In *The European Debt Crisis: The Greek Case*, Simitis agrees that modernization indeed did not go far enough in tackling the lack of competitiveness. But this was certainly not due to his leadership. Rather, the "causes of the crisis are rooted in the country's backwardness" (305), unfavorable "mental attitudes and behaviours" (316), inefficiencies and a "lack of expertise" (310) on the part of the public administration and political leaders other than him, or simply "the shortcomings of Greek society" as a whole (62). Either way, considering the rationality of the capitalist growth paradigm and the neoliberal principle of competitive uncertainty inherent in any neoliberal critique, it is doubtful whether reforms ever go far enough: for his agenda's twenty-year anniversary, Simitis (2017, 11) acknowledged, "There is no 'end' date to a project of modernisation."

Because neoliberalism is hostile to political discourse, most of these critiques committed to the explicit and transparent character of measurements and rankings (Simitis being an exception, as his book is more of a defense of his administration). This is due to the fact that neoliberalism makes normative rather than ontological claims about the pervasiveness of economic rationality (Brown 2005). The neoliberal critique of the Greek crisis therefore inevitably reiterates previous claims: a lack of competitiveness, an inefficient public administration, "overregulated" markets, an expensive welfare state, etc. By critiquing the crisis in economized terms against a neoliberal benchmark of constructed metrics, this line of critique serves two purposes. The first purpose is to provide intelligible, technical data on complex social relations (what in the previous chapter I called "the logic of numbers") in order to render the crisis manageable. This serves to bolster the immanent validity of neoliberalism's quantitative methodologies of audit and valuation. The second purpose is to anchor and justify the existence of neoliberalism through permanent criticism of governmental action and intervention, often in relation to the neoliberal principle that the market can offer solutions to situations caused by the market in the first place (Mirowski 2014). In both purposes, economized critique seeks to strengthen the imaginary of neoliberalism as a norm. What is often rather conveniently forgotten here is that by virtue of its sovereignty and authority, it is the state that creates the conditions for the market to be able to offer any solutions at all.

Finally, what neoliberal critiques gloss over is that to argue for an (economic) order in which competition is paramount inevitably means to argue for inequality. This is because competition assumes a paradoxical combination of equality and inequality, where contestants are *"formally equal at the outset and empirically unequal in the conclusion"* (Davies 2014, 37). "Formal" equality is merely defined through "fairness" in assuming competition. The fact that competitors usually start with resources that are unequally distributed among themselves is of little or no concern. What is at issue, then, is whether we want to play a game that is only worthwhile for a few.

Surprisingly, left-wing critiques do less questioning of neoliberalism than one might think. Regardless of how rigorous a point these critiques from the Left make when they say that Greece is far from exceptional, and that any explanatory account of the crisis needs to be embedded within the systemic failures of the eurozone (Laskos and Tsakalotos 2013a, 2013b), or when they point to center-periphery inequalities in the European Union due to the competitive advantages enjoyed by countries at the center (Lapavitsas et al. 2010), they take the competitiveness paradigm as a given. So when economists (both neoliberal and left-wing) point to the macro-economic "imbalances" in the eurozone or elsewhere, (e.g., Laskos and Tsakalotos 2013a, 82f.; Petrakis 2012, 340; Varoufakis 2011, 61) as the reasons for the ensuing crisis, they are pointing to the intrinsic or immanent outcomes of the economic game. Drawing on aggregate metrics such as GDP, sentiment indicators, or business climate indicators, these critiques speak the language of neoclassical economics, thus reproducing the logic of numbers. The underlying presumptions of such critiques are based on the unfairness of the current political-economic system. This, however, makes these critiques essentially liberal in spirit—merely reproducing the sovereignty of neoliberal principles as much as their methodologies (Davies 2014). As Luc Boltanski and Ève Chiapello (2017, 29) argue, "The price paid by critique for being listened to, at least in part, is to see some of the values it had mobilized to oppose the form taken by the accumulation process being placed at the service of accumulation." Critiques need to be susceptible to their reproductive qualities and therefore ought to be explicitly alter-neoliberal in spirit if they are to function as public pedagogy and are to limit the reproduction of neoliberal norms and principles.

Unsurprisingly, and arguably also due to the uninspiring, liberal nature of left-wing critiques that can barely be read as a radical alternative, the neoliberal critique succeeded in hegemonizing the ways in which the crisis has been confronted. In the end, the crisis has been entrusted to those who created it, which, as Max Haiven and Alex Khasnabish (2014, 31–32) point out, has consequences for the ways in which it is popularly perceived and signified: "Rather than challenging the status quo and setting the stage for a radical unsettling of it in order to make room for something new, the crisis trope encloses our collective imagination of what is possible, narrowing it to focus on the crisis as defined by those with the power to proclaim it."

Indeed, the ways in which political elites framed the crisis was really through discourses of anti-crisis. Instead of radically imagining alternatives, where principles and techniques of evaluation would be subjected to critique and debate, continuous state intervention and executive decisions are intended to defend the status quo and prevent the moment of radicalized judgment so inherent to crisis. Anti-crisis perpetuates an imagination that limits normative expectations of what is possible to what is necessary. Worsening economic and social conditions weigh heavily on individuals, which has the effect of lowering their expectations and guiding their conduct by threat rather than opportunity, in ways that strengthen rather than undermine the principles of the status quo. Anti-crisis, therefore, is to subject individuals to a regressive signification of crisis. Twenty-five-year old Petros, who is about to graduate from university with an economics degree, provides a telling example.

> [Crisis] is a violent displacement of normalcy and of reality. So in this period that we are talking about a logic that is harshly, harshly personal is being consolidated. You know, things are very difficult! Exactly because of this I need to study, to finish quickly, to get a Masters, to find a specialization, to do special seminars, to work so I can enter my industry as soon as possible so I can build my CV. And then I will see whether I can accomplish something. (Petros, personal communication, February 9, 2017)

In this regressive signification of crisis, people are to bear the brunt of its cost and try harder, trusting in authority's assertion that they indeed "lived beyond their means," that "we all ate together,"[1] and therefore "there is no alternative" to the "measures"—that is, a stricter, harsher adoption of the reforms of neoliberal modernization. For individual conduct, as Petros's example shows, this calls forth a stricter adherence to individualized subjectivity: increase human capital to be competitive amid ever increasing uncertainty. It is in an overwhelming feeling of paralyzing uncertainty, in the fear, stress, and anxiety born of uncertainty, that obedient service to the narrative of anti-crisis is rooted (Bauman 1999). In that sense, anti-crisis is much closer to a Schmittian (2007) state of exception than to crisis. It is still radically extraordinary, but without the possibility of alternative judgments. Instead, the extraordinariness of the situation is decided upon and enforced by sovereign executive authority, rather than by democratic debate (Davies 2014, 177). When European and Greek political leaders repeatedly pronounce the need for exceptional measures to tackle the crisis with an utterly detailed roadmap and contingent prior actions that must be completed before the payout of each tranche of loans, they are micromanaging the country's government by force of continuous executive decision. The meticulous, technocratic micromanagement of crisis serves to debar or delay judgment, for fear that the status quo would otherwise be destroyed. This signifies what Boltanski (2009, 104) calls "truth tests," where institutions *make visible the fact that there is a norm* in order to stabilize it. This is to render reality complete, closed in the sense that "this is all there is" (Susen and Turner 2014). Any critique that goes beyond self-responsibility and technocratic reform-implementation is rebuked as "impractical" or "unrealistic." As a discursive tool—very much resonating with modernizers' mocking of the search of alternatives to neoliberal modernization—this narrative effectively refutes any deviance, opposition, and resistance to what are Benthamism-inflected modes of action from the outset.

But as for a large number of people, including all of my interlocutors, there is no upside to the way the crisis is being managed, it becomes

---

1. A few months prior to Greece's first bailout package in 2010, PASOK veteran Theodoros Pangalos asserted in Parliament that everyone, not just politicians, bore the responsibility for the squandering of public money.

88 Paradoxes of Emancipation

increasingly difficult to sustain a narrative of "no alternative." The neoliberal justification for austerity as a way for Greece to exit the crisis—that is, increasing competitiveness by cultivating quasi-market conditions—was undermined by the fact that there is less and less to compete over. This refers to the unfulfilled promise that economic certainty can be achieved by competing for middle-class belonging. Petros offers a striking analysis regarding the limits of that paradigm.

> The ideology is deeply rooted in the brains of . . . a generation who has . . . learned that, you know, gradually generations get better, that the child needs to study hard to be better off, to get a good job. . . . Yes, [my parents] told me too. But . . . in Greece we're in a phase where youth unemployment . . . is at 50 percent. That means one out of two are out of a job. . . . This means that an expectation of Greek society that was upheld at least for thirty years has collapsed. We're not talking about how it's in tatters. It has already collapsed! (Petros, personal communication, February 9, 2017)

The justification of neoliberal crisis management for austerity being "necessary" dwindled as the crisis deepened. "The tale goes," thirty-three-year-old freelance journalist Thodoris tells me, "that austerity will make Greece better so people will be better off and can consume as they did before the crisis. But as the years pass, they have less and less money to live off" (personal communication, August 28, 2016). For an increasing number of people, it becomes impossible to sustain themselves, let alone compete for middle-class belonging. Not only does the belief in the (competitive) game—the *illusio*, as Pierre Bourdieu (2013) famously calls it—lose its appeal. By bailing out banks and as a consequence socializing the cost of the financial crisis downward, liberal values of opportunity, fairness, or the freedom of the market are effectively thrown overboard. With the rules of the market suspended, the justice of inequality can no longer be legitimated as fair, let alone just. Instead, state bailouts, austerity, and structural adjustments ensure that the winners of competition will always be the same, as will the losers. In effect, the anti-crisis management of the Greek crisis undermines competition's very conditions of possibility.

"Waking Up"   89

For my interlocutors, these contradictory developments cast doubt on the justifications for status quo crisis management, leading them increasingly to view crisis through what I call the progressive signification.

Progressive Significations

In the progressive signification of crisis, normative expectations are rendered so very fragile that previously doxic assumptions are elevated to the level of discourse, where they can be challenged (Crossley 2003). This signification builds strongly on Bourdieu's (2013, 168–69) crisis theory:

> The critique which brings the undiscussed into discussion, the unformulated into formulation, has as the condition of its possibility objective crisis, which, in breaking the immediate fit between the subjective structures and the objective structures, destroys self-evidence practically . . . the would-be most radical critique always has the limits that are assigned to it by the objective conditions.

Rather than what Bourdieu dubs "objective crisis," my interlocutors show how the progressive signification of crisis has as the condition of its possibility disbelief about, and a distancing from, the ways in which elites present crisis to us. This allows individuals to engage with what I call the previously unthought-of: an experience that transcends normative expectations and allows what was previously doxic and tacitly internalized to be reevaluated. Here, the possibility of critique and resistance is stimulated in ways that are susceptible to the radical imagination. The experience of crisis-derived hardship forces individuals into questioning the very norms they are subjected to and are subjecting themselves to. To my interlocutors, the material consequences of crisis enable what Boltanski (2011) calls a metapragmatic kind of critique: a meta-evaluation of not only the status quo of the crisis but also the order that is to be restored and perpetuated through austerity. In this regard, former manager Lukas rather agitatedly remarks:

> Do you see in this perpetual contest . . . some sort of progress for humans? I don't see that at all! I could . . . work eight to twelve hours in

a purely hierarchical environment. That means referring to those above me and those above me referring to the owners or shareholders . . . for half my life. In order to achieve what? To pay back the loan I took out for the house and the car, and to have consumer goods that others like me produce, who live the same lives. Do you see any meaning in this entire situation? (Lukas, personal communication, February 23, 2016)

As crisis abruptly displaces normative expectations, the rationality of these expectations themselves, and the practices that render them manageable, come under scrutiny. Following on from this critique, crisis comes to be signified through its creative and imaginative capacities.

We have come to the point where we in the [activist] groups say among ourselves that the crisis is a fucking important opportunity. If it were not for the crisis, none of this, not Syntagma, would have happened. The way we think, the way we consume, the way we live would have never changed. "The crisis is an opportunity," we often say. Not that we're happy. We don't say we're happy, of course. But we say, "Thank goodness the crisis exists." Because inside that crisis the people get worried, they start to think. (Katerina, personal communication, October 19, 2014)

The radical imagination of the Syntagma Square occupation signifies precisely this change in "the ways we consume and live." That is, profoundly alternative ways of practicing (alter-politics), and a distancing ("people get worried") from the status quo (anti-politics). In effect, the progressive signification of crisis is a key condition of possibility for such a process to unfold.

At the heart of this process lies the spatial manifestation of the progressive signification of crisis. In the introduction to this book, I elaborated on the claim that the subject is not the foundation of political (or other) practices, but rather its formation ought to be traced in these practices. I clarified that while the subject is an immanent effect of practices, this does not mean that it is entirely produced by the status quo of power and knowledge, governmental rationalities, and disciplinary technologies. Instead, the (politicized) subject is constituted in practice against, and in confrontation with, the practices of power. Because "it really does matter *where* the subject is" (Pile 2008, 214), and because "we usually experience ourselves, and other things, in relation to places and spaces" (Malpas 1999, 10), the next part of this chapter illuminates how these practices constitute and are manifested in space. From a dialectic viewpoint, space is the product of (space-making) practices, but it also influences our practices. Space prestructures, stabilizes, and gives durability to "doing" practices, which in turn allows the subject to be traced through these practices. This claim is grounded in the consideration that the temporality of occupations of squares, as a recurring space reproduction, allows newly conceived practices guided by alternative sets of norms and ethical principles to those of the status quo to become routine.

Approaching the Syntagma Square occupation as a liminal spatiality that is both a (structural) consequence and an (anti-structural) answer to the crisis in Greece allows us to think more carefully about the conditions of possibility for what my interlocutors refer to as "waking up": the emergence of the radical imagination (chapter 3) and the political quality of subjectivation that ensued from "demystifying" critiques of the status quo (chapter 4). Both are formative phenomena for the transformative experience with regard to the subjectivity my interlocutors narrate. This is because, as Steve Pile (2008, 214) claims, by "thinking through the spatial metaphors that can so easily become the common sense of how subjectivity is understood (the where you are from), new visions of the predicaments and joys of subjectivity can be produced."

The Spatiality of Syntagma Square

> We were sleeping a long time. As Greeks. The Greek people were sleeping. I told you: Bouzouki joints, credit cards and coffee shops. . . . Syntagma was a big bang inside the crisis, where many people woke up and decided to unite in order to change all that. (Maria, personal communication, February 10, 2016)

In her analysis of representations as affectively charged, anthropologist Begoña Aretxaga (2005, 201–5) convincingly illustrates that metaphors

92   Paradoxes of Emancipation

are not simply representations detached from social reality. Rather, metaphors "do" things: they organize and disguise (unconscious) significations; engender and enact political affectivities. Maria's use of "sleeping" and "woke up" is very much metaphorical, signifying the Syntagma Square occupation as a transitioning from unawareness to awareness. From an empirical viewpoint, Maria's example seems to suggest that sleeping signifies modernization as a period of unawareness—of ignorant consumerism, overt leisure, and credit culture (chapter 1).[2] "Waking up" points to the fact that Maria and my other interlocutors did not make sense of the crisis through what I earlier dubbed regressive signification, despite the elite's concentrated efforts of anti-crisis management and discourses. Conceptually, this metaphorical transitioning from unawareness to awareness can be read as a rite de passage similar to Arnold van Gennep's (2011) and Viktor Turner's (2008) theorization. This allows the Syntagma Square occupation to be viewed in its liminal and anti-structural capacity: as a transitory space that is "neither here nor there; . . . betwixt and between the positions assigned and arrayed by law, custom, convention, and ceremonial" (Turner 2008, 95). Structured by the significations of crisis ("big bang inside of crisis"), norms and expectations are negotiated creatively in such a liminal space, allowing the emergence and prefiguration of alternative, unthought-of practices and imaginations (chapter 3). Furthermore, drawing near to what Jacques Rancière (1999) describes, the political quality of subjectivation (chapter 4)—what my interlocutors refer to as "political maturation" against the practices of power—emerges precisely in situations of "being-between," which are, by definition, liminal.

A spatial approach to these considerations is justified, not least due to my interlocutors' own narratives: their talk of the square having an "inside" and an "outside," an "upper" and a "lower" part, indicates their awareness of spatial categories. Many mentioned in passing the word *space* (*Chōros*), whereas others, like Lukas, explicitly urged me not to "underestimate the spatial order" (personal communication, February 23, 2016). Apart from

---

2. It would be interesting to consider here whether this is sleeping or that which brings about the very unawareness of sleeping.

these more explicit empirical hints, a spatial approach also allows the inter-relationship between the practical, material, and affective aspects of "the social" to be taken into account as well as its structuring and structured capacities as to experience and subjectivity. At the epistemological heart of this approach lies the study of the social in its (Bourdieusian) dialectics, reconciling the relationship between structure and agency. Social phe-nomena become socially produced situations (Clarke 2005)—structuring and structured in practice—which transcend the normative assumptions of macro-meso-micro levels of analysis. Simply put, this is to say that crises structure spatialities and are structured by spatialities, spatialities structure subjectivities and are structured by subjectivities. And subjectivities there-fore structure crises and are structured by crises. While there is some dis-crepancy between the relatively circular conception of reproduction and Bourdieu's recognition that social structures are constantly in process and subject to change, situations of conflict, struggle, and change are ordinary features of processes of reproduction, where inventive actions "can both modify existing structures and generate new ones, breaking the 'circle' of reproduction" (Crossley 2003). In Bourdieu's (2013, 20) own words, "When-ever the adjustment between structures and dispositions is broken, the transformation of the generative schemes is doubtless reinforced and accel-erated by the dialectic between the schemes immanent in practice and the norms produced by reflection on practices, which impose new mean-ings on them by reference to alien structures." As I argued in chapter 1, neoliberal governmentality creates conditions of competitive uncertainty that are to mold a neoliberal subjectivity. This is because structures act as norms and rules that condition habits of thought and action. But as crises are inherently liminal situations, where subjects can become aware of the constructed nature of previously held doxic assumptions (what I call the progressive signification of crisis), the structuring quality of crises is marked precisely by the anti-structural—that is, by the now visible multiplicity and incommensurability of rival normative expectations. In structuring spatial-ities and subjectivities, crisis reproduces this multiplicity and incommensu-rability in practice. Subjects, with their ordinary conduct in turmoil due to the uncertainties of crisis, collectively produce spatialities that are expres-sions of, and answers to, both this turmoil and (the uncertainties of) crisis.

In abstract terms, the social orderings of such spatialities are a radical departure from the orderings of the status quo, not least due to the act of occupation itself: an extraordinary, often extrajudicial disruption of public order. The empirical characteristics of a given spatiality are contingent upon the specific affective, material, cultural, political, and historical qualities of a set of spatial categories. These categories consist of place, space, presence and space-making practices, and stasis and territoriality. Methodologically, these categories are derived from my interlocutors' meaning-making practices as well as previous and abducted theoretical considerations and similar observations in analogous empirical cases, such as the Tahrir Square occupation. They are constitutive of liminal spatialities and are crucial components for understanding the conditions of possibility for "waking up."

Place

The physical location of Syntagma Square as a place is the material prerequisite for the production of spaces. As sociologist Thomas Gieryn (2000, 473) notes, place "stabilizes and gives durability to social structural categories, differences and hierarchies; arranges patterns of face-to-face interaction that constitute network-formation and collective action; embodies and secures otherwise intangible cultural norms, identities, memories and values." In this sense, place prestructures the social production of space. Similar to Bourdieu's (2013, 169) observation that "the would-be most radical critique always has the limits that are assigned to it by the objective conditions," the material and symbolic characteristics of place do indeed play a limiting role in imagining, practicing, and experiencing space.

Syntagma Square is no exception to this. It received its name—*Syntagma* is the Greek word for "constitution"—in 1843 as a result of the 3 September 1843 Revolution. The Athens garrison of the Hellenic army, supported by a large crowd of ordinary people, gathered in the forecourt of King Otto's palace to demand a national assembly to work out a constitution; they also demanded the departure of the Bavarian officials who were dominating the country's government. The demand for a constitution was successful, and as a result, Otto later changed the forecourt's name from

Palace Square (Plateia Anaktorōn) to Constitution Square (Plateia Syntagmatos, using the adjectival form of *Syntagma*). Today, Otto's palace has been repurposed as the seat of the Greek Parliament. There are some intriguing, not-so-hidden symbolisms in this brief historical excursus. To my interlocutors, the role of the German government in managing the Greek financial crisis was reminiscent of the policies of the German-led monarchy of the nineteenth century. Their negative impressions also drew on the history of the cruel occupation of Greece by the Nazis through most of World War II (Mazower 2001). Indeed, the fact that the Greek Parliament—outside which tens of thousands of people during the 2011 occupation vehemently but unsuccessfully protested against the implementation of the government's measures—was once the residence of an autocrat paints an uneasy picture of the symbolisms of authority and representation. Lastly, the notion of Syntagma Square as a symbol of "granting" a constitution to the people raises the question of whether positive, constitutional rights—formed by power relations of state-institutional arrangements—can truly ever be the basis for emancipation (Foucault 2008).

I leave it to the reader to engage further with these considerations. The takeaway, however, should be that the role of place for contestation is significant beyond its functional purpose as a mere locality where protesters voice their demands and persevere with their struggle.

> It could not have happened somewhere else, because Syntagma Square symbolizes many things. First of all it has consolidated itself in the consciousness of the people as the "square of popular claims." All the protests that are going on always pass by here. So in some way this raises questions regarding people's consciousness. It is the square that claims must end up in. And of course the Voulē [Parliament] is opposite it. This too is important. They [protesters] feel that their message, even if they cannot hand it in personally, will be received through the windows by those inside— which is true. (Vasilis, personal communication, October 24, 2014)

Apart from the physical and infrastructural, place holds symbolic, historical, political, and therefore affective significance (chapter 3), which influences the social production of space. Similarly, as Aggelos points out:

96   Paradoxes of Emancipation

> I think that the fact that [the occupation] happens in front of the parliament is important; that it happens in front of where decisions are taken, important ones. It would have been different in Omonoia [the second most iconic square of central Athens]. But in front of the parliament, I think . . . it's symbolic, but also real. There were attempts to get in there and to burn it down [in a humorous tone]. (Aggelos, personal communication, January 26, 2017)[3]

Building on the work of sociologist Asef Bayat (2009), I argue that protesters' symbolic, affective, and functional associations with, and significations of, Syntagma Square, offer insights into why they chose this place for their contestation over others. First, apart from the historical significance of the square, the downtown area of Athens houses key political institutions symbolizing state power. Syntagma Square has been described as the "imagined centre of the nation" (Hager 2011, 551). Regarding institutions, apart from Parliament facing one side of the square, the Ministry of Finance is also right by Syntagma. The Megaro Maximou, which is the official seat of the prime minister, is less than six hundred meters away. Immediately adjacent to Syntagma Square is the five-star hotel Grande Bretagne, which has a long history of housing political and military elites and was a sort of unofficial residence of the Troika. Apart from this authoritarian significance, Syntagma Square's importance stems from uprisings that occurred in the area, other than the 3 September 1843 Revolution. Violent clashes erupted during the December events of 1944, which started in Syntagma Square, between members of the Greek left-wing resistance and the British troops who had entered Athens with the support of the returning Greek government. More recently, Syntagma Square was at the heart of the 2007 protests against the government's poor handling of countrywide

---

3. In an analogous manner, during the Egyptian uprising of 2011, protesters set the headquarters of the then-ruling National Democratic Party on fire, "Which they identified as a symbol for the corrupt, authoritarian rule responsible for their grievances. Setting the building on fire contributed to the protesters' perception that power structures are negotiable, as the regime was metaphorically slowly 'burning down'" (Soudias 2014, 118).

forest fires[4] and was an important locus of the 2008 Athens riots. Secondly, mobile crowds can rapidly assemble and disperse at the square via its adjacent avenues and side streets. This relates to people's familiarity with the area, and happened on multiple occasions when police officers raided the square with tear gas, and points to the tacit knowledge of and familiarity people have with the area. Syntagma Square also serves the function of an infrastructural intersection for mass transportation and communication networks, facilitating easier access and escape for potential protesters while being at the center of media attention. The Athens bureau of the Associated Press is within walking distance of Syntagma Square, and Reuters even has its offices right by the square. This allows protesters to project their discontent beyond their immediate environment.

In this sense, place is a unique material formation which, if we take Gieryn seriously, has implications for the "tacit" or "spontaneous" acknowledgment (chapter 3) of why discontent unfolded in Syntagma and not elsewhere. Thirty-two-year-old anarchist architect Panagiotis remarks, "The first protest in Syntagma was . . . against the King . . . and I believe since then there was such a, you know, 'knowledge' that the protests end up in Syntagma" (personal communication, October 6, 2014).

Despite the durable and stabilizing characteristics of place, its social construction needs to be conceived of as a process. In light of Athens' creeping neoliberalization during the modernization period, it is worth mentioning how the area around Syntagma Square has been transformed. With the pedestrianization of nearby Ermou Street, Syntagma Square became little more than a throughway to access more easily venues of consumption. Syntagma Square, Dimitris Dalakoglou (2013) rightly observes, was advertised as the "square-display of the capital city" and became "a neoliberal public space proper, where few people would sit or stand if they

---

4. "There was a precedent [to the 2011 Syntagma square occupation] in 2007, when there were large-scale [forest] fires. . . . Through blogs, etc., a nonpartisan protest had been organized in Syntagma, which was very large. There was no real content, it just had to do with the forests. . . . But there were many references [to this in the Syntagma square occupation in 2011], at least in the ways in which this whole thing was depicted in the media" (Panagiotis, personal communication, October 6, 2014).

were not consuming something in the coffee shops of the square or participating in carefully orchestrated and controlled events." Merely a locus of
leisure, Syntagma Square has been stripped of its metaphysical qualities,
reduced to the merely physical: subjects are encouraged to use the square
"passively" (for lack of a better word), through walking, driving, watching,
consuming, as an inherently depoliticized place. Lukas recalls, "One of the
first basic things that was gained was the reappropriation of public space.
Previously in Syntagma Square, people passed by and didn't even stand
still. It was a transit zone" (personal communication, February 23, 2016).
The construction of such "non-places," to use the term of anthropologist
Marc Augé (1995), was a common development in the renewal of central
Athens throughout the period of neoliberal modernization. Non-places
are assigned, classified, promoted, "where the habitué of supermarkets,
slot machines and credit cards communicates wordlessly, through gestures, with an abstract, unmediated commerce; a world thus surrendered
to solitary individuality, to the fleeting, the temporary and ephemeral"
(78). Considering this, it is of little surprise that my interlocutor Thodoris says, "Syntagma? Its best use was a meeting point to go have a beer"
(personal communication, October 17, 2014). The extended occupation
of Syntagma Square broke with this normative expectation, as the active,
participative use of Syntagma Square transformed the square's meaning
and repoliticized it. The process of this transformation is grounded in the
production of space.

Space

Assuming that place is indeed "the order of things without movement or
action" (Ismail 2006, xxxvi), space, as an analytical category, signifies the
characteristics of place laid out earlier, including movement or action.
As mentioned before, space is conceived in its dialectics as a structuring
and structured structure or, put differently, as the relationality between
space and human agency (Lefebvre 2007; Soja 1980, 1998). Stamatis, a
seasonal waiter in his mid-forties who had little protest experience prior
to Syntagma, offers a good example of the occupation's spatial dialectics.

> How can I say? . . . It generally had a changeable character. This means its character changed continuously. It wasn't a steadily organized structure. . . . Basically it didn't have an organized structure. It was a—how should I put this?—an organism. Imagine an organism that reacts to stimuli. (Stamatis, personal communication, February 3, 2016)

Stamatis's metaphor drawn from biology naturalizes space as something given. His tacit assumption of Syntagma Square's structuring qualities resonates with Trevor Barnes's (2002) claim that biological metaphors in the social sciences often point to the inherent functions of social phenomena. Relatedly, Stamatis's metaphorical use of "organism" and "stimuli" points to scholarly works in critical geography and urban sociology, which assume that people act according to intersectional positions such as gender, class, sexuality, race, physical ability, or age "within" and in reaction to space, but also create and modify particular spaces to express their own needs and desires (e.g., Gottdiener and Hutchinson 2010). A Lefebvrian (2007, 36–37) conception underlines this processual and dialectic character of space. In his own words, the "'object' of interest must be expected to shift from things in space to the actual *production of space*." Here, spaces are constructed through social relations, especially practices, and structures. Acknowledging that spaces are experienced in multiple ways, Lefebvre (33, 38–39, 245) identifies the triad of conceived space (representations of space), perceived space (spatial practice), and lived space (representational space); he sees a unity between the (abstract) imaginative, the (concrete) material, and the social (see also Elden 2004; Martin and Miller 2003). Squares and streets have been conceived—that is, designed and planned by experts through labor, technology, and institutions. The ways in which they are designed and planned are intended to ensure a particular kind of order. They are perceived in everyday life in their materiality and physicality. The meaning of, and affectivities toward, such spaces, however, are adapted and transformed as they are lived by social actors. Lived space, then, is where perception and conception meet and interact, where "the imagination seeks to change and appropriate" (Lefebvre 2007, 39). This conceptual view is a case in point for the transformation of Syntagma

Square from non-place to the spatial manifestation of the radical imagination (chapter 3). Conceived as a forecourt to King Otto's palace, how the square has been popularly perceived has been in flux ever since: living Syntagma Square as a space of contestation, a meeting spot, a transportation hub, a throughway for leisure, and yet again a space for contestation offers but a few examples of this ongoing process. With the beginning of the Syntagma Square occupation, the square has been lived as a space of resistance, as one of contestation against the status quo and for something else entirely, despite its initial conception.

Presence and Space-Making Practices

A key premise for the transformation of spaces with regard to occupations lies in bodily, extraordinary presence (Schumann and Soudias 2013). By being present in Syntagma Square, protesters take part in the production of spaces and transform them in practice. To give an example: forty-one-year-old private English tutor Viktoria describes the very beginnings of the Syntagma Square occupation. Her decision to go was made at the Spanish embassy in Athens' Thisseio neighborhood, during the solidarity protests with the Spanish Indignados.

> We went there [Syntagma Square] at 1 am. Some set up a tent. I went home to sleep with the purpose of getting up early so as to begin. We didn't have a plan. We didn't know. . . . And the next morning it was raining. I remember that well. I get up and go to Syntagma. There weren't any people. Not even the Spanish came in the morning. There were two people from the group of Thisseio who only brought a small tent and a small table. I brought my laptop. We set up the laptop. Just three people. (Viktoria, personal communication, October 22, 2014)

Merely by being present in the square, and through such seemingly mundane space-making practices as setting up tables and laptops, Viktoria and her comrades began transforming the setup and meaning of Syntagma Square into something else. A few hours in, passersby started perceiving the square differently; they got curious and engaged in conversations with those who had recently turned into occupiers. So did an elderly woman, Viktoria recalls:

> "What will you eat?" she says. "We will buy something," I tell her. She says "I will go cook with my women friends and I will bring you [food]." And she brought us Tupperware. And so the grandmother with her friends started the next group, which is the catering and cooking group. (Viktoria, personal communication, October 22, 2014)

This may seem banal, but it underlines the relevance of presence as the prerequisite for space transformation. To be present allows for interactions and highlights the possibility for contemplation, discovery, epiphany, or (radical) imagination (Bamyeh 2013; Schumann and Soudias 2013). The formation of various structures and groups such as the medical clinic, the popular assembly, or the group of political economy are space-making practices that produce Syntagma Square as a space with particular sets of norms and guiding principles. To put it in more Lefebvrian terms, through such practices, protesters use Syntagma Square in a manner other than its initial conception, turning the square into something else entirely, appropriated in use. The square's "orderly" use of merely passing by or meeting up with friends changes toward an "exceptional" appropriation with changing practices, symbols, norms, discourses, and moral principles. These are broadly made up of an egalitarian and antiauthoritarian ethic.

Beyond the active and engaging potentialities of presence, there is also a more passive quality to it that finds its formulation in affect. A simple, but telling signifier in this regard is the phrase *I was there*, repeated by many of my interlocutors.

> The reason I went is basically that something was going on there [said with enthusiasm]. Something was going on and many people went, and I also wanted to be [there]. So that was the first move. I felt good being there, okay? And even if you didn't speak. I sometimes just went and observed the people. This made me feel better. . . . I don't know. (Maria, personal communication, February 10, 2016)

Feeling good through simply being there fosters affectivities between occupiers but also toward the square itself, which my interlocutors find difficult to fully "discursivize." The sensual and bodily experience of being present in a shared space allows for the generation of affective bonds and commitments that contribute to the enduring spatial reproduction of the occupation of the square. These sorts of affective commitments further a sense of shared ownership over space that has territorial implications regarding a perceived "inside" and "outside," and perpetually made my interlocutors return to the square. This is not least because, as Alain Badiou (2005, 256) points out, "Fidelity to the site is . . . in essence, fidelity to the event." These processes are not uncontested. The presence of protesters (and the space transformation that comes with it) jeopardizes the use of these spaces according to their initial conception (conceived space) and calls authorities to the scene to enforce "public order" through repressive policing strategies in an attempt to quell divergence.

Stasis and Territoriality

Without presence social space cannot be produced, but it is in and of itself not particular to protest occupations, as it also occurs in, say, marches or demonstrations. What distinguishes occupations is that, as Thodoris puts it, "In the first few days, there were people *coming by,* ok? At some point people came *to stay*" (personal communication, October 17, 2014; emphasis added). This distinction has concrete implications for the temporality of presence. Lukas corroborates this viewpoint, describing the occupation

> like a public space in the everyday. The protests are another thing. Protests occurred in the entire decade, in the entire twentieth century and the twenty-first century. . . . But Syntagma as a static gathering of people, to such an extent, has not occurred since the political gatherings of the eighties—which wasn't even the reappropriation of public space, it was an occasional occurrence. . . . So this was a thing that was achieved after 2011. De Facto. (Lukas, personal communication, February 23, 2016)

What Lukas refers to as "everyday" and "static" describes presence beyond the ephemerality of protest marches. This signifies what the ancient Greek notion of stasis seeks to capture. Costas Douzinas (2013, 153) frames stasis as "upright posture, standing tall and serene, holding your stance." Stasis allows for the recognition of one's own strength (Tsavdaroglou 2017), as it "creates both a space for reflection and a space for revolt, but also an affective comportment of standing and standpoint" (Butler and Athanasiou 2013, 151). As opposed to protest marches or demonstrations, the stasis of occupations allows practices to be perpetuated and made routine. Stasis, in turn, allows for the development of an extraordinary everyday that parallels the quotidian. A practice-theory approach toward subjectivity argues that it is precisely because of such processes of routinization that meaningful guidelines for subjectivity can emerge.

> This entire thing, let's call it "Syntagma Square," was a crucial factor, an important moment. I mean, my life took a turn. There was something before, but it *asphalted* the change of my way of thinking and all that. (Maria, personal communication, January 27, 2016; emphasis added)

Metaphorically, Maria's choice of the word *asphalted* conveys the fixing, the internalization, the routinization of her changing practices in quite literal ways. What is more, stasis allows for both prolonged processes of territorialization that foster a sense of ownership over place, and simultaneously deterritorialization that seeks to overcome the status quo order of place altogether.

> I was always there. The developments gave you a sense of duty: that you have to stay. And this wasn't a duty that somebody else assigned to you. Everybody assigns it to themselves. (Lukas, personal communication, February 23, 2016)

The assertion of attachment and responsibility ("sense of duty") and an almost militaristic collective self-subjection ("everybody assigns themselves") resonate with Robert Sack's (1993, 19) definition of *territoriality* as "the attempt by an individual or group to affect, influence, or control people, phenomena, and relationships, by delimiting and asserting control over a geographic area." Elaborating further, Lukas explains that the importance of this "sense of duty" lies in the contested nature of territorialization:

It is very important that despite the repression, people didn't leave! If people don't leave, at some point, the forces of repression get exhausted. There were days when they were lying on the ground. Madness. I mean, from the exhaustion. Because they were on duty seventeen to eighteen hours. (Lukas, personal communication, February 23, 2016)

Territorialization, then, is not a unilinear but rather an interactive and relational process. Protesters' appropriation of place and production of spaces of resistance are challenging state territoriality. This brings the police to the scene, more often than not bringing with them a range of repressive strategies. The state's actualities of domination and subordination build on its control over territory. The police are agents of enforcing this control. They are given a set of legal and coercive powers to enforce control in terms of Foucaultian (1995) disciplinary power. They represent authority through their physical presence at places and use their powers to (re)produce and maintain spaces according to particular sets of norms that can be broadly subsumed under status quo public order.[5] Maintaining public order remains fundamental because it is "the test of a government's capacity to govern" (Anderson 2011, 155). Therefore, security forces attempt to prohibit protesters from constituting spaces of resistance through their very own territorialization so as to maintain public order—that is, the capacity to govern. Steve Herbert (1997, 6–10) notes:

> Territorial control is an inherent outcome of the social organization of the police . . . modern policing has meant the development of a capacity to intrude into and control space . . . officers can, when necessary, secure control of the flow of action in space. The police . . . are expected to be effective agents of territoriality, to be able to control social action by controlling area.

5. A discussion on the conception and practice of "public order" is beyond the scope of this book. For this, I suggest turning to Anderson (2011), who offers an exciting account of the term in his analysis of the French police.

The notion of social control in relation to Foucaultian governmentality exposes territoriality as a means of subjectification: of ensuring the docility of subjects in relation to the orders of the status quo. Many policing strategies involve enacting boundaries, restricting access, and using force to create and maintain public order. Sack (1993, 327) notes, "Social power cannot exist without these territorial rules. Territorial and social rules are mutually constitutive." The state's authority and existence is dependent on "the capacity of the police to mark and enact meaningful boundaries, to restrict people's capacity to act by regulating their movements in space" (Herbert 1997, 13). To lose territorial control, therefore, also means to lose authority and sovereignty. For example, once Syntagma Square was taken over by protesters, the threshold for extending their discontent beyond the square was significantly lowered; occupations proliferated as even public buildings and ministries were occupied (Douzinas 2013). Underlining the importance of stasis, Thodoris illustrates how the contestation over territorialization materialized in the square:

> When the police tried to evacuate the square, there was this point when you have to take the square. You have to own the square. So you have to get back the square, which is very interesting. It's something that you cannot do at a general strike, for instance, or at demonstrations. (Thodoris, personal communication, October 17, 2014; emphasis added)

In this sense, space-making practices and stasis further a claim to ownership over territory that physically locates autonomy (away from state authority). But not everybody was happy with the underlying implications of social control for protesters' very own territorial claim, as Irini, an environmentalist activist and street market vendor in her late forties, shows. Talking about the square's "defense group," she states:

> They brought their tents and in them they had their laptops. . . . Then they established the defence group, so they would protect their laptops that were in their tents. They walked by, like cops, looking inside the tents [said with disgust]. This is when the system divided us. And this is

106   Paradoxes of Emancipation

when it was taken from us. Because when we are cops, we are divided. (Irini, personal communication, February 3, 2016)

For Irini, the compartmentalization of the Syntagma Square occupation into groups eventually led her to stop going to the square. Her reference to being "divided" can be signified as a result of this compartmentalization. Each group in the occupation had its own location and role in the square. And with this place and division of labor—in addition to the de facto social-control mandate of the defense group—comes a sort of micro-territoriality that, paradoxically, reproduces the very logics of social control Irini sought to challenge with her participation in the first place. In this sense, to occupy Syntagma Square means not only to physically locate autonomy from social control by state authorities, but to aspire to autonomy from social control altogether. What Irini's dissatisfaction shows is that by producing spaces, protesters do not merely strive for reformist change or other forms of reproducing the status quo along different political lines. Rather, such spaces are expressions of a struggle for alternative sets of practices and orders—what I referred to in the introduction as radical imagination and what others have called "experiments in living otherwise" (McKay 2005), "radical political imaginaries" (Hage 2015), or "heterotopias" (Castro Varela and Dhawan 2006; Foucault 1986). That is to say, that with the territorial comes the ideational, which is one reason why contention over space is a direct challenge to state control and authority. But it is also a contentious issue with regard to how to imagine and practice radical alternatives that minimize the reproduction of the orders of the status quo.

The Upper and the Lower Square

As protesters territorialize Syntagma Square and practice the spatial production of the square, they are increasingly confronted with the radical changing of norms and expectations. In Petros's own analysis:

You move in a delimited space within a contemporary society—because contemporary society . . . can limit your movement in de facto ways—without you ever realizing that. You work, you go home, you go to sleep, you walk on the sidewalks, you cross the traffic light when it's green. When it's red you stop, right? When you are so violently moved towards another direction, . . . when you see that this thing can actually happen . . . before that I hadn't thought that such a thing can happen. And I don't think anybody did. That through a movement . . . the everyday life of a city can be so violently disrupted. (Petros, personal communication, February 9, 2017)

Petros's considerations provide us with telling insights as to the relation between crisis, normative expectations, and spatial production. In pragmatist thought, there is the assumption that while individuals possess a critical autonomy, they nevertheless remain limited in the types of actions, decisions, statements, and routines available to them. Such "conventions" (Boltanski 2012) exist as sets of rules that condition and limit the forms of thought and conduct available to people ("without you even realizing it"). As Petros's example shows, however, in situations of crisis, people indeed possess the ability to question and penetrate normative orders. This is indicative of the fact that expectations extend beyond the tramlines laid down by any single (moral) system and that taken-for-granted norms and "truths" are contingent (Davies 2014, 31). After all, the taking over of Syntagma Square in and of itself is a disruption of public order, and therefore, a "violent disruption," as Petros would have it, of a normative expectation in everyday life through a collective and participatory out-of-the-ordinary process. It underlines my previous considerations regarding the transition from unawareness to awareness, grounded in the metaphors of "sleeping" and "waking up." Describing Syntagma Square as an "earthquake," former advertising executive-turned-solidarity-economy-activist Andreas offers another instance as to the violent disruption of normative expectations:

If for a hundred years you have your mind closed, and then after a hundred years you open it, what comes out of it is . . . almost delirious, I mean crazy! But this was beautiful, because there was such passion in the square. (Andreas, personal communication, February 11, 2016)

In line with these empirical observations, crisis structures the out-of-the-ordinary use of Syntagma Square and the ensuing construction of space as a situation in which doxic assumptions become visible. The visibility of these previously taken-for-granted assumptions relative to the realities of practicing the unthought-of constructs Syntagma Square as a liminal spatiality: a temporary reversal of, or even an expulsion from, the social order; a transitional time in which taken-for-granted norms, rules, and cultural templates of what is conventional, appropriate, and justified can be collectively and creatively (re)negotiated. Being "on the limit" is genuinely a situation where "anything is possible!", as Turner (2008, 94) puts it. In the case of my interlocutors, the liminal character of the occupation reproduces the structural characteristics of the progressive signification of crisis, in that the opportunity for critical reflection and debate upon previously unquestioned assumptions is made possible, precisely because "the 'fit' between objective structures and subjective expectations is broken" (Crossley 2003, 47). Panagiotis points out:

> Also for the politicized, Syntagma touched on the established order of things. It did make some people get out of what they were used to. . . . Because in protests there is a habit that, when repeated, sets some regularities. It generally surprised many different and heterogeneous people. (Panagiotis, personal communication, October 6, 2014)

On the one hand, Syntagma Square, in its stasis capacity as a prolonged out-of-the-ordinary copresence of thousands of individuals, signifies a situation in which many "different and heterogeneous" normative expectations slip out of alignment with the actualities of the space, thereby shocking individuals out of their habitual acceptance of taken-for-granted norms and into a more critical attitude. These processes enable the unthought-of: an experience that transcends normative expectations and allows for reevaluation of what was previously doxic and tacitly internalized. In this regard, Lukas remarks that "what is going on exceeds what you considered acceptable and normal until then. . . . Perhaps because humans need to expose themselves to something different from what they have lived until that moment, so that they can really change" (personal communication, February 23, 2016).

On the other hand, Bourdieu (2013, 169) reminds us that crisis "is a necessary condition for a questioning of doxa but is not in itself a sufficient condition for the production of a critical discourse." Therefore, although the production of liminal spatialities can enable the radical imagination (chapter 3) and demystifying critiques of the status quo (chapter 4), it does not have to do so. The spatial demarcation of the upper square and the lower square are case in point. In this regard, the particular ways in which crisis is signified and the guiding principles of how spatial reproduction is practiced are empirical questions that lie at the heart of understanding why the two squares were so radically different in their imagining (of alternatives) and critiquing the status quo.

The so-called lower square is Syntagma Square proper. The upper square is the smaller rectangular area on the other side of the broad Amalias Avenue. It is bounded on one side by the avenue and on the other by the Parliament building. The two squares were territorially and ideologically demarcated, varying in the ways in which respective participants practiced protest and the production of space, critiqued the status quo, and imagined ways of coping with, and overcoming, crisis. In broad terms, for those below, the upper square was where right-wing and fascist ideologies were dominant. For those above, the lower part was a stronghold of the left, especially the Coalition of the Radical Left (SYRIZA) and the anarchist milieu (Bakola 2017, 98).

Practicing the Upper Square

As early as May 22, protesters congregated in the upper square. Along its railings, stands, and pavilions of such diverse groups as the three hundred Greeks—who were collecting signatures to hold a referendum to abolish parliamentary privilege and the memorandum, and to chase the International Monetary Fund out of Greece—and priests of the Orthodox church were set up side by side. According to Stavrou (2011, 33), the groups in the upper square formed "the conservative block" of Syntagma. Similarly, Roussos (2014, 61) describes those participating in the upper square as "people coming from the conservative space of the center-right or the popular right, disappointed voters" of the two major parties—conservative New Democracy and social democrat Panhellenic Socialist Movement (PASOK)—in addition to people who had not previously taken part in either formal politics or protests. But there are also accounts of openly fascist groups (Bakola 2017, 174).[6] From the perspective of the lower square, those above were usually looked down on.

> Now, at Syntagma Square, and this is very interesting, there were two different portions of people. The one portion of the people was in the upper part of the square. They were called "indignants." In the lower part of the square you had "our space," to put it that way. OK? In the upper part of the square, there were people who complained about what was going on, essentially against the crisis. They . . . banged saucepans, they did the *Mountza*[7] and such things. (Aggelos, personal communication, January 27, 2016)

The upper part has been described as having a carnivalesque mood and a more "stadium-like" atmosphere and "psychology" (Stavrou 2011, 32). In the narrative of my interlocutors, the upper square was one of bodily practices and protest rituals, such as chanting, clapping, cheering, and dancing. By blowing whistles, banging saucepans, yelling loudly against the "thieves" and "traitors" inside Parliament, and chanting, "Let it burn, let it burn, the brothel called Voulē," a cultural performativity of body politics by those in the upper square created a liminal, bodily communality similar to that seen in parades, festivals, or sports events. This performativity not only signals inclusion by those participating, but is also a way of engaging with politics by way of gesture and affect, rather than by words

---

6. "There was a very big difference. They [in the upper square] were nationalists, fascists. The wider left was below. . . . I mean, one guy said, "We need to get rid of the migrants," the other guy said, "I want to beat the guy who wants to get rid of the migrants" (Panagiotis, personal communication, February 17, 2016).

7. The *Mountza* is a very long-standing, everyday gesture of insult in Greece. The gesture is practiced by holding one's palm toward somebody else in order to express condescendence. It is an affective display of anger, disdain and, above all, indignation (Tsomou 2014b, 121).

"Waking Up" 111

and verbal discussion. "The protesters here seem 'properly' enraged. They are done discussing; they simply want to shout against the 'thieves' and the 'liars' inside parliament" (Hager 2011, 552). Indeed, whenever forums of discussion were attempted in the upper square they fell apart due to a lack of interest and participation (Stavrou 2011, 34).[8] In this regard, Tsomou (2014b, 125) observes the upper square's "hooliganist-aggressive performativity" was appealing to, and compatible with, regressive forces, precisely because they sought to drive the affective dimensions of anger and indignation in a more nationalist and fascist direction. Waving the Greek flag and singing the national anthem, as recurring discursive and symbolic performances in the upper square, created a sense of "communitas" (Turner 2008) held together by "Greekness" and latent ethnocentrism. This served the purpose of unifying against the perceived neocolonial assaults of institutional Europe as well as the political class that had "betrayed" them.

Relating these observations back to Turner's (2008) work on liminality, the upper square also signifies an anti-structural state, one that is "betwixt and between" and inherently transitory. Keeping in mind the etymology of liminality as derived from the Latin word for threshold (*limen*), liminality can lead from one structure to another but can also lead back to the same. Chanting "thieves," "traitors," or "liars" suggests a broken promise, an expectation toward state-institutional arrangements that has not been met. As a critique, it is immanent: it seeks the reestablishment of an order and the satisfaction of a demand prior to the crisis, rather than a radical departure from it. In this sense, the ways in which the upper square performed contestation denotes a performative display of what I have previously termed a regressive signification of crisis. The

---

8. A few times, political figures such as former MP Georgios Karatzaferis of the then-governing Popular Orthodox Rally (LAOS) came to the upper square to give speeches. Vasilis remembers that "Karatzaferis came and held an event during this time, saying that we should not leave the square to the left. That we shouldn't bestow the square to the left. So later, in some way, there were more right-wing, let's say, voters" present in the upper square (personal communication, October 24, 2014). In the past, Karatzaferis has frequently sympathized with the racist and now outlawed Golden Dawn party and engaged in antisemitic slurs (Nedos 2005).

112   Paradoxes of Emancipation

insecurities and uncertainties conditioned by neoliberal modernization and aggravated by the crisis perpetuate an imagination that limits normative expectations of what is possible to what is necessary. This imagination diminishes expectations and guides conduct through threat, rather than opportunity, in ways that only strengthen, rather than undermine, the orders of the status quo. Cloaked in an amalgam of ethnocentric and conservative values, such a critique seeks to find meaning, security, certainty, and order by returning to a mythical moment prior to the crisis—an illusionary past that never existed. By not engaging in discussions, all that participants of the upper square are left with is affect: anger and indignation against "those above" and joy and pleasure within their communitas. Despite the liminal character of the upper square, the near absence of articulated ideas and (political) proposals arguably impeded their transformation, making it difficult for the radical imagination to emerge and "demystifying" critiques to be generated.

Practicing the Lower Square

Thirty-six-year-old refugee activist and café co-owner Eleftheria, who took part in the lower square, notes that the two squares "rarely interacted. Some from the upper square sometimes came down out of curiosity. But they never took part in our actions" (personal communication, October 6, 2014).[9] In my interlocutors' perceptions, it was the lower square that went beyond mere bodily presence and affect and came to mean political vision, organization, and assembly.

> In the lower part of the square, the choice was more collective and directly democratic. This means, groups started being created. The

---

9. Such an account raises the question as to how my interlocutors were able to recognize participants of the upper square. Their criteria of distinction are often vague, and their accounts would often remain on an affective and aesthetic level and dependent on particular markers. Examples include the short haircuts of participants (they were mostly male in my interlocutors' perceptions) of the upper square, their aggressive posture and vulgar expressions, and their carrying of the Greek flag or other national symbols.

artists' group, the economy group . . . many different groups. We decided to live there, to put up tents and try to function collectively and in an organized way . . . different from those banging saucepans and complaining. So it was a different approach. That we can do things here and now. Whereas the [people] above where like, "We will kill them . . . and what have they done to us!" . . . On the one hand there is the confrontation without [said with emphasis] a proposition for something new. And then there is the "we can here and now do things." So, I was participating in the lower square. There, where you had self-organization. It's organization within groups, with large assemblies where everybody could speak and take decisions in a more direct, democratic way. (Aggelos, personal communication, January 27, 2016)

Aggelos, like most other interlocutors,[10] generally views the upper square in negative terms. While this may not necessarily tell us something about the "realities" of the upper square, the way in which my interlocutors represent it as a contrast provides us with insights into their own expectations and ideas about politics and the political, their signification of the crisis and, therefore, their (changing) position as subjects. Practicing "something new" provides a glimpse into the radical imagination of the lower square's practices, where self-organization and direct democratic practices constitute a radical departure from the ways in which we usually go about our everyday.

Conditioning Possibilities

This chapter dissected the relationship between significations of crisis and the spatial production of the Syntagma Square occupation as the conditions of possibility for the emergence of the radical imagination. Despite the fact that crises are inherently liminal situations, they do not necessitate the emergence of radical critiques, judgments, and alternatives to cope

---

10. Viktoria offers another example: "They were just up there nagging. They didn't have anything to offer. And they also had a violent behaviour. I mean, they made this *Mountzōma*" (personal communication, October 22, 2014).

114 Paradoxes of Emancipation

with and overcome crisis. Instead, the ways in which crisis comes to be signified by subjects tells us a lot more about the potentiality for the emergence of the radical imagination and demystifying critiques of the status quo. The ways in which political elites justified and managed the Greek crisis is really signified by anti-crisis. Analogous to a Schmittian (2007) state of exception, anti-crisis is radically extraordinary, but without the possibility of alternative judgments. Instead, the extraordinariness of the situation is decided upon and enforced by sovereign executive authority in an effort to uphold the *illusio* (Bourdieu 2013) and delay critique or even debar it entirely.[11] In this narrative, to overcome the crisis individuals must adhere to the immanent logics and measures of neoliberalism in even stricter ways, reducing what is possible to what is necessary. In effect, this is to nudge individuals toward a regressive signification of crisis, demanding that they subject themselves to a neoliberal (governmental) rationality in ever more competitive, flexible, and resilient ways.

But as anti-crisis suspends market rules, it also strips competition of its alleged fairness, undermining competition's conditions of possibility. For my interlocutors, therefore, in addition to the increasing precariousness of life, the "belief in the game" loses its appeal precisely because neoliberalism's anti-crisis signification is unjustified. This forces upon them reconsideration, allowing for the emergence of what I dub the progressive signification of crisis. Here, normative expectations are rendered so very fragile that previously doxic assumptions are elevated to the level of discourse, where they can be critiqued. In this progressive signification of crisis, my interlocutors can conceive of the previously unthought-of, where possibility is stimulated in ways that are susceptible to the radical imagination and demystifying critiques of the status quo.

The significations of crisis found their spatial manifestation in the Syntagma Square occupation.[12] Here, what allows the origination and rou-

---

11. "Leibniz, for instance, interpreted 'the suspension of judgment (*epoché*) as "doubt" and doubt as an involuntary state of ignorance which leaves us at the mercy of impulses originating in the passions'" (Bauman 2008, 59).

12. It could be argued that anti-crisis, too, was spatially manifested in the Syntagma Square occupation: the police also took part in the production of space marked by the

"Waking Up" 115

tinization of practices reproducing space lies in occupation's stasis. Intertwined with place, presence, and territoriality, stasis allows space-making practices to be routinized in ways that render them quotidian. Whereas the upper square was marked by a regressive signification of crisis that reproduced logics of the status quo, the lower square's progressive signification of crisis laid the groundwork for the emergence of the radical imagination.[13]

---

constitutive spatial categories I have elaborated on throughout this chapter. The police's mandate of social control, grounded in its monopoly of force, allows extraordinary ways of conduct—that is, the use of violence—without allowing alternative judgments as to the legitimacy of using force. Because the occupation of Syntagma Square is extraordinary and extrajudicial, the police's efforts to enforce order through violence are simply viewed as "necessary."

13. Dimitriou (2014, 76) offers a further intriguing conceptualization in this regard, attributing to the upper part of the square a Dionysian character and to the lower part an Apollonion one. The Dionysian was the part of excess and "bodily gestures, movements, songs, cries and chants. The second one represented metaphorically the mind within the body, hosting people's assembly and the movement's camp." In this reading, the Dionysian character can be viewed as escapism similar to excess and intoxication.

3

Aspiring the Utopian

The Alter-Politics of Radical Imagination

When asked what encapsulates the importance of his experience in the Syntagma Square occupation, Stamatis replies:

> There, I found a new structure in my life. . . . I was in a phase, at a turning point in my life. . . . Because the model, at the time, of the economy—that we work, make money, spend it and so on and so forth—the consequences started to show. I needed to find some stability, some other way in my life. Because otherwise, OK—what should I do? Turn nuts? Should I commit suicide? [laughs and knocks on wood]. (Stamatis, personal communication, February 3, 2016)

The material realities of the Greek crisis brought Stamatis to question the ways in which he was going about his everyday. Facing a turning point in his life, arguably because his ordinary conduct did not fit these new realities, his participation in the Syntagma Square occupation provided him with a sense of certainty and stability. Additionally, throughout our conversation it became clear that taking part in the occupation essentially made him feel better. Instead of what I dubbed as the regressive signification of crisis in the previous chapter, where what is possible is reduced to what is necessary, out of the fear, stress, and anxiety born of uncertainty, Stamatis perceives crisis in its creative and imaginative capacity. In this progressive signification of crisis, his participation in the Syntagma Square occupation allowed him to envision radical alternatives to the status quo in practice.

From a cultural studies viewpoint on practice theory, practices are guided by normative conditions of what is, intersubjectively, appropriate action. Integral to any practice, these norms are learned as knowledge, and acquired by experience and discoveries of how to do things (Wallace 2008). According to Andreas Reckwitz (2002, 249), practices are a "routinized type of behavior which consists of several elements, interconnected to one other: forms of bodily activities, forms of mental activities, 'things' and their use, a background knowledge in the form of understanding, know-how, states of emotion and motivational knowledge." A practice—for example, a way of setting up a working group in Syntagma Square, of discussing politics, of consuming, of taking care of oneself and others—forms a conglomerate of those activities that Reckwitz refers to, and cannot be reduced to any single one of them. That is to say that these activities form practice as something that is understandable (to others) and "held together" by tacit, methodical, and interpretative knowledge (Reckwitz 2003). Beyond single acts, practices are marked by routinization and habitualization. In short, actors tend to repeat, and therefore, reproduce, practices.

As argued in the previous chapter, situations of crisis are liminal in nature and require embedded or "context-sensitive" significations, which, depending on how precisely crisis is signified, "force" reinterpretations onto practices, effectively breaking with sole reproduction. In other words, the extraordinary event of the Syntagma Square occupation as a structured result of, and a structuring answer to, the ongoing crisis in Greece confronted routinized practices in ways that broke through "ordinary" patterns of habits of thought and action. This allowed practice to be reconsidered and modified.

In Syntagma Square, these reconsiderations were codified from the outset in the first call to action, dated May 20, 2011. Issued on Facebook, supposedly by three young people wanting to express their indignation about the economic crisis in Greece (Stavrides 2012, 586), the call proclaims that "today's young people are not like the previous ones," as they are marked by "a new mentality and a different ideology which will bring radical changes to our society" (quoted in Giovanopoulos and Mitropoulos 2011, 278). Seeking to mobilize people for May 25, the first call

118   Paradoxes of Emancipation

proposes an explicitly nonviolent protest, without leaders, with no flags to be displayed, and where parties and party-adjacent organizations were not welcome. People are called upon to take part in the protest as individuals and are held "responsible for their words and their actions." The event was to be spontaneous, "without schemes and plans" (278).

Nonviolent action, the role of parties and flags, as well as the call's reference to spontaneity and a "new mentality" can be read as a set of codified precursor norms for how social relations and forms of organization could be practiced differently. As I argued in the introduction to this book, the radical imagination is characterized by a certain balance between anti-politics and alter-politics (Hage 2015), where anti-politics signifies the act of distancing from the existing order, and alter-politics aims at providing alternatives to that order. Throughout this chapter, I seek to lay bare the ways in which the latter was practiced in Syntagma Square.

First, I argue that the radical imagination of the Syntagma Square occupation can be broadly subsumed under an antiauthoritarian and egalitarian ethic (Breton et al. 2012), guided by principles of equality, collectivity, mutual respect, autonomy (from the state), self-governance, self-organization, and solidarity. In that sense, these principles stand in stark contrast to the neoliberal precepts and individualizing subject positions during the period of modernization I elaborated on in chapter 1. What is more, these principles shape and are shaped by my interlocutors' practices and imaginaries of what a better society may look like (alter-politics), their demystifying critiques of status quo state-institutional arrangements (anti-politics; see chapter 4), and their self-proclaimed (re)formation of subjectivity (chapter 5). Therefore, my second argument is that the conditions of possibility for the transformative character of participation in the Syntagma Square occupation lay precisely in the prefigurative layout of how these principles are practiced. If thinkers like Alain Badiou (2005) and Jacques Rancière (1999) are right to assume that equality is the ontological basis of radical politics itself, then the ability to practice equality in the here and now (i.e., prefiguration) allows for grasping the transformative character of these practices as to subjectivity. This is to say that by practicing the change that is desired, (re)formations of subjectivities emerge in prefiguration. Prefiguration, therefore, must not be thought of as either a way of doing practice where means are ends or the attempt to establish alternative forms of organization. Rather, they must be conceived in their synthesis, linked by the radical imagination. In a nutshell, the radicality (in the literal sense of "root-breaking") in the radical imagination lies precisely in that it prefigures alternatives that are ontologically and epistemologically so fundamentally different from the status quo, that it not only challenges but also consciously minimizes the reproduction of status quo values.

To develop these claims, this chapter investigates the practices and affectivities my interlocutors highlight, in order to abstract from them the underlying ethical and moral normative principles that guide their practices. From a practice theory standpoint (Bourdieu 2013; Reckwitz 2002), how my interlocutors "do" practices tells us something about the underlying, guiding (ethical, moral) principles of their undertaking. The totality of those practices produces the spatiality of the Syntagma Square occupation, building on the constitutive spatial categories I elaborated on in the previous chapter. Therefore, inquiring into those principles that guide the practices of the square allows one to abstract what kind of radical imagination the occupation signifies in terms of (ordered) spatiality.

The first part of this chapter takes a closer look at the precursor norms of the occupation. These norms, in effect, helped overcome intersectional divisions and societal cleavages in the Syntagma Square occupation through the emergence of egalitarian guiding principles from the start of the occupation. Furthermore, the call for spontaneity allowed prefigurative practices, where change is lived in the here and now, to be generated. The second part elaborates on the ways in which Syntagma Square—as a structured spatiality—has been constructed in practice. Here, I will show that practices were guided by equality and mutual respect, collectivity, self-governance, self-organization, and solidarity. The third part of this chapter investigates the affective dimensions of these practices, in order to make sense of my interlocutors' narrations of bonds and attachments to each other, to the collective community, and to the occupation of the square. Conceiving affect as "thought in action," I claim that practices constitute the situated environments through which we experience ourselves affectively. The affective attachments my interlocutors speak of so passionately are grounded precisely in the antiauthoritarian and egalitarian character of the occupation's radical imagination. In a word, by virtue of the egalitarian and antiauthoritarian character of the radical imagination, the ways in which my interlocutors experience the Syntagma Square occupation affectively is also marked by equality and collectivity.

Precursor Norms

The precursor norms of the Syntagma Square occupation can be read as a rupture with the norms of the status quo of everyday life. As I argued in the previous chapter, the immanence and relative stability of routinized habits of conduct and normative expectations can be attributed to the square's stasis: a prolonged temporality of presence that enables *longue durée* social processes, allowing alternative sets of practices to be originated and to become routine. "Back then, it was everyday life," Petros recalls (personal communication, February 9, 2017). After all, the fact that the Syntagma Square occupation was sustained by protesters for over two months allowed it to become a temporary, everyday spatiality with relative (anti-)structuration, intersubjective comprehensibility, and a normative layout vis-à-vis what is, or is not, appropriate action. The internalization of precursor norms of nonviolent action, the refusal to have any political party present, or to have flags of nation-states or political organizations was to establish an inclusive, egalitarian character for the occupation from the outset.

The first norm relates to nonviolent action. That first Facebook post clarified that "whoever wants to provoke any kind of problem and use any kind of violence, to hit NOT ATTENDING and stay at home" (quoted in Giovanopoulos and Mitropoulos 2011, 278). It is fair to say that this norm was largely upheld in the first weeks of the occupation and only came to an end when the policing strategy toward the occupation changed to violent repression from June 15 onward. While the role of violence as antipolitical practice in the face of police repression will be dealt with in more detail in the following chapter, it should be stated that taking a nonviolent approach to protest is to enthuse more people into participating (e.g., Chenoweth and Stephan 2011). "To be united," Viktoria remarks, "we had to be nonviolent. So this was the first thing that was set up" (personal communication, October 22, 2014). The refraining from forceful methods was not consensual for all of my interlocutors, however. Kostas, an anarchist sound engineer in his mid-thirties, views violence as a productive force in certain situations.

> Regarding violence in Syntagma: There were many pacifists. OK, so? I mean, do we know that it works with violence? Have we ever seen it work with violence? Are we so sure about violence? I am telling you that as somebody who is with violence. I believe that through violence things can be done. But I'm not going to have a problem with others who don't want violence. So I accepted that in the beginning. [They] chose another path, so okay. (Kostas, personal communication, February 17, 2016)

Even though Kostas does not categorically reject the use of force, he gave way to the square's nonviolent approach, at least before the police repression began, out of mutual respect for the expectations of other participants. If violence is viewed as an authoritarian, sovereign relationship that violates the autonomy of others (Newman 2010, 131), then setting nonviolence as a norm is a stance against subordination and domination. As Thanos remarks, "I disagree with violence, whoever produces it. I consider violence authoritarian and fascist, even from the anarchists" (personal communication, February 3, 2016). Nonviolence, here, seeks to further inclusion of those who do not want to take part in violent actions for whatever reason. Simultaneously, it structures a more egalitarian approach to practices. On the other hand, Thanos's account runs risk of partly reproducing state-derived definitions of violence and nonviolence (chapter 4).

The second norm relates to the refusal to have any party presence in the square. The marker my interlocutors used to express this was simply "no parties." Any expression of political parties—be it symbolic, material, or discursive—was considered objectionable in the square. Journalist Vasilis, keen on offering his own analysis, explains that this had to do with the political mood at the time.

> There was a climate . . . during that time . . . where participating in an organized action peaked. I mean for either a party or a leftist group. Because they had all decided on a particular stand towards things: "I can take part in an action, but I want it to go this way." The other, which might even be the adjacent party ideologically speaking, would likewise say, "I'm taking part, but I want to go in that direction." So this created a spectrum [of opinion] and it came to a point where they could never discuss anything. . . . They had chained themselves to an opinion, all of them. And nothing progressed. [In Syntagma], in the early days, there was this "no parties, no unions" thing, in order to break exactly this thing. (Vasilis, personal communication, October 24, 2014)

As party politics in representative democracies is based on competition, refraining from showing and expressing party affiliation was arguably intended to overcome a likely deadlock in discussing political ideas that was foreseen from the outset. "Syntagma in the beginning had the logic of 'white shirts'—no party symbols," fifty-six-year-old anti-consumerist activist Anastasia remarks. "So there was this logic of distinguishing itself from the old parties, of finding a new solution" (personal communication, March 28, 2016). Her statement is indicative of the structure of the radical imagination: framing it as a departure from conventional party politics, Anastasia explains that people were allowed to take part in the events of the square as individuals, but not as affiliated to a party. This suggests the antipolitical component of the radical imagination. "To find a new solution" suggests alter-politics; that this norm was to envision politics radically differently from status quo, representative democracy. Just as with nonviolence, the refusal to allow party politics a presence in the square was meant to produce Syntagma Square as a more inclusive and egalitarian space. Arguably, this was an attempt to underline the commonalities of participants, rather than the differences.

The third norm relates to the role of flags. While my interlocutors were all, without exception, against the display of party flags, the role of the Greek flag was more contentious. For those interlocutors identifying themselves as part of the anarchist movement (such as Lukas or Panagiotis) or the radical Left (Thodoris), the Greek flag is a repugnant symbol, as it symbolizes the dividing and conquering of subordinate groups. When asked about his sentiment toward the Greek flag, Thodoris simply replied, "I hate it" (personal communication, October 17, 2014). Others, who describe themselves as having had a less refined "political identity" prior to their participation in the Syntagma Square occupation, had a more complicated relation to the "no flags" norm. Thanos is case in point:

> Look, the flags of the parties, I didn't like. None. And I think everybody was united on this. . . . They didn't want parties. That is to say, nobody wins, to get votes from what was happening. Except for [the fact] that when a Greek flag, or an anarchist flag, or a red leftist flag came up, I had no problem with that. It's within the frame of human expression. And I like free expression, as long as it's not happening so someone can profit from it, such as a party, or whoever else might profit: if Coca-Cola had come and advertised on the square, for example, that would have bothered me. It wouldn't be selfless. But if that didn't exist, I had no problem with symbols. Neither do I think somebody has the right to tell somebody else to not have symbols. He can just not show symbols. He has no right to tell somebody else what to do. (Thanos, personal communication, February 3, 2016)

Thanos's approach toward the role of flags in Syntagma Square reveals the relation between precursor norms and the guiding principles underlying the practices of the Syntagma Square occupation. He first points out the intersubjective consensus among occupants ("everybody was united on this") with regard to not allowing party symbols to be displayed. He rationalizes this norm with his interpretation as to what these symbols mean: parties are organizations that want to maximize their shares in Parliament, to gain electoral votes; they want to utilize "what was happening" as a resource to further their agenda. This gives us a glimpse as to Thanos's underlying ethics: to gain something from the Syntagma Square occupation is morally reprehensible and ought to be precluded by (ethical) norms and principles. Here, he draws on the no-flags norm to essentially safeguard against parties having a presence. This shows that the lines between two apparently opposing precursor norms—for and against flags—are in

124   Paradoxes of Emancipation

fact blurred, arguably owing to the fact that both norms rest on egalitarianism and antiauthoritarianism. But as Thanos moves on, he offers us a further qualification of the no-flags norm. It is not flags per se he considers problematic, but the meanings they convey. By not taking issue with anarchist and Left flags, he tells us what was acceptable in the lower square, which was driven by more left-wing and anarchist ideas. It is worth noting that the anarchist black flag, as well as the anarcho-syndicalist red-black flag, have long stood as symbols of universally negating the authoritarian, hierarchic, and exclusivist character of all national flags (Shantz 2009, 73). For Thanos, this falls within the guiding principle of free expression. Peculiarly, however, he includes the Greek flag in his list, despite its exclusivist character. This points to the paradoxes of using exclusivist symbolisms in an effort to further an inclusivist agenda. Finally, by offering a counterfactual example ("if Coca-Cola came and advertised"), he orients the no-flags norm around another principle: selflessness. What is implicit in his statement is that whatever is not selfless, is morally reprehensible. To be selfless means to have or show great concern for others and little or no concern for oneself. What becomes evident here is that the *we* is treated as more important than the *I*—a theme I will develop in in this chapter with regard to the affective dimension of practices. That is to say that doing something for the greater good is more virtuous than doing it out of self-interest. By treating the Coca-Cola Company example as analogous to party symbols, he shows that parties in his view cannot be selfless: here, both are competitive, utility-maximizing organizations.

All these precursor norms are intended to challenge forms of domination and subordination—be it nationalist ideas, competitive party politics, or the undermining of individual autonomy through violent force—in ways that further notions of inclusion, openness, and equality from the outset. In this sense, they prestructure the radical imagination of the Syntagma Square occupation around an egalitarian and antiauthoritarian ethic. At the same time, however, the ways in which these norms are enforced is by sanctioning deviant practices, as Panagiotis recalls:

> Oftentimes you would see fights between people there. Not big ones, more like vehement discussions. This occurred due to how the protests

Aspiring the Utopian   125

were set up: No violence, no parties. So if you had a political identity, you needed to somehow leave the party out. So when somebody, especially in the early days, was handing out flyers of political organizations, others would walk up to him and tell him to stop. (Panagiotis, personal communication, October 6, 2014)

The paradox of establishing and practicing an antiauthoritarian ethic, broadly conceived, by exercising certain forms of authority poses a dilemma that is not easily overcome, and inevitably also has exclusionary consequences. For Cornelius Castoriadis (1998), who views imaginary institutionalization as the basis for direct democracy, humility and self-limitation are central notions for democratic self-understanding. If the community is supposed to maintain its norms, it cannot show hubris in relation to them. Kostas's acceptance of nonviolent action despite his personal stance toward violence is a case in point. In the sense that these precursor norms further equality, rather than inequality, they are a radical departure from ordinary conduct. Arguably, the reason they were largely upheld throughout the course of the occupation lies precisely in the fact that they offer a radical alternative to the status quo. This points to the importance of occupiers' ideological "fidelity" (Badiou 2005) to the radical imagination of Syntagma Square, as the majority of occupiers accepted the precursor norms as "resonant" with (Rosa et al. 2016), or at the very least not contradistinctive to, their own ethic.

Spontaneity

The proliferation of norms does not appear out of thin air. They stem from experiences of previous practices (Wallace 2008). Some interlocutors had been participating in various radical movements prior to their exposure to the Syntagma Square occupation.

These movements in which I was—for example the eco-communities group—they were already formed in Athens and couldn't wait any more for something to happen . . . to change the societal situation. So these groups already followed the logic of direct democracy with assemblies.

126   Paradoxes of Emancipation

They didn't have a presidium, they didn't have, I don't know, hierarchies. . . . This was the mature thing, which came to the square. And then we talked about direct democracy there. Because we had direct democracy in the eco-communities and at the Kafeneion[1]. . . . And they also brought it to the square. OK, up to a point. The politics continued to be tense. But there was a direct democratic *attitude*. People couldn't come as [members of] parties. We accomplished this. (Andreas, personal communication, February 11, 2016; emphasis added)

Viktoria adds that those first people participating in the lower square were

already "hooked," as we say. That means that they were already in groups. They were in the position to make a proper assembly. . . . So we discuss properly . . . and it turned out that we agreed on many things, such as that at this point, we must not focus on flags or on parties. We must be united, nonviolent. So these were the first things that were set out. (Viktoria, personal communication, October 22, 2014)

Direct democratic practices, the refusal to include party politics, and an anti-nationalist agenda expressed by the rejection of the Greek flag were precursor norms that arrived in Syntagma Square by way of being practiced by those who already had prior movement experience. According to Nicholas Apoifis (2016), the anarchist, antiauthoritarian milieu in Greece[2] had a particularly important influence on the occupation in this regard, which supports my argument that the Syntagma Square occupation rests on an egalitarian and antiauthoritarian ethic.[3]

1. The Kafeneion, or Café at the Academy of Plato, is a collective café established in 2009 that served as a precursor of Athens' mushrooming social and solidarity economy spaces.

2. Peculiarly, except for those self-described anarchists, all my other interlocutors decisively refused this label for themselves, despite their practices in the square. This may well have to do with the negative ways in which anarchists in Greece are framed in everyday life (Kotronaki and Seferiades 2012).

3. In the following chapter, I will take a closer look at those self-described "apolitical" interlocutors who had little or no protest experience prior to the Syntagma Square occupation.

A key organizational characteristic in these milieus is that of spontaneity. Many interlocutors pointed to the fact that "everything happened on its own" (Lukas, personal communication, February 23, 2016), and generally showed appreciation toward the spontaneous practices of the square. However, "even in self-organization," Aggelos remarks, "spontaneity needs organization (personal communication, January 27, 2016). In this sense, it can be said that spontaneity was routinized. It is not that the various kinds of practices in Syntagma Square erupted spontaneously, as much as that there were individuals—some with veteran experience in radical movement politics—who deliberately argued for spontaneity, as opposed to more structured methods of mobilization. As established earlier, the initial Facebook call to action explicitly asked for actions to be "spontaneous and not planned." In this sense, and despite the egalitarian character of the occupation, there were individuals who, because of their experience and background, had a disproportionate influence on the shape and character of the occupation as a whole. Viktoria tells me how her friend Haris, whom she describes as an anarchist, is such an individual.

> Haris . . . knew his job . . . I mean, he played a very big role in the square. . . . I mean, he brought tarps and organization. We set the tarps up. And under the tarps we made the first group. It was the reception group with the purpose that for each person who came, they would give us their name, they would tell us some. . . . I don't know, expertise and such. And we would then see what other groups [we would need] to establish. Haris brought many such ideas [to the square]. (Viktoria, personal communication, October 22, 2014)

This raises another question regarding more symbolic forms of authority grounded in personal experience and how they relate to the egalitarian and antiauthoritarian ethic of the Syntagma Square occupation. To argue for spontaneity as a method requires some rudimentary sort of planning and organization, which may be detrimental to the ethical precepts of those participating. In consequence, however, the call for spontaneity as opposed to conscious planning allowed for many of the practices of the occupation to be prefigurative in nature.

Prefiguration

For Katerina, "all the actions that occurred were crucial. In my eyes *they* were the revolution" (personal communication, October 19, 2014; emphasis added). Arguably, the revolutionary aspect of these practices was the prefigurative layout on which they rested. Prefigurative practices have been embraced, especially by anarchism, feminism, and the radical Left, to highlight that political action should already embody the values and norms of the type of society one seeks to build (Cornish et al. 2016; Holloway 2010; Polletta and Hoban 2016; Trott 2016).[4] Instead of more structuralist-reformist agendas that hope for a revolutionary vanguard to seize structures of power,[5] or look to political parties or unions to leverage reforms within the status quo ante,[6] prefiguration pursues the creation of a new society by developing counterhegemonic institutions and interactions that already embody the change that is desired. This is implied when Kostas refers to the Syntagma Square occupation as an opportunity "to create structures outside of the state . . . for the people to finally believe that things can be done differently" (personal communication, February

---

4. For a detailed account of the history of prefigurative politics since nineteenth-century anarchism, see Haiven and Khasnabish (2014, 244ff.).

5. The newspaper of the Communist Party of Greece, for example, argued that the square could not provide any alternative political suggestions beyond the immediate rejection of the government and the austerity measures. Effectively, it viewed protesters as in need of "enlightenment" and the guidance of a vanguard (Prentoulis and Thomassen 2014, 213–14).

6. Panagiotis reveals that not everybody was favorable toward the prefigurative layout of the occupation. Having had a skeptical stance from the outset and participating more as an observer, he remarks: "For me, that what has value is the spirit and the trend of thinking and imagining a popular discourse collectively. . . . And if you will, this discourse had content, but only for the people of Syntagma Square, and not for a trade union official, or a political organization, or the working class" (personal communication, October 6, 2014). Panagiotis credits the collective radical imagination in and of the square. But with his political orientation being more vanguardist, he was reluctant to take part in the occupation more actively, forming—together with Thodoris—the critics of the transformative capacity of prefiguration.

17, 2016). In a word, they are a test of the future today. For Aggelos, it is an amalgamation of these considerations that made him sustain his participation. In Syntagma Square:

> You feel that you are in a space where there are people you can maybe communicate with and who maybe want the same things you want. And the only thing you need to do is to communicate what you want, what you consider to be a good thing to happen. Here and now. Practically, all together. . . . This I can say kept me in the square. . . . There are various ways for people to do things. Here and now. Outside of companies, outside of the monopolies, outside of the existing market system. (Aggelos, personal communication, January 27, 2016)

Often grounded in antiauthoritarian and anarchist thought, prefigurative practices transcend our evaluation and distinction of political practices regarding the here and now and planning toward a distant future (van de Sande 2013) in such ways that "means and ends become, effectively, indistinguishable . . . in which the form of the action . . . is itself a model for the change one wishes to bring about" (Graeber 2009, 210). Referring to taking action "outside" the market system, Aggelos reifies precisely the desire to take part in counter-hegemonic practices that follow different logics of social organization than those set by the status quo. In more Weberian terms (1978), prefigurative politics are therefore reminiscent of a "value-rationality," in that action is guided by values rather than by instrumental efficiency. This, in turn, underlines the claim that the Syntagma Square occupation offers a radical alternative to the more utilitarian and, by extension, neoliberal logics of conduct. It is because practices in Syntagma Square were prefigurative in their ontological layout, which is to say that the change that is desired is intrinsic to "doing practices," that they produced the spatiality of the square as a radical imagination. Therefore, because prefiguration means "to anticipate or enact some feature of an 'alternative world' in the present, as though it has already been achieved" (Yates 2015, 4), it must not be thought of as either a way of doing practice where means are ends or the attempt to establish alternative forms of organization. Rather, the practices in the square must be conceived in their

130   Paradoxes of Emancipation

synthesis, linked by the radical imagination. "It was one small society," Viktoria remarks. "It was how an autonomous society with human rules could function" (personal communication, October 22, 2014).

The Practices of the Radical Imagination

The precursor norms facilitated the imprinting of an egalitarian character on the square from the outset. The call for spontaneity rendered the practices of the square prefigurative. This section carves out the guiding principles of these practices. From a cultural studies point of view, practices are a routinized type of behavior that is understandable (to others) and held together by tacit, methodical and interpretative knowledge (Reckwitz 2003). The ways in which practices are "being done" allows for inquiring into their underlying moral principles. This, in turn, enables the radical imagination to be abstracted, to tackle the question: What kind of (ordered) spatiality does Syntagma signify? In line with this chapter's argument, the practices I will shed light on are guided by the principles of mutual respect, self-governance, self-organization, and solidarity.

Mutual Respect

On the first day of protests, May 25, 2011, many people initially congregated in Syntagma Square out of curiosity. In the beginning, they wanted to speak. "More and more [people] came," Eleftheria recalls, "and all they wanted was to speak out: 'I want to speak out and get it off my chest'" (personal communication, October 6, 2014). Individuals felt an urge to express themselves, to voice their opinions, frustrations, and desires, to communicate with each other.

> So what I think happened a lot especially in the beginning of Syntagma, was that in a society where people didn't listen to each other, as if there was a switch flipped, suddenly they listened to what you told them. I mean, it was the first time where, at least for me—and I am fifty years old, okay?—you saw a large group of people gathering, and anybody could get up and say something—even if what he said doesn't mean

anything to you—and you listen to him. I don't believe this has happened before. And this I believe created a bond between the people. And in some way people looked at each other very benevolently. . . . I mean they were very amiable. Whatever somebody may have said, the others listened to it. And you felt like they listened to you. They didn't wait until you finished, so they can say their own things. That was a very important innovation of Syntagma, which I would say occurred automatically. It happened due to the attitude of the people, mostly. (Vasilis, personal communication, October 24, 2014)

The importance of getting to know each other, of people voicing their opinions and being listened to, resonates among all of my interlocutors. Stepping forward visibly, and raising their voices without succumbing to paralyzing impotence and fear is indicative of practices that radically depart from the regressive signification of crisis I elaborated on in the previous chapter. The benevolence and amiability that Vasilis and other interlocutors highlight, assume that this process goes against "a new obsession with power, one which assumes that its only purpose is to triumph over others" (Liebsch 2016, 73). Additionally, Vasilis's metaphor of a "suddenly" flipped switch underlines the unexpectedness of this process—a rupture from everyday life where the people inside the space of Syntagma Square went about practices differently: mutual respect for each other's opinions furthered affective bonds among participants. Some of the more veteran activist interlocutors referred to this communicative process as "psychotherapy," where, rather therapeutically, protesters got their frustration out of their systems before they could engage in the more political practices of the square. Interlocutors also emphasized how this notion of communication is a departure from their experiences prior to their participation in the Syntagma Square occupation.

Until then, I had known a society where, inside an apartment building, one didn't know who lived next-door. This is something I didn't like and I still don't like. Since then, I have become a lot more gregarious, for example, and more extroverted. (Thanos, personal communication, February 3, 2016)

Studies in psychology (Cherniss 1972; Whittaker and Watts 1971) and social movement studies alike (Profitt 2001; Shriver et al. 2003) have shown how communicating and voicing one's opinion during protests increases self-confidence. Maria, for example, describes herself as not having felt smart enough to take part in political discussions prior to the Syntagma Square occupation and during the early days of the occupation there.

> I was embarrassed to speak. These were very much unknown things for me. . . . I was embarrassed, because I didn't have any political opinion. . . . I thought that a person like me doesn't have anything to say, to offer. . . . And I'm telling you I was very reticent in the beginning. I didn't speak a lot. Now, I can't stop. (Maria, personal communication, February 10, 2016)

Work on gender-role devaluation (Nutt 1999, 133) has indicated that there is a "lack of power as a loss of voice" arising from sexist experiences in everyday life, where women practice "self-silencing" (Akarsu and Sakallı 2021) in response to feeling unintelligent, subordinate, incompetent, and overpowered. Although Maria does not explicitly refer to gender roles, her initial subject position in Syntagma Square points to many of the attributes that Nutt describes. After all, "capitalism is not a system separate from patriarchy but a form of patriarchy itself" (Sotiropoulou 2016, 61). The more Maria participated, however, the more confident she felt speaking out. This relates to Cary Cherniss's (1972) work on how exposure to taking part in protests encourages women to move beyond normative gender roles. In this light, Maria's speaking can be signified as a tacit renegotiation of and departure from normative gender roles in Syntagma Square.

The exposure to a situation in which my interlocutors found common ground with many others (regarding their vulnerabilities and demands) rendered a previously held expectation about society obsolete. The ways in which individuals communicated in Syntagma Square was a significant departure from the depoliticized subjectivities of neoliberalism (chapter 1), where ignorance is praised as "the appropriate state of a dedicated market participant" (Mirowski and Nik-Khah 2017, 32). Instead, interlocutors highlight how much they value communicating collectively in a drive

Aspiring the Utopian   133

for change. In this regard, a key practice that my interlocutors emphasize is that of *Zymōsē*, which literally translates as "fermentation." Metaphorically, however, it signifies a change-directed discussion, or more accurately, a discussion within a political or social space that prepares for a situation to be changed.

> There are some things words cannot explain. It is called Zymōsē. This process I cannot describe as anything other than a mutual influence. There's a lot to learn. As long as you admit to it, which is the first stage. And the great joy is to accept that there are people who can influence you, who you didn't even reckon, who influence you *positively*—who bring you forward. (Lukas, personal communication, February 23, 2016; emphasis added)

Pointing to the dialectic and democratic nature of Zymōsē ("mutual influence"), Lukas highlights a practice that allows for the collective radical imagination. The ways in which Zymōsē ought to be practiced is to accept that experiences of other people can be beneficial for one's own development. In this sense, it feeds into the imagination of what else is possible.

> There needs to be a discussion, a Zymōsē. I mean, a political idea that is consolidated is dead. Let's go bury it. Ideas need to be alive to be ideas, to be politics. Because otherwise they are not politics, they are ideology. Fascism and such bullshit. "I am right, I am more right than you are." (Kostas, personal communication, February 17, 2016)

First off, Kostas distinguishes Zymōsē from the more competitive notion of winning arguments ("I am right"), where the former is a collective and consensual process while the latter is combative or confrontational. More importantly, however, Zymōsē, in Kostas's conception, can be read as a radical departure from a neoliberal understanding of politics. As opposed to conceiving of politics as a latently teleological, economized, and rationalized implementation of "best practice," which, in effect, reduces politics to mere technocracy, Zymōsē is a prefigurative approach to politics that is not consolidated, but is "in-the-making" on principle. It must be

134   Paradoxes of Emancipation

so in order not to be "dead." If politics requires Zymōsē—a collective, change-directed discussion—so as not to be "fascism," as Kostas tells us, then politics requires democratic principles as its condition of possibility. As Jacques Rancière (2011a, 79) puts it, "It's what keeps politics from simply turning into law enforcement." Zymōsē opens up possibility and imagination precisely because it redemocratizes politics through prefiguration.[7] In this regard, Lukas adds that "what is going on there [in Syntagma Square] is way too strong to not influence you. This Zymōsē, if you're open and let it get inside of you, is very strong" (personal communication, February 23, 2016). The openness derives from the "attitude" that Andreas and Vasilis referred to earlier, which may well be the result of the relationship between progressive crisis signification and the egalitarian character of the precursor norms reproducing Syntagma's spatiality. With regard to subject formation, Steve Pile (2008, 211) notes that "what is important is not so much the formation of something identifiable—nameable—called the subject: the 'location' that we use to 'site' ourselves. Instead, it is the radical openness of the self to others, and the constitution of the self always in relation to others, that is important." In this sense, my interlocutors were open to listening to each other, rather than trying to win arguments and impose their opinions. The collective nature of change-directed discussions (Zymōsē) underlines that the radical imagination is not an individual resource, but rather a collective process (Haiven and Khasnabish 2014) in which everybody can be equally involved. This brings to the fore the next principle: that of self-governance.

Self-Governance

Sited by the fountain of Syntagma Square, the popular assembly was at the heart of the encampment, both territorially and organizationally. During the opening meeting of the occupation on May 26, proceedings were held from 10:00 p.m. until 1:00 a.m., with a total of eighty-three speakers, consisting of students, the unemployed, private sector workers, homeless

7. In chapter 4, I pay close attention to the processes of politicization that my interlocutors describe.

Aspiring the Utopian 135

people, and many others (Break the Blackout 2011). The minutes of that constituting assembly reveal a wide array of proposals and topics: occupying the square until the government steps down, calling for the "plutocratic system" to collapse, claiming that representative democracy is neither just nor equal, expressing joy about the unity of those in the square, calling upon people to look their neighbors in the eyes in order to overcome the indifference created by consumerism, and many more. For three straight hours, everybody present was allowed to have their say.

> If you want my opinion, and this is very important Dimitris, the great difference with regard to the other squares was the popular assembly. Nowhere was the popular assembly so massive, with discussions every day and for at least three hours with so many people, discussing everything. Everybody could put forward whatever topic they wanted. And when the popular assembly accepted it, it happened. It wasn't like somebody set an agenda, as it was, for example, in Spain. Here, the most inapt [person] could make proposals. These proposals could be voted on and included in the agenda. So it wasn't decided in advance. And this created such a massive phenomenon. (Vasilis, personal communication, October 19, 2014)

Vasilis eagerly emphasized the words *everybody*, *everything*, and *every day* in our conversation, highlighting the inclusive and collective character of the assembly. Moreover, by underlining that the agenda was not "predecided," Vasilis indicates the prefigurative and spontaneous approach toward agenda-setting. Drawing on a method used in Athenian democracy in the sixth century BCE, those who wanted to speak were selected by lottery. In the Syntagma Square occupation, each speaker were given a piece of paper with a number on so as to wait their turn. They had three minutes in which to share their opinions and ideas. Agreement, disagreement, etc., were mediated through the use of sign language. As long as the precursor norms outlined earlier were followed, everyone present could participate on equal terms in the assembly. Once again, the aim of these procedures was to create Syntagma Square as a spatiality that is as inclusive and open as possible for participants, minimizing the hierarchical and authoritarian elements of political practices.

136   Paradoxes of Emancipation

"What the square wanted is: 'We decide, without parties, without representatives'" (Alexandros, personal communication, March 28, 2016). Alexandros's remarks hint at the principle of self-governance and direct democracy, where people have a direct say in decisions that affect their lives. These practices were not exclusive to the organization of the general assembly—they were also integral to the working groups of the square.

> I have to tell you that a big element that remained in our minds is the element of direct democracy. That is to say *how* we express opinions, *how* we decide, *in what way* we take our decisions. In this, the Spanish helped a lot, and generally in all the groups they took part in. Their role was crucial in inspiring and transmitting what they knew. So in our group [the time bank] there were four Spanish people. So we began holding meetings and slowly we produced a text that went through the general assembly, informing the people that our network had been formed. Then we had a small table in the square where we gave people information about our idea. And slowly we tried to put this idea into practice. That is to say, we researched all the possible ways in which we could exchange services and goods. There are many, many ways. And we decided finally that a "time bank" is the most effective and the quickest instrument to turn this [idea] into practice. So in our meetings, we're talking about meetings where we were sixty to seventy people only for the time bank, there was a lot of participation. We took suggestions for discussions from the people, we told them about what the time bank is, with the logic of building a website so as to operate later on. Of course the square finished before that, unfortunately, but the website went online. But whatever data we gathered, we used later on. So there was continuity. The way we held our meetings for the time bank was just like in the general assembly. This thing was fantastic. At each spot in the park you saw circles, groups, holding meetings for certain issues or certain actions. It was a very beautiful moment. (Katerina, personal communication, October 19, 2014; emphasis added)

By pointing to how practices are being done ("how we express opinions," "how we decide"), Katerina offers us her own analysis as to the guiding principles of practice, grounded in self-governance. Her reference to Spanish activists underlines how the radical imagination begins in experience (Paulson 2010). Through Zymōsē (here referring to large and collective meetings), the time bank, as a practice of reciprocal exchange of services using units of time as currency, emerged as an idea. By producing texts and taking part in the popular assembly, this idea materializes in practice. Referring to the time bank as a "network," Katerina clarifies the group's grounding in self-governance. As Marina Prentoulis and Lasse Thomassen (2012, 177) clarify, the network metaphor expresses "the aim of horizontal relations among autonomous individuals and groups of individuals," underlining the egalitarian character of this principle. Sending representatives from the network to the popular assembly, however, posed a dilemma as to the direct democratic principles of practices. In response, protesters set up Direct Democracy, an open, thematic group that was to research and propose concrete actions for implementing the principles of equality, justice, and freedom through self-organization and self-government.

Basing decisions on self-government is a critical departure from status quo politics of parties and representation, (that might be called "government by others"). Self-government is guided by a different form of political organization outside formal political institutions. To say that practices were driven by self-government is therefore to contrast them with the representative and hierarchical parliamentary politics we have grown so accustomed to.[8] Direct democratic principles challenged this widely held normative expectation of what democracy means, as Kostas shows:

> You said, "Direct democracy," and people said, "But we have democracy!" They understood it differently. So there was a direct democratic discussion around this topic. It shifted a lot. Some parts of the anarchist movement came closer to direct democracy, some parts of the Left came closer to direct democracy, ordinary people came closer to direct democracy and so on—which I like. (Kostas, personal communication, February 16, 2017)

8. The value my interlocutors give to self-government needs to be seen against the backdrop of the increasing depoliticization and crisis of (neo)liberal democracy.

138   Paradoxes of Emancipation

The ways in which self-government is negotiated is through direct democratic discussions, bringing us back to the notion of Zymōsē. This highlights the prefigurative character of practices in Syntagma Square, where means and ends are effectively indistinguishable, where the future vision of a direct democratic society materializes in practicing direct democracy in the present. The routinization inherent in practice exposes participants of the occupation to a reevaluation of what democracy entails ("But we have democracy!"), precisely because the square's radical imagination differs significantly from the workings of the status quo. It forced many of my interlocutors to reconsider the ways in which they practice. Katerina provides a telling example:

> Before 2011 I was used to taking responsibility, as I told you, to taking a leading role in anything I did. When I started working collectively this was causing me problems, because I had this leadership thing. The others freaked out some times. They thought, "Who's she now? Who does she think she is? Does she think she's the leader?" And many people didn't like me, even. And they didn't know me because it was in the beginning when people were getting to know each other. So they said various things [about me]. I realized [that] from . . . the negative energy from some people. And slowly, slowly, I said to myself, "Katerina, it's true. You talk a lot. It's true that you're not the only one here, there's a group. Listen to the others a bit. Give them space and time." So I started becoming a bit more collective, to try and improve this part about me, to not be a leader as much. Because now we are talking about another situation: We are talking about a horizontal, equitable [situation]. How will it work if I'm always the one who talks and speaks up and the others follow? It doesn't work like that. It isn't nice. So I realized this is an element of myself I need to improve in some way. And those around me helped a lot by telling me. (Katerina, personal communication, February 11, 2017)

In the early days of the Syntagma Square occupation, Katerina went about the activities in the square in the ways she was accustomed to. She took the lead. One way of signifying Katerina's experience is that because the square was anti-hierarchical and leaderless in its layout, fellow occupants confronted Katerina about what they perceived to be authoritarian practice. While taking on a dominant role in organizing may be Katerina's tacit attempt to renegotiate gendered inequalities in voicing ones position, the very notion of "having this leadership thing," as Katerina puts it, runs risk of reproducing a "masculine ethic" of leadership and domination (Billing and Alvesson 2000). This is to say that Katerina's routinized habits of thought and action clashed with the collective, horizontal, and equitable realities of the Syntagma Square occupation. A second way of signifying her experience, however, is that Katerina's (self-) criticism about her behavior may also be grounded in the fact that even progressive and open processes, such as Zymōsē, may latently rest on gender perceptions of hegemonic masculinity (Christensen and Jensen 2014). Here, Katerina's taking on of a leading role may have been viewed as an affront by other participants, precisely because they have tacitly habitualized men's patriarchal dominance over women. Going back to Viktor Turner's (1986) work on experience and subjectivity, however, what matters in this observation is not necessarily what "really" happened, but instead what kinds of guidelines emerge for how Katerina signifies her experience: as a reflexive subject, she questioned the doxic assumptions she held about being a leader and elevated them to the level of discourse, where she critiqued and changed them. This process, in her view, was supported by "those around" her. With that change in practice, she altered her subsequent practices toward more, collectivist, direct democratic, and anti-hierarchical principles. In effect, this process can be signified as a prefigurative change of subjectivity in practice, where Katerina subjects herself more thoroughly to the principle of horizontalist self-government.

Self-Organization

If self-governance describes practices based on the principle of people having a direct say in decisions that affect their lives, then self-organization means they are the main participants in the application of these decisions. An important expression of self-organization in the square was the "open" groups that, as their label signals, aspire to overarching inclusion of those willing to take an active part in the occupation. Working autonomously and reporting to the popular assembly, they consisted, at the peak of the occupation, of nineteen working groups and twelve thematic groups (Giovanopoulos and Mitropoulos 2011, 341). Ranging from dealing with organizational, infrastructural, and provisional matters, such as technical support and food, to thematic discussions on gender relations and work and unemployment, these groups signify a self-organized envisioning of a better society in practice.

> A thing that was very interesting was the groups that worked autonomously, and simultaneously cooperatively. That was something very magical. We said, for example, that we need a text. As we said this sentence out loud, it was already finished. We said that this text needs to be translated, and it was translated [laughs]. We said we needed food to be made. The food was ready. So as the wish for something was expressed, they carried it out instantly. (Andreas, personal communication, February 11, 2016)

Counter to central planning, Andreas's example shows how autonomous self-governance and self-organization functioned due to a tacit, mutual awareness ("instantly") of what was needed for the occupation to be sustained. "As if you push a button, and then everything began to unfold automatically," Eleftheria points out similarly (personal communication, October 6, 2014). Arguably, this tacit knowledge can be understood as a result of the (temporary) internalization of spontaneity as a method, alongside the adherence to the collectivist principles of the square. Related to this, Andreas's appraisal of the seemingly automatic functioning of the square may also be understood against the backdrop of a Greek state that, in the collective imagination and in the context of austerity measures, does not seem to function as desired, nor provide what its populace expects. At an earlier point in the conversation, Andreas underlines this assumption by saying, "We want to do something, because we cannot wait any more. We don't have the resilience to wait. Time passes, and we don't do anything. The state doesn't do anything. And nothing happens" (personal communication, February 11, 2016). Self-organization, therefore, needs to be seen beyond its ideational grounding in an antiauthoritarian ethic.

Against the backdrop of ever-decreasing welfare and social needs provision by the Greek state due to austerity, self-organization is also an answer to this reality; a coping-mechanism against the precarization of the livability of a common life (chapter 4). It may have been similar considerations that drove Katerina's way of thinking about self-organization:

> How are we going to help each other? How are we going to solve our problems on our own, without needing the state? So the self-organization, I would say, was a very important element that excited me and made me more active at some point. (Katerina, personal communication, October 19, 2014)

What both Andreas and Katerina show is that they are not aiming to seize control of the state in order to bring about change. Instead, practicing self-organization ("how are we going to") is a radical departure from being reliant on the state. While it may be merely a way of getting by in times of crisis, much in the sense of Asef Bayat's (2009) work on the "quiet encroachment of the ordinary," it also allows the limits of state power to be glimpsed. Assuming that the power of the sovereign state resides in the fact that we do not know how powerful it really is (Davies 2014), the radical imagination of Syntagma Square practiced as an extraordinary spatiality that is temporarily out of reach (of the social orderings of the state) makes the limits of statehood momentarily visible. This relates to what Veena Das and Deborah Poole (2004) capture with their notion of the state's "margins:" sites of disorder where the state is unable to impose its order fully (chapter 5).

A very prominent expression of self-organization that left a significant impression among virtually all of my interlocutors is the episode of the cleansing of the square on June 15, 2011. That day, police officers violently raided the occupation after a forty-eight-hour general strike had culminated in a large demonstration in Syntagma Square. Although protesters were chased away three times and driven into the many side streets adjacent to the square by police officers using batons and tear gas, they each time succeeded in reclaiming the square. On their return, protesters cleaned the debris from the day's clashes with the police, Katerina recalls.

142 Paradoxes of Emancipation

> [The police] threw a lot of chemicals. . . . It was a mess. There were so many chemicals that you actually could not breath. It was in the atmosphere. What did we do? All of a sudden one or two people . . . said, "Guys, let's create a chain." And a human chain from the fountain to the top [of the square] was created. They [laughs] filled up small bottles with water and one gave it to the next and we threw water on the ground on the upper [square], where there was a mess from the chemicals. We wanted the chemicals not to get up in the air. . . . Imagine cleaning the entire square. . . . You had two rows. . . . One [person] gave the bottle to the next [person] and the last one emptied it in the streets. Then we returned the bottles from the return [line]. (Katerina, personal communication, February 7, 2016)

And:

> This was very moving. You see people all over sudden collaborating in a very human way. Others tried to find bottles to fill them. This was very moving. There I truly felt this human solidarity on a very creative and simple level. As if this was a very simple procedure. This was really one of the very good moments of the square I think. It worked very beautifully. . . . It was very touching. I felt very connected with these people, without knowing them all. This moment united us—I don't know how to tell you—substantially. We said, "No, we'll find a solution" [laughs]. "Fuck you guys, throw [chemicals] at us as much as you want." I remember that day there were so many chemicals that you could not breathe, which is why this need to do something came about. . . . And then of course we followed them and helped just like many others . . . the line went up to . . . the cordon that they [cops] erected in front of the Voulē [Parliament]. This self-organization, for me, is the most important thing that happened. (Katerina, personal communication, February 7, 2016)

Katerina describes the self-organized practices that day as unthought-of (chapter 2), spontaneous ("all of a sudden"), collective, and driven by the need to clean, and therefore maintain, the square occupation. The practice of handing bottles to each other, as equals in a chain, is figurative for the necessity to work together in order for the occupation to function. The practical need to clean the ground they were occupying also suggests occupants' sense of ownership and territorialization (chapter 2). My interlocutors recount that after the cleaning the occupation had been restored totally to its initial state. This suggests the need to restore the status quo of the occupation—the order of the "extraordinariness." The recurrent reestablishing (and therefore reproducing) of the Syntagma Square occupation in the face of perpetual police attacks renders the occupation as a spatial structure worth keeping: one that offered stability and lasted even throughout repression.

In the face of tremendous police violence, the ways in which self-organization is practiced by principles of mutual aid ("helped just like many others"), collaboration, and solidarity leads Katerina to render this experience exclusively in positive affective terms ("very moving"). This sense of affection and ownership also resonates beyond my interlocutors. As one participant describes, it was "as if they cleaned a child that has fallen ill and now is getting better. They replanted the trees . . . picked up the trash. It was the most beautiful action I have ever seen" (quoted in Papapavlou 2015, 234). This affective attachment furthered a sense of collectivity ("This moment united us") and belonging ("I felt very connected with these people"), as Katerina tells us, that sustained the occupation beyond the material needs of necessity toward more ideational ways of doing things together and for each other.

Solidarity

Katerina's example is only one of many in which the principle of solidarity, marked by benevolence for others, mutual aid, and support, has been rendered of particular importance by my interlocutors. Solidarity materialized in many of the square's practices: from the catering group receiving food donations and providing up to two meals per day not only for those participating in the groups but also for the public at large and performing artists such as the musical trio Tiger Lillies and the Théâtre du Soleil, who performed for free to express their solidarity with those occupying the square. Eleftheria, when asked what the opposite of solidarity is, quickly replied, "Competition" (personal communication, October 6, 2014). Indeed, solidarity is detrimentally opposed to the competitive-individualist ideas of

144   Paradoxes of Emancipation

neoliberal reasoning. Friedrich Hayek (1992, 80–81), for example, belittles solidarity as "a remnant of the instinctual, and cautious, micro-ethic of the small band." Such a view is in line with the curious neoliberal belief that collectives are symptomatic precursors of a dictatorship of the masses (Hayek 2005). From the vantage point of crisis in Greece, however, solidarity becomes an alternative horizon; an antidote to the alienation and individualization experienced since the period of neoliberal modernization, and to the "indifference of state bureaucratic culture" (Rakopoulos 2016, 145). Practically, solidarity is sourced in the commonality of vulnerability: the precarization of the livability of a common life in the face of crisis and uncertainty about the future. Maria was impacted severely in this regard:

> I moved out of my apartment, I lost my job, I didn't have money. I needed to change habits and [my] way of life. I couldn't sleep. I was stressed. I had a racing heartbeat. I wasn't well psychologically. And all that [her experience at the Syntagma Square occupation] helped me. . . . I started to become more active, and started to see things differently. I helped other people. Through this, I helped myself. . . . I liked that there were other people who were going through the same things I was going through. (Maria, personal communication, February 10, 2016)

Maria's example shows how situations of crisis force upon people a reconsideration of practices ("habits") and consequentially subject positions ("way of life"). The underlying violent displacement of Maria's reality needs to be seen against the backdrop of the grim realities of financial and economic distress and the underlying psychosomatic symptoms ("I had a racing heartbeat. I wasn't well psychologically") that it causes (Adams 2016; Davies 2015a; Han 2017). In Syntagma Square, Maria witnessed the commonality of vulnerability ("other people who were going through the same"), which rooted practices of mutual aid and solidarity. In line with Burkhard Liebsch's (2016, 73) theorization that the politicizing subject "must learn from the negativity of what can only be tolerated with difficulty, or not at all," Maria's reconsiderations of practice ("become more active") led her to radically imagine alternative ways of confronting the status quo ("see things differently") through practices guided by the principle of solidarity. In line with my theorizations on the progressive signification of crisis, what Maria's example shows is that although neoliberalism is intellectually and ideationally a project that breaks down solidarities, the material realities it produces for many people in effect undermine that very agenda. In pragmatist terms, then, the conceptual relevance of solidarity lies in what it "is" for my interlocutors in relation to what solidarity "does" in terms of its (observable) consequences (Papataxiarchis 2016).

In this regard, apart from economic vulnerabilities, solidarity is also an effect of police repression (Aslam 2017; see chapter 4). In the face of perpetual tear gas attacks by police officers and their attempts to evacuate the square from mid-June onward, pharmacists provided free medication for the square's wounded, young women and men ran up to protesters to squirt them in the face with Maalox as an antidote to the tear gas, and the more combat experienced among protesters defended the square in the "defense group" and beyond. For Marili, this showed "unbelievable solidarity between the people who were here. [I felt] that I wasn't alone, that I will be defended by the others. That we are a group. So this thing that would happen, we would deal with collectively" (personal communication, March 28, 2016). Violence, therefore, set in motion another commonality of vulnerability, but simultaneously—as Stavros Stavrides (2012, 594) remarks—the "solidarity developed in practice gave people the means to confront violence."

> So some cops came and drove us out. There you had this magical thing that happened, that when somebody fell, as he was falling, [people] helped him up and carried him. They didn't wait for somebody else to take him. "I don't take him, somebody else will." No! As somebody fell, if I was close by, I took him . . . to protect him. And it was as if we all were one thing. (Andreas, personal communication, February 11, 2016)

As my interlocutors' practices in the square were based on solidarity, their exposure to violence evoked reactions guided by that same principle. Protesters took care of themselves and of each other due to the collective experience of violence. At the same time, as Andreas shows us, being on

146   Paradoxes of Emancipation

the receiving end of violence furthers a sense of *Communitas* (Turner 2008) ("We all were one thing"). And it does so despite the fact that what authorities seek to accomplish when deploying violence is to disperse and break resistance.

In sum, the precursor norms and practices of the Syntagma Square occupation structured a spatiality that had an egalitarian and antiauthoritarian ethic. The radical imagination here is made up of the guiding principles of that ethic: collectivist in nature, equality and mutual respect, self-governance, self-organization, and solidarity provide a fundamental alternative to the workings of the status quo. The departure from the normative principles of the status quo furthers the formation of affectivities that are intrinsic to, and expressive of, the radical imagination of Syntagma Square.

The Affectivities of the Radical Imagination

> This [thing] that the others also told you—that if you haven't lived it you cannot understand it—that is something all of us who lived through Syntagma have. What I want to say is, it was something absolutely *experiential*. And I believe that it had to do with the aura that the people who participated had, where you suddenly felt—and I emphasize the "suddenly"—that you participated in a community—which in Athens hasn't happened before. (Vasilis, personal communication, October 24, 2014; emphasis added)

A common trait among my interlocutors was that they struggled to find words to describe their experiences in Syntagma Square. Unable to fully discursivize and rationalize what they have lived through, they draw on metaphors of the arcane and the mystical to make their experiences understandable to others. As I outlined in the previous chapter, metaphors "do" things: they organize and disguise (unconscious) significations, and they engender and enact political affectivities (Aretxaga 2005). Vasilis speaks of an "aura" and others have used the word *magical* to describe what they have lived through in the square. In his work on authenticity, Walter Benjamin (2008) highlights the reverence and "unique existence" of artistic objects, attributing to them an aura that remains hidden and only visible, and hence accessible, to the esoteric few. Similarly, "magic" can be viewed as something that is inexplicable in scientific terms—that is, the scientific knowledge we have available to us today. So when my interlocutors describe their experiences as "magical," they might associate with them a "noticeable experience of deep inner change, or a knowing, or a sense that something significant has happened" (Hume and Drury 2013, x). As a metaphor, both magic and aura are something my interlocutors understand, but cannot (yet) make understandable to others, with the noticeable exception of those esoteric few who participated in the collective experience at Syntagma Square. Vasilis's emphasis on the term *suddenly* signifies, by definition, an experience that comes about quickly and unexpectedly: unthought-of. In this sense, my interlocutors' use of metaphorical categories is an attempt to make discursive something that is still prediscursive; grounded in affect, rather than deliberate reason (Schumann and Soudias 2013).

Scholarship in social movement studies has examined the affective dimensions of protest, especially love[9] of the group (Berezin 2001) and hatred[10] for outsiders (Mann 2004; Scheff 1994); both feelings are said to maintain protesters' enthusiasm and commitment. Protesters seem to be strengthened when they share emotions in response to events and to one another—what James Jasper (2011, 294) calls "shared" and "reciprocal emotions." In much work on the sociology of emotions as well as social

---

9. "The good days were like when you're falling in love. I thought, 'This is it! I want to keep it'" (Eleftheria, personal communication, October 6, 2014). Feminist theorist Lynne Segal (2017, 26–27) notes that "falling in love" was a common metaphor used by those involved in second-wave feminism. "It is when more inclusive spaces open up for particular groups of hitherto marginalized or subordinated people to find themselves anew, in affirmative identifications with one another."

10. "When I see the police clean the square, I feel hatred. This frightens me. I cannot always get hit. [I'm afraid] that I won't just be somebody who accepts being hit. That I will be transformed into a beast. That is to say that this behavior may force me to be even more violent than him [referring to the police] (Andreas, personal communication, February 11, 2016).

movement studies there is a tendency to distinguish between seemingly direct emotional responses, such as sensations or reflex emotions, and more enduring and conscious emotional states, such as affective commitments or moods (Flam and King 2005; Jasper 2007, 2011; Pearlman 2013). While there may well be an analytical benefit to the compartmentalization of these categories for some studies, for the purpose of investigating meaning-making practices of lived experiences, I agree with Sara Ahmed (2014, 40) that this separation is an artificial one, as even seemingly direct responses actually evoke past histories, both bypassing consciousness through bodily memories.

> Certainly, the experience of "having" an emotion may be distinct from sensations and impressions. . . . But this model creates a distinction between conscious recognition and "direct" feeling, which itself negates how that which is not consciously experienced may itself be mediated by past experiences . . . this analytic distinction between sensation or affect and emotion risks cutting emotions off from the lived experiences of being and having a body.

As I am indeed interested in lived experiences and their transformative character for my interlocutors' subjectivity, I suggest one should think of the social construction of emotions, sensations, affects, etc., in terms of their affective dimension in practice (Scheer 2012). Nigel Thrift's (2008, 175) work on affect and nonrepresentational theory lays the groundwork for how to sensitize the concept, defining affect as a *"form of thinking, often indirect and nonreflective true, but thinking all the same."* Just like the metaphor "aura" indicates, affect can be viewed as a way of thinking about sensations that we do not (yet) have the language to describe. It allows what would otherwise elude language to be captured. Brian Massumi (1995) refers to this as the "autonomy of affect." "Similarly," Thrift (2008, 175) says, "all manner of the spaces which they generate must be thought of in the same way, as means of thinking and as thought in action."

Conceiving affect as "thought in action" intersects with my previous considerations of practice. Doing work and creating together in Syntagma Square signifies the perpetuation of practices over time, as protesters form and experience affective bonds with each other but also with the spatiality of the square occupation itself (the latter of which furthers the possessive claim toward territory I elaborated on in chapter 2). In other words, practices constitute the situated environments through which we experience ourselves affectively. They shape "feelings towards each other, as well as towards ideas, activities and objects" (Feigenbaum et al. 2013, 17). Syntagma Square has been associated with a lasting and "positive" affective climate along such lines as happiness, euphoria, and optimism (Davou and Demertzis 2013, 110). My interlocutors point out a variety of affective dimensions that they attribute to the occupation experience. The coding process revealed the central affective dimensions to be "belonging" and "being among like-minded people," "feeling united," "not feeling alone anymore," "trust," and "feeling *Omopsychia*," which translates literally as "same-soulness."

"Belonging," much as in the case of solidarity, is the inverse of, and stems from, the shared negative experiences of precarization and uncertainty about the future as a result of the crisis (Lorey 2015; Wright 2010). In the words of fifty-four-year-old nursery school teacher Kyriaki:

> What I liked especially about the square? I like that I saw, finally, that there were many people, *just like me*, who weren't satisfied with things. And you saw that they all went to show their presence . . . against the things that they weren't satisfied with: In government, in their lives, in their jobs, in their wages, with the taxes, in education, in health first and foremost. (Kyriaki, personal communication, October 19, 2014; emphasis added)

This commonality of vulnerability and the sense of deeply rooted dissatisfaction with the status quo brought for my interlocutors a sense of going through shared hardship. Others, such as Aggelos, referred more explicitly to this affective dimension:

> Basically, I think, that for me, now that I think about it, what it did to me, why I wanted to be there, was more . . . that I felt I was *among people* who also wanted things to happen here and now. Not just to complain.

> And that *inside* of all the things that were going on in the square, you
> could find crazy people, like me, who want to do something after the
> square. [This is] something that happened . . . I mean, I felt that there
> were people with whom I could communicate. (Aggelos, personal com-
> munication, January 27, 2016; emphasis added)

In the words of feminist theorist Sara Ahmed (2014, 4), a sense of belonging is "a mark of one's own presence," where being among like-minded
people provides affective commitments that tend to persist (Vestergren et
al. 2017). Intersectionality-informed approaches show that belonging is far
from hardwired and very much positioned vis-à-vis gender, ethnicity, sexuality, age, physical ability, amongst others (e.g., Youkhana 2015). In this
light, it is far from likely that more marginalized groups, such as migrants,
experienced the same sense of belonging in the square that my interlocutors' attest.[11] But here too, what matters with regard to subjectivity, is
what kinds of meaningful guidelines emerge from how my interlocutors
claim belonging has informed their experience in the square, rather than
how things "really" were "back then." In a similar vein, my interlocutors
illustrate belonging through their affective attachments toward the square
itself. Andreas remarks, "It was magical. We had a space where we felt it
was ours. We lived there. If you live there, if you hold assemblies and if you
discuss there, it is yours in some way" (personal communication, February
11, 2016). This attachment furthered my interlocutors' (tacit or explicit)
territorial claim toward the spatiality of Syntagma Square (chapter 2).

The egalitarian character of the precursor norms and the antiauthoritarian character of the square's practices also furthered a sense of unity
among my interlocutors.

> You felt that you entered a utopian space. That means everybody had
> goodwill. How should I say this now? With an open mind. We all were
> like, we were like siblings. Nobody asked all these miserable things that

---

11. This is especially pertinent against the backdrop of the xenophobic discourses
of the upper square, and studies that point to racist attacks against migrants there (Kaika
and Karaliotas 2014).

the Greeks ask: "Where are you from? Who are you? And why?" Nothing. You came here as equals. (Vasilis, personal communication, October 24, 2014)

The sense of belonging and feeling equal was difficult for Vasilis to put into words ("How should I say this now?"). Precursor norms contributed to overcoming the more divisive characteristics of identity constructs and allowed for a sort of openness and egalitarianism among participants. In its prefiguration ("here and now"), it was also an escape from an increasingly frustrating reality.

> THANOS: I wanted to participate in something massive, to protest. . . . I mean, I was very depressed and pressured. And I wanted to find relief for this somehow.
> DIMITRIS: Depressed with what?
> THANOS: With the situation, as it has enfolded. . . . So for me [the Syntagma Square occupation] was a way out. . . . I was looking for something, somewhere to go, something to do. (Thanos, personal communication, February 3, 2016)

The underlying assumptions of "a way out" may well be framed in psychoanalytical terms as escapism, signifying a retreat from unpleasant realities through diversion or avoidance, often related to feelings of depression or general sadness (Stonebridge 2016). But much in line with Paul Ricoeur's notion of productive imaginaries (2008), Thanos's pointing at "doing something" does not signify resignation and retreat, but rather a progressive signification of crisis that links prefigurative practices to the radical imagination.

As opposed to the processes of individualization under neoliberal modernization that furthered a general sense of loneliness (Davies 2011; Cacioppo and Patrick 2008; Monbiot 2016), the sense of belonging and unity in Syntagma Square made my interlocutors point to how they did "not feel alone anymore." Katerina remarks that

> the most important thing is that I didn't feel alone. I mean, the loneliness . . . of the type . . ."it's me and I am fighting alone". . . . This

loneliness can also be harmful, because you say to yourself, "Fuck, what am I doing? I'm alone. What will I change all alone in this world?" This didn't exist. We were many. This loneliness didn't exist. . . . I always say, that the most important thing, for me, is that I learnt to trust the people around me and to not feel alone in this world [and] that I want to change. (Katerina, personal communication, October 19, 2014)

The antiauthoritarian and egalitarian guiding principles of the radical imagination in Syntagma Square furthered a sense of collectivity that can be seen as a radical departure from the described loneliness prior to my interlocutors' participation in the Syntagma Square occupation. As feminist scholar Lynne Segal (2017, 69) argues, joy arises from moments of collective existence precisely because they overcome "the individuating principles that have become so prominent in modernity." Relatedly, this newly found collectivism furthered the feeling of "trust" among protesters.

One thing I would like to tell you, another thing that the square left me with, is that I learned to trust people a lot more. I have become friends with people who I know won't betray me. . . . I trust people a lot more than before. I don't look at them suspiciously. You know, kind of "What does he now want to gain from me?" (Thanos, personal communication, February 3, 2016)

The notion of belonging and being among like-minded people furthers trust. Jeff Goodwin et al. (2004, 419) note, we "trust those we agree with, and agree with those we trust." Trust persisted through the duration of the occupation (and beyond, as Thanos's example shows) and allowed mutual acceptance of ideas and opinions.

All these affectivities among protesters, as well as the space of the square occupation and its ideas, practices, and principles, furthered a particular sense of community among my interlocutors.

It's magical, without understanding the "why": Connecting with people and feeling like you are in a group. . . . Such magical . . . *Omopsychia*. . . . That people want to belong to a group and feel they have something in common with the others. (Thanos, personal communication, February 3, 2016)

Thanos offers yet another example of the pre-discursive dimension of affect that eludes explanation and therefore obliges him to draw on the arcane ("magical") to make his experience understandable to others. The sense of community he tries to convey is rendered through use of the term *Omopsychia*. Literally meaning "same-soulness," it signifies a sense of togetherness and unity that is perhaps best captured with the term used by Aristide Zolberg's "moments of madness." In explaining his concept, Zolberg (1972, 106) describes how the "moment of immense joy, when daily cares are transcended, when emotions are freely expressed, when the spirit moves men to talk and to write, when the carefully erected walls which compartmentalize society collapse, is also a moment of political harmony." Zolberg's conception indicates an underlying liminality and therefore overlaps with Viktor Turner's (2008) notion of *Communitas*. As such, both frame radical departures from our societal everyday vis-à-vis structure, differentiation, and hierarchical systems of politico-legal-economic positions, and instead signify an unstructured, or rudimentarily structured and relatively undifferentiated, "communion of equal individuals" (Turner 2008, 96). "It was," Andreas remarks, "as if we all were one thing" (personal communication, February 11, 2016). By virtue of the egalitarian and antiauthoritarian character of the Syntagma Square occupation, it comes as little surprise that the ways in which my interlocutors claim they experience the occupation affectively is also marked by equality and collectivity. Some of my interlocutors describe this experience as moving from an individualist subject position to a more collectivist one.

The square is something that overwhelmed me. I moved out of my "I." Whether I wanted to or not, I moved out of my "I." Because I got excited, because I was charmed, because I was open, because it was that state of political maturation? Because I was thirsty and I didn't know it? I moved out of my "I." I joined a "we," which I didn't determine. This in itself can move you forward a lot. . . . The "we" brings you forward. The "I" is a systemic autism. . . . It is very comfortable to be millions of

154 Paradoxes of Emancipation

"I." The "we" is what is very exciting. (Lukas, personal communication, February 23, 2016)

By definition, *overwhelming* is something that is very large in effect and difficult to fight against. It indicates the transformative quality of experience that my interlocutors highlight. Bringing back to mind the dialectical argument I presented in the previous chapter, space as a structuring and structured structure is the product of practices, while at the same time, space shapes practices and the experience thereof, which maintain and reproduce space. Lukas describes an almost involuntary transformative process as to experiencing and living through the Syntagma Square occupation. In his attempt to make sense of it, he describes his openness to the experience, which I argue was facilitated by an egalitarian ethic. He also describes a sort of willfulness ("thirst") to the process from the outset, which arguably is grounded in the progressive formation of crisis. Here, individuals reconsider and reinterpret ordinary habits of thought and action in ways that are conducive to the radical imagination: that things could be radically different. In effect, Lukas affectively describes a change in his subjectivity from previous individualism toward subsequent collectivism. He attributes a normative positivity to the latter in demarcation to the (morally) "wrong" values of the former ("systematic autism"). In this sense, Lukas offers us a stark critique of the individualisms so inherent in neoliberalism. In the same vein, it is worth considering whether the ways in which the Syntagma Square occupation is experienced affectively also signify a departure from the capitalization of emotions—a resource for gain and maximization (Adams 2016; Davies 2015a; Ehrenreich 2010; Han 2017). In any case, the sense of community and collectivity that my interlocutors describe stands in stark contrast to the neoliberal ideal of competitive, individualist subjects.

New Answers to Old Questions

How do we respond to the extraordinary challenges of crisis? How do we position and organize ourselves in the face of worsening economic conditions? How do we take care of ourselves and others? The Syntagma

Square occupation ought to be seen as an answer to these questions. In this chapter, I tried to disentangle and lay bare the radical imagination of the Syntagma Square occupation in order to make sense of the transformative quality of the participation experience that my interlocutors describe. Grounded in an intersectionally positioned understanding of experience, my interlocutors' euphoric and valorizing accounts of the practices in Syntagma Square signify their ethical aspiration and guidelines regarding subjectivity, rather than fixed and positivist representations of how things actually played out in the square. With this in mind, the radical imagination of the Syntagma Square occupation rests on an egalitarian and antiauthoritarian ethic. This is to say that in its spatial dialectics, the imagination of Syntagma Square was shaped in practice but also shaped practices in the "spirit" of the radical imagination, thus maintaining and reproducing space in ways that allow subjectivities to be collectively transformed.

Practice theory informs us that this process does not appear out of thin air, but instead rests on previous experiences and practices. As I have shown in this chapter, there were veteran activists taking part in the occupation who argued for egalitarian and antiauthoritarian principles over other kinds of principles. Related to this, spontaneity as a mode of organization did not come about coincidently, but was instead advocated from the outset by some of the more veteran activists with previous experiences in the anarchist movement. In effect, spontaneity renders the practices of the square prefigurative in their ontological layout. Here, means and ends are effectively indistinguishable and practices embody the change that is envisioned. It is because of the prefigurative layout of practices that change is experienced in the moment of practicing. This allows for the radical imagination to be lived and experienced in prefiguration. As Lukas remarks in this regard, "If the individuals produce collectives and collectives produce squares and uprisings and this happens in a somehow similar temporal momentum, the dynamics that can be released are unfathomable to the fantasies of even the most optimistic revolutionary" (personal communication, February 23, 2016). It is important to highlight that the ways in which my interlocutors narrate their selves during the period of neoliberal modernization (chapter 1) and crisis (chapter 2) must be viewed precisely as a (partial) result of the collective experience of the radical imagination Lukas points to.

Specifically, the radicality in the radical imagination lies precisely in that it strongly departs—ontologically and epistemologically—from the experience of the status quo, particularly the period of neoliberal modernization: it not only challenges but also minimizes the reproduction of status quo values. This occurs in four interrelated ways. Regarding egalitarianism, the precursor norms of dismissing violence, party involvement, and the display of flags contributed to the occupation's open and inclusive character in an effort to overcome societal cleavages from the outset. This is a first departure from the justice of inequality as the "common condition" (Minogue 1989, 100) set by the status quo of neoliberal everyday life.

As inherent guiding principles to my interlocutors' practices in the square, equality and mutual respect, self-governance, self-organization, and solidarity mark the radical imagination as grounded in an antiauthoritarian ethic. These principles signify a second departure from the status quo of neoliberal everyday life. They do so because self-governance stands in stark contrast to competitive representation; because solidarity forms the antithesis to competition; and because self-organization signifies attempts to enact practices that are autonomous from the centralist authority of the state.

The egalitarian and antiauthoritarian character of the Syntagma Square occupation not only shaped the ways in which my interlocutors radically envisioned and practiced in the square but also the ways in which they experienced it affectively. The guiding principles of the occupation furthered a sense of belonging, like-mindedness, and, consequently, *Communitas*. This signifies a third departure from neoliberal everyday life, as collectivism trumps notions of individualist subjectivities.

The radical imagination of the Syntagma Square occupation also significantly departs from utilitarianism, upon which neoliberal reasoning rests. Utilitarian theories, such as Jeremy Bentham's (1876) Greatest Happiness Principle, view people's aspirations as fixed, and external to action. They do not view expectations and aspirations as derived from or changing through experience. Rather, they see them as an expression of universally valid principles derived from logical deductions or anthropological presumptions (Beckert 2016). Utilitarianism axiomatically considers that action is taken to obtain positive future sensations. The radical imagination of Syntagma Square, however, is alter-neoliberal in its ontological layout: inconceivable and incomprehensible from the viewpoint of either the state or neoliberal practices. This signifies a fourth departure from neoliberalism.

Finally, the radical imagination of Syntagma Square also departs from Marxist theorizations of change. As David Graeber (2002, 2009) points out, Marxism has tended to be an analytical discourse about revolutionary strategy. The radical imagination of Syntagma Square, on the other hand, was basically an ethical discourse about revolutionary practice. The basic principles of self-organization, self-governance, solidarity, equality, and mutual respect are essentially moral and organizational.

With the alter-political quality of the radical imagination extracted, the next chapter attends to the antipolitical quality. This quality is marked by the practices and experiences of my interlocutors in Syntagma Square as to their exposure to, and critique and analysis of, those forces perpetuating the status quo: the state.

4

Challenging the Dystopian

The Anti-Politics of Demystification

Fleeing the clouds of tear gas spreading through Syntagma Square during the clashes on June 28, 2011, Katerina sought shelter in the adjacent area around the popular shopping street Ermou. Police units of the infamous DIAS (Hellenic Police Motorcycle Unit) squad were chasing protesters through the many alleyways. "There were two on each motorbike," Katerina recalls. "The one in the front was driving, the other in the back . . . with the baton. And they all get off their bikes and start hitting whoever they find in front of them—whether it was a child, a grandfather, a grandmother. They didn't care" (personal communication, October 19, 2014). Desperately trying to escape the beatings, Katerina fled into a restaurant where the owner hid her in a basement closet. Police did not stop short of entering the premises and the owner had to yell furiously for them to finally leave. "I felt that what I live is not something natural," she recalls. "And it reminds me a lot of the stories of my father from the Polytechneio.[1] I realize that what I live, this is not a democracy" (personal communication, October 19, 2014).

Katerina's account begins with an uneasy affective description ("felt") of a situation she deems extraordinary ("not natural"). Trying to make sense of this situation and being aware of her father's experience

---

1. Katerina refers to the Athens 1973 Polytechnic University uprising against the Greek military junta of 1967–74. The uprising escalated when a tank crashed through the university gates and killed more than two dozen people.

with state violence during the military dictatorship, Katerina views her experience as analogous. With this authoritarian framing in mind, her experience of being exposed to the violence of those very forces that claim to serve and protect her led Katerina to question a doxic assumption she had held about institutionalized democracy in Greece. When I ask her during a later conversation what it is that she is living, if it is not a democracy, Katerina replies, "It is authoritarianism and fascism with a very nice face on the outside. It looks democratic" (personal communication, February 7, 2016).

Katerina's account is paradigmatic of my interlocutors' experiences with the state during the occupation, as their views shift toward perceiving contemporary Greek state-institutional arrangements as authoritarian precisely because of the ways in which these arrangements present themselves in public. What this chapter seeks to investigate is the relationship between my interlocutors' negative experiences with "the state"[2] during the occupation and the political quality of subjectivation. Conceptually, investigating my interlocutors' meaning-making practices of their experience with repression really signifies studying their (shifting) imagination of the state in their critiques. I claim that my interlocutors essentially "demystify" (Abrams 1988) the state in their critiques. Katerina's metaphorical use of "face on the outside" points precisely to the demystifying yet disillusioning character of such experiences. As I seek to render the political subject meaningful not as the foundation of political (or other) practices, but rather by tracing its formation in these practices, I further argue that the critiques that emerged from my interlocutors' experiences with the state solidify into the emergence of meaningful guidelines as politicized subjectivity. These processes become all the more pertinent and intelligible against the backdrop of my interlocutors' experience with, and practice of, the alter-political qualities of the radical imagination of the Syntagma Square occupation (chapter 3). To put it another way, the experience of state repression constructs an almost Manichean juxtaposition between the aspiring equality and self-governance of the

---

2. I use "the state" and "state-institutional arrangements" interchangeably.

160   Paradoxes of Emancipation

Syntagma Square occupation, and the subordination and domination by the Greek state.

I will first elaborate on conceptual discussions about the imagination and demystification of the state, and how I can study "it" through my interlocutors' (meaning-making) practices. Second, I will briefly describe how state repression unfolded during the occupation in the two paradigmatic episodes of June 15 and June 28–29, events in which Athens witnessed forty-eight-hour general strikes. The stand-offs between the police and protesters, and the ways in which violence unfolded, are marked precisely by the territorializing aspects of spatial production I elaborated on in chapter 2. Third, I will shed light on the discursive and practical consequences of being exposed to this repression for both my interlocutors and the occupation as a whole. The experience of repression shifted discourses and practices of violence away from the initial nonviolent stance of the "quiet days" (Papapavlou 2015), and impacted the overall composition of participants as a group in ways that allowed the presence of party cadres, especially those of the Coalition of the Radical Left (SYRIZA), to increase. This, in turn, brought to the fore the struggle between retaining the radical imagination of the square and returning to the more "ordinary" street politics prior to occupation's inception. Fourth, I will examine in detail the critiques that my interlocutors developed as a result of these conflictual developments. I will show how my interlocutors essentially demystify the state, focusing on its actualities of domination and subordination. From these processes and observations, I can make sense of my interlocutors' narration of transformative experience regarding what they refer to as "political maturation." This allows us to then put forward a theorization of the political quality of subjectivation.

Demystification

In his groundbreaking work on the difficulty of studying the state, historical sociologist Philip Abrams (1988) insightfully concludes that the state "is not the reality which stands behind the mask of political practice" (82). Instead, it is "itself the mask which prevents our seeing political practice

Challenging the Dystopian   161

as it is." It is "a bid to elicit support for or tolerance of the insupportable and intolerable by presenting them as something other than themselves" (76)—namely, legitimate, impartial domination.[3]

In ordinary times, the invocation of the ordering role of the state as legitimate or justified silences protest and normalizes state repression. And even if frustration is voiced and protest unfolds, more often than not, critiques of state-institutional arrangements rarely ever rattle their ontological foundations. As I claimed in chapter 2, when protesters in the upper square are frustrated about corruption and patronage in Greece, or express grave disappointment about politicians by calling them "traitors" or "thieves," what they do is critique particular aspects of state-institutional arrangements in relation to their "shortcomings." Such a critique can be framed in Boltanskian (2011) terms through the "practical register," in that it is immanent to the state: it demands from the state, broadly conceived, that it should function and operate "properly." Thomas Blom Hansen and Finn Stepputat (2001) conceptualize this way of going about critique as the paradox of the state: while the authority of the state is constantly questioned and functionally undermined, it remains the central addressee of claims. This paradox has to do with the persistence of the imagination of the state as an embodiment of sovereignty, representation, social order, stability, and authoritative institutions. It remains pivotal in understanding of what society "is." For J. P. Nettl (1968), this ordering role for the state is presumed precisely because our imagination of it is deeply

3. I depart here from more statist approaches to the study of the state as well as political systems theorizations in comparative politics and functionalist political science (Almond 1988; Easton 1981). This has to do, above all, with this literature's scientistic presumptions that often add to the—deliberately (see Almond and Verba 1963; Loewenstein 1944) or not—naturalization of the state. Instead of assuming a naturalness of the state in the pursuit of rendering meaningful what the state "is," I argue here to shift the attention to how the state presents itself. Much in line with my abductive analysis' pragmatist approach to study meaning in consequences, I draw close to studies from sociology, history, and anthropology that conceive the state (as a figure of thought) as a structural, "metaphysical effect of practices that make such structures appear to exist" (Mitchell 1991, 94). This allows the state to be studied by way of how it is imagined by my interlocutors.

incorporated in habits of thought and action. The seeming impossibility of extracting ourselves from the state rests on the (often violent) force of its performance, which frequently leaves us with "an obsessive attempt at interpretation, at translation of mere force into the language of reason" (Aretxaga 2003, 407). It is because the state is presumed to be a justified formation of social orderings that we rarely ever come to question what lies at its core.

To demystify the state, then, we need to make the invisible visible, by elevating the doxic to the level of discourse. Arguably, only then will we be able to assume the state to be an exercise of legitimating the status quo ante; an exercise of an otherwise illegitimate and unacceptable domination. Pierre Bourdieu (1994, 4) assumes that in order to "have a chance to really think a state which still thinks itself through those who attempt to think it, then, it is imperative to submit to radical questioning all the presuppositions inscribed in the reality to be thought and in the very thought of the analyst." What this requires, is to recognize the cogency of the imagination of the state as an object of study, while at the same time not "*believe* in the idea of the state, not to concede, even as an abstract formal-object, the existence of the state" (Abrams 1988, 79).

Crises are situations that facilitate such considerations, where the everyday basis of the legitimacy of the state can be foundationally questioned. To be a radically "metapragmatic" (Boltanski 2011) critique, one that demystifies the state, it must be a ruthless assault on the state's claims to be a justified ordering role of moral (and other kinds of) regulation as well as its assertion that it pursues the common interest. In line with the work of anthropologists Veena Das and Deborah Poole (2005, 6), the locus for such critiques to unfold can emerge in the state's social and spatial margins—"sites of disorder, where the state has been unable to impose its order." My interlocutors' space-making and territorializing practices that I elaborated on in chapter 2, and their prefigurative practicing of the radical imagination that I investigated in chapter 3, can signify the Syntagma Square occupation as a marginal space—one where the state, temporarily, is caught off-guard and loses territorial, and therefore social, control. The state's violent attempts to reinstate its vision of order and to control subjects through repression allows the focus to move "from the analysis of the state to a concern with the actualities of social subordination" (Abrams 1988, 63). The ways in which my interlocutors signify and draw conclusions from their experiences with state repression denotes just that. They break with the paradox of the state, albeit in varying degrees. By questioning the safeguarding role of the police, the democratic nature of representation, the ordering role of state institutions overall, they question, in the end, the instruments used to justify subordination and domination and, in turn, the central mode of subjection.

Police Repression

As occupants were for weeks diligently prefiguring a radical alternative to the status quo in Syntagma Square, it was only a matter of time before the state would react to this development in one way or another. In the square, the ways in which this reaction was anticipated evolved around discussions of state repression. Some participants initially did not believe the police would dare to use brute force against a peaceful protest. Others, with previous experience of repressive methods, were convinced police reactions would be fierce and discussed different ways in which protesters could prepare against such an attack. Meanwhile, various protest actions started being planned in anticipation of June 15, the day on which Parliament was to discuss the first set of austerity measures. Unions announced a forty-eight-hour general strike against the vote, hoping to bring the country to a virtual standstill. In Syntagma Square, the Action Group for the Memorandum was set up to plan and coordinate activities for the day. Eventually, the square's popular assembly on June 10 circulated a call for protests to support the strike. For the general strike specifically, the call stated three main meeting points: in front of Parliament, at the Evangelismos metro station, and at Panathenaic Stadium, with the purpose of encircling Parliament and preventing MPs from entering the building to vote. While Syntagma retained its peaceful and nonviolent character until June 15, the square's vivid opposition to the austerity measures soon brought police repression to the scene.

Violence Is Coming

On June 15, police preempted protesters' attempts to block access to Parliament by temporarily shutting down Evangelismos and Syntagma metro stations and cordoning off large areas around Parliament with riot police. As a result, most protesters were unable to access the scheduled meeting points and converged on Syntagma Square. Maria Papapavlou (2015, 225) notes that protesters congregating on June 15 were from all different backgrounds and ages. From hospital workers to socialist youth to hotel porters, people were in a rather festive mood and good spirit. Things changed when some protesters tried to break through police cordons to reach the Parliament building. Riot police responded swiftly with large amounts of tear gas, literally poisoning the atmosphere. As most participants fled from the violence into the square's many side streets, the colorful scene was transformed into a foggy battlefield, with police officers in full riot gear facing off protesters: the police destroying everything they came across in the square and protesters throwing at the police whatever they found in front of them. As I argued in chapter 2, for the police, the protesters' attempts to get to Parliament were a direct challenge to their role as enforcers of social control and public order and had to be met with repressive policing strategies. For protesters, the forceful denial of access to Parliament had to be resisted through their own attempts to control space by tactics of territorialization and deterritorialization (Soudias 2015, 2018). During the violent episodes, members of the occupation's general secretariat perpetually repeated, in calm voices and using their loudspeaker system, "We do not leave the square. Calm. Cool. We are all together. We stay here. The square belongs to us. We do not retreat" (quoted in Papapavlou 2015, 225), highlighting their possessive claim on the square. In the midst of all the commotion, many of my interlocutors recall a man playing the Cretan lyra.[4]

---

4. The lyra is a three-stringed instrument, played with bow, typically used to play rhythmic Cretan music.

As this happens, everybody starts leaving. To protect myself, I also slowly leave. . . . The guy who was playing the lyra continued to play. I was leaving and said to myself, "what is he doing?" I saw that there was a lot of tear gas. There was a cloud [says it anxiously]. But he continued to play. He didn't stop. As I was leaving and I saw that the music continued to play, despite the very intense incidents, I said to myself, "Where am I going now?" So I started looking into how I could return [to the square]. . . . The guy played steadily until the air cleared up a little and the people reassembled. This is when he stopped. And this guy then was vomiting all over. . . . Because he got hit really badly by the tear gas. . . . And whenever I remember it and think about it, I get goose bumps. Even now. It was a very intense event. I mean, an incident of bravery where I felt that, OK, we can fight for this issue. And we can endure it and fight for it and we can be steady in what we want and believe in. That we want to have value inside of a democracy. (Thanos, personal communication, February 3, 2016)

My interlocutors attribute a particular importance to this episode. First of all, the lyra player's act of "bravery," as Thanos put it, enthused people into returning to the square to sustain their participation, as they saw what their fellow protesters were willing to take in their determination to hold on to what they valued. At the same time, playing music and dancing are practices defying violence as well as a tactic to retain territory through stasis (chapter 2) without acknowledging violence through counterviolence. This is to say that despite repression, protesters managed to uphold the radical imagination in the sense that they did not reproduce "ordinary" reactions of violence, which only reproduce and legitimate state power, but instead some radical and creative alternatives to it. The affective attachment to the square, expressed in practices of dance and music, culminated with the self-organized cleaning I outlined in the previous chapter. Here, protesters formed human chains, passing water bottles to wash away any toxic leftovers of the tear gas from the ground in the square. And after a long and tiring day of fights, destruction, and reconstruction, the occupiers decided in the popular assembly to skip the general meeting and clear their heads with more music and dance (Papapavlou 2015, 244).

166 Paradoxes of Emancipation

The Free Besieged

After the excessive violence of June 15, then–prime minister Georgios Papandreou sought a vote of confidence on June 21 in order to garner support for his policy of austerity (Traynor and Smith 2011). In response, the square's popular assembly voted "no confidence," as "those who created the problem cannot solve it." In the spirit of the square's radical imagination, the resolution added, "To their violence we respond: Our weapon is our solidarity and our souls" (quoted in Giovanopoulos and Mitropoulos 2011, 287). Unaffected by the protests in the square, Papandreou survived the vote even as violent clashes between police officers and protesters were taking place right in front of the Parliament building. Just a few days later, in anticipation of the scheduled parliamentary vote on the memorandum for the Economic Adjustment Programme for Greece, a second forty-eight-hour general strike, from June 28, brought Athens to a standstill. Similarly with the previous general strike, the plan was to block the vote on austerity by peacefully surrounding Parliament and impeding entry (Markantonatou 2015, 202). The police response this time was tactically similar, but differed so immensely in intensity and excessiveness of violence that it alarmed even Amnesty International (2011, 2012). With batons and over one thousand rounds of tear gas used (Mason 2013, 101), police violence left more than five hundred people injured after the two days of clashes (Sotirakopoulos and Sotiropoulos 2013, 449). "In substance," Andreas recalls, "it was a siege of the square" (personal communication, October 24, 2014).

When Viktoria and I went on an ethnographic walk through the square together, she recalled the events of June 28–29 vividly: public transport workers had defied orders to shut down Syntagma Square metro station, arguing that it was a necessary exit for protesters.[5] Police officers armed with tear gas and batons charged against protesters seeking refuge in the station, risking the consequences of people falling down the stairs

---

5. These workers were allegedly later dismissed from their jobs for defying orders. According to Viktoria, protesters collected money for those who got fired due to this act of solidarity (personal communication, October 22, 2014).

and suffocating from tear gas in the confined underground space. There, shopkeepers opened their stalls, which then were used as areas for first aid and medical assistance. As the police continued to drive people down into the station with batons and tear gas, the space became so crowded that public transport workers had to use the station's PA system to call for the police to stop, as people risked falling onto the rail tracks, where trains were running normally. Enraged by the crude violence, some elderly people attempted to climb up the stairs of the underground station in order to stand up to the police and "defend their children"—referring to the majority of young protesters. Worried about their safety, younger protesters tried to stop those "grandparents" from going, but they simply replied, referring to their experiences during the military junta, "We have had our share of beatings in this country. Don't worry about us." Managing to break through the smoke screen, these elderly men and women started angrily yelling at the police, asking whether they had no shame, to gas the ones they ought to protect; some even pushed police officers. After that, Viktoria tells me, the police interrupted their attacks in the direction of the station, as if they respected the authority of those elders. Hundreds of people, barely able to breathe, tried to return aboveground, where the air was a little more breathable (Viktoria, personal communication, October 22, 2014). While protesters were suffocating and being beaten, in the safety of the parliamentary compound their representatives voted in favor of the Troika's midterm plan. As police attacks continued ceaselessly, it became abundantly clear that the goal was to besiege and destroy the Syntagma Square occupation by brute, indiscriminate force.

Experiencing the State

From the pragmatist viewpoint that informs my abductive research strategy, to make sense of social phenomena is to trace their consequences. The occurrence of violence, and the injurious ways in which mass media and political elites went about framing it, especially after June 15, had consequences for a variety of factors within the occupation as a whole. These consequences relate notably to changing discourses and practices of violence as well as the overall composition of participants in the protests.

168   Paradoxes of Emancipation

I argue that state violence introduced a shift away from the egalitarian and antiauthoritarian practices of the Syntagma Square toward more ordinary reactions akin to "traditional" modes of contestation in Greece (e.g., Kousis 2015, 150–59). That is to say that violence tarnished the radical imagination of the occupation that had become an everyday feature of the peaceful gatherings prior to June 15; it turned practices away from prefiguration toward more reactionary and tactical ways of coping with the state.

Significations of Violence

The topic of how to anticipate state repression had become a dominant issue discussed in the lead up to June 15. According to Papapavlou (2015), many participants initially did not believe the police would dare to use brute force against a peaceful protest. Others, with previous experience of repression, were convinced police reactions would be fierce, and suggested different ways protesters could prepare for it. Consequently, two contesting discourses emerged in Syntagma Square, for and against the use of violence in the face of police repression. Despite the fact that those voices justifying the use of force increased from June 10 onward—a reversal of the trend of previous weeks—the resolution voted on in the popular assembly for the actions on June 15 explicitly stated that protests would remain peaceful. As violence did break out despite this initial nonviolent stance, subsequent discussions in the popular assembly increasingly dealt with issues of violence (Papapavlou 2015, 253). Viktoria recalls:

> Violence is a virus. With the outbreak of the first violence, the people got stubborn. They wanted to "eat the cops" [says it emphatically], let's say. I mean, at one point on, our assemblies changed and we talked about what we would do to the cops. How we would defend ourselves, how we would keep hold of the square. So we got into a war-like situation. (Viktoria, personal communication, October 22, 2014)

Viktoria's talk of a "war-like situation" indicates how violence forces on the occupation a shift in expectations and practices. Practices in Syntagma Square changed from a prefigurative to a more tactical layout in an effort to secure territoriality. As Michel de Certeau (2002, 37) notes in this regard, "The space of a tactic is the space of the other. Thus it must play on and with a terrain imposed on it and organized by the law." As its own defined place is under attack by the authorities, protesters' practices become more tactical and reliant on opportunities (Soudias 2014). But through this, they are also reactionary, forsaking the precursor norms (nonviolence; see chapter 3) and guiding principles (chapter 3), in the hope of thwarting attacks and defending the square. In a sense, this signifies a state of exception within a state of exception, as the state managed to force upon the Syntagma Square occupation its own game; its own norms and principles by way of violent repression. As part of this trend, and often explicitly grounded in Karl Marx's (1887, 534) declaration that "force is the midwife of every old society pregnant with a new one," discussions in the square shifted toward justifying certain forms of violence in the face of police repression, as Zoe explains:

> Violence became somehow legitimate. The media framed us as rioters. Slowly though, other people came down to the square and saw what was really happening. The police were continuously charging against us brutally, while the media was misrepresenting us. People realized the police were at fault and therefore using violence against them, in defense, became somehow legitimate. (Zoe, personal communication, October 2, 2014)

That is to say that the precursor norm of nonviolence was scrutinized and situationally compromised by my interlocutors in light of police repression, and elite and media frames. For Étienne Balibar (2015), violence can be justified if it is a response to an original, unjustified moment of violence.[6] In this regard, the very notion of violence was questioned, as this quote from a male participant who spoke in the popular assembly on June 22 shows:

---

6. When counterviolence exceeds that moment of violence, Balibar (2015, xii) speaks of "cruelty," which can never be justified.

170   Paradoxes of Emancipation

> If I attack the police, am I being violent? If I help my fellow man, whom the cop is going to hit and I hit him, am I being violent? If . . . he goes to hit me and I hit him, am I being violent? What I would like us to think about individually is where does violence stop and where does solidarity begin. (Quoted in Papapavlou 2015, 254)

By reframing nominally violent acts as practices of solidarity in the face of repression, this account is evidence of the complex struggles of signification. From this viewpoint, and against the background of the commonality of vulnerability among protesters, an antiauthoritarian perspective on violence offers an analytically fruitful point of departure. Here, the normative evaluation of what signifies violence and nonviolence is grounded in their codification in law. This is to say that the law makes some forms of violence visible and renders them illegal (e.g., throwing rocks at police officers) or legal (e.g., policing protesters), while it renders other, more structural forms of violence invisible (e.g., the consequences of structural racism, gender discrimination, poverty, austerity, and other forms of harm created by inequality; see Graeber 2012). First, this means my interlocutors' binary distinction of violent and nonviolent needs to be understood in its immanence in the law. This distinction does not allow for questioning its immanence as the very condition of possibility upon which the binary rests, which is precisely why my interlocutors' reproduction of this binary points to how they have internalized it. Second, from the viewpoint of the law, if the legal order is the basis of the status quo, then the very questioning of its legitimacy is understood as violence (Rammstedt 1969). This is to say that the law takes a tautological form, as Walter Benjamin (1978, 281) shows:

> The law's interest in a monopoly of violence is not explained by the intention to preserve legal ends but, rather, by that of preserving the law itself; that violence when not in the hands of the law, threatens it not by the ends that it may pursue but by its mere existence outside the law.

For even if nominally nonviolent acts are practiced merely to reveal shortcomings and failures of the status quo, when they do not follow legally sanctioned venues (such as Parliament), authorities frame them in their violent capacity—that is, their violation of the status quo. Taking this line

Challenging the Dystopian   171

of thinking further, to suggest a nonviolent approach to bringing about radical systemic change can be rendered inconsequent as it nips the entire undertaking in the bud. In Lukas's words:

> Large-scale changes, historically, haven't been achieved peacefully, unfortunately . . . If one thinks about [the fact] that the state holds the monopoly of violence, what can be the answer? What is the answer to the monopoly of violence? What is the answer to a militarized, repressive mechanism? A two-day strike? Five protests? Ten protests?" (Lukas, personal communication, February 23, 2016)

On the one hand, as ethical beings, my interlocutors negotiate the very definitions and significations of violence between emancipation and reproduction. Yet their struggles of signification are limited by the contradiction as to the subordinating and authoritarian nature of violence that I elaborated on in the previous chapter. Insofar as an antiauthoritarian and egalitarian ethic affirms the freedom, equality, and community of all beings in the world, physical violence and other forms of repression could not possibly produce positive effects to that end. The point here is not to make a moral claim as to whether violence is universally right or wrong, nor that all kinds of violence are the same. Rather, it is to make visible the paradoxes and uncontested reproductive consequences that underlie my interlocutors' understandings and justifications of violence, in a way that acknowledges, yet carefully scrutinizes, the structuring reality of the binary between violence and nonviolence.

However tacit, it is arguably due to these reasons that the role of violence remained a contested issue throughout the course of the Syntagma Square occupation. Viktoria and Thanos, for example, continued to advocate and practice a nonviolent stance in this vein. Others, however, point to how in fact the practices of the square became more violent. Lukas, referring to nonviolence, explains:

> So, alright, it's a nice message. But in practice, on the streets, on the 15th we got beaten. On the 16th we got beaten again. On the . . . 28th of June: "Should we maybe also [says it emphatically] throw one [stone]?" On the 29th: "Guys, things weren't pacifist." Half the square was with

172 Paradoxes of Emancipation

> the Black Bloc and got into fights with the cops! We were there, we saw that. (Lukas, personal communication, March 28, 2016)

By engaging in running battles with the police, throwing stones and Molotov cocktails, and setting up burning barricades, violence was practiced far beyond the stereotypical "usual suspects" of the anarchist milieu, stigmatized by many in Greece as violent instigators (Apoifis 2016). Kostas remembers protesters' willpower and commitment: "People were decided. They were rebellious and wanted to participate. The violence gets real! I mean, you see barricades being set up, you see stones being thrown" (personal communication, February 17, 2016). These practices show that violence was increasingly viewed as a justified means to thwart police attacks. At the same time, and this is much in line with my previous considerations regarding the role of violence as the commonality of vulnerability for furthering solidarity (chapter 3), Kostas also notes that violent practices furthered a sense of collectivity: "It's also a psychological thing. You say, 'I do something together with others. I am here and throw the stone, but the one behind me also wants to'" (personal communication, February 17, 2016).

Arguably, what the contentious and changing discourses and practices of violence in the face of state repression indicate is not merely something that simply addresses questions of legality, tactics, or even violence. It is about the very ways in which my interlocutors imagine the stakes at hand, the nature of state-institutional arrangements and the status quo, and the most promising route to change. At the same time, however, the shift away from the more prefigurative practices toward engaging in violence led many participants increasingly to stay away from Syntagma Square. This had consequences regarding the composition of participants and related to this, how ideas of change shifted in the square.

The Creeping Rise of Party Politics

After June 28 and 29, as more and more people stayed away from the occupation due to violence,[7] it became clear to my interlocutors that the

---

7. "I think that after a while things started to become unpleasant, because the [number of] people started to decrease. And as you were going there—without doing anything,

number of people affiliated to parties increased in the square (Bakola 2017, 92). "In the assemblies, for example," Aggelos remarks, "there was a political hijacking. That means, people from parties who wanted to push their agenda, with 'this is how it has to be done.' They didn't function collaboratively any more" (personal communication, January 27, 2016). Putting blame on SYRIZA for "hijacking" the occupation was a theme that resonated among all my interlocutors. In what they see as a strategic "infiltration" of the square, my interlocutors emphasize the consequences it had for the practices of the occupation.

> SYRIZA [people] entered the groups in heaps. And they started to do whatever they wanted. I mean, they tried to make it theirs. They have this tendency. . . . They did not respect the decisions of the assembly. They brought in many of their people, in order to get the majorities they wanted. So they were promoting SYRIZA. . . . They didn't respect the people in the groups. They brought about disharmony. And the people who saw that parties were going down [to the square] got pissed off slowly and started to leave. And then they [SYRIZA supporters] were the only ones left. We brought new people to the groups and they would say, "We don't need more people, we're good." But we weren't working like that! (Viktoria, personal communication, October 22, 2014)

Perceived as undermining the established guiding principles of collectivity, equality, and mutual respect, the actions of party supporters appeared to my interlocutors to be marked precisely by the kinds of practices that the radical imagination of the Syntagma Square occupation was trying to overcome in the first place. My interlocutors point out that there was a return to the accustomed practices of party politics, in which, arguably, the ultimate goal is to generate votes.[8]

---

ok? You didn't break anything, or anything like that, they [the police] fired tear gas. And the people started to leave, of course. You couldn't stand that" (Kyriaki, personal communication, October 19, 2014).

    8. "Let's not hide behind the tear gas. The political hijacking has a name. It was SYRIZA, who basically had networks in all the movements from below. And as we speak . . . it showed that they sucked and milked the movements from below to generate votes. And they managed just fine" (Lukas, personal communication, February 23, 2016).

174 Paradoxes of Emancipation

> Instead of trying to create structures that would last into the future, they all [referring to parties] tried to get something out of [the occupation]. . . . Organizing its members to get a vote. . . . I mean, this assembly could have dealt with how to build, for example, an open university—outside of the state, outside of the system, and so on. How, for example, a social clinic can be built, and so on. Instead of creating that in Syntagma, SYRIZA took the idea and built social clinics by SYRIZA—with the politics of Syntagma, the project of Syntagma, that of participation, direct democracy, common decisions. (Kostas, personal communication, February 17, 2016)

Although one may assume that SYRIZA having taken some of the ideas of the occupation and put them into practice would be met with approval, my interlocutors view this development with disdain. This may well have to do with the precursor norms dealt with in the previous chapter, in which parties were barred by protesters from taking part in the activities of the square, precisely because of their presumed motives to competitively maximize their shares of potential votes. As I will show, my interlocutors' contempt for existing political parties must also be seen in light of those parties' incorporation into state-institutional arrangements.

Between Returning and Retaining

As violence came to Syntagma Square, and as the overall number of participants decreased and parties (especially SYRIZA)[9] increasingly influenced

---

9. Although to a lesser extent, my interlocutors also bemoaned the role of the extraparliamentary, anti-capitalist Left party Front of the Greek Anti-Capitalist Left (ANTARSYA). Thodoris provides a curious example during the popular assembly. As mentioned in the previous chapter, those who wanted to speak in the assembly were selected by lottery. They were given a piece of paper with a number on it so as to wait for their turn. "The ANTARSYA members, many of them ask for a paper. They take the paper, they gather the papers together and give them to one person so he can give a thirty-minute long speech. Actually that's how all the extra-parliamentary Left works. . . . What was interesting, is that it was not accepted [by the popular assembly]. It was booed. Apart from those who were doing it, [that is,] the members of ANTARSYA, the others were against it" (personal communication, October 17, 2014).

Challenging the Dystopian   175

the practices of the square, the adherence to precursor norms that was meant to ensure the egalitarian and antiauthoritarian character of the occupation slowly started to erode. Christos Giovanopoulos (2011, 57), who was part of the communications group, remarks:

> When the momentum of the "new" together with the people started to separate from Syntagma Square and the composition of people in the square changed . . . the return to old ways of doing things was visible . . . Or the "new" was trapped inside old schemes and truths.

Aggelos, who had been a lively participant in the square's activities from the start, left precisely because of these factors, only a month into the occupation.

> This is exactly when I separated, because I saw that it [the Syntagma Square occupation] was going in a different direction. It was going in an extreme, leftist—not Left!—leftist direction, which was more in line with party ideology. This is a weird form of fascism. I mean, that some people assume the right that "this is ours now!" (Aggelos, personal communication, January 27, 2016)

As though Syntagma Square was taken from him, Aggelos describes the ways in which the practices of the occupation as to mutual respect shifted toward the dominance of particular interest groups, something akin to party politics. This, for him, in turn tilted the egalitarian character of the square toward more authoritarian tendencies ("a weird form of fascism").

As a consequence, with the arrival of repression, the ways in which practices took place in Syntagma Square shifted. As many people abstained from participating due to violence, and party politics surged in the square, practices subtly shifted toward more ordinary modes of political practice: tactical, hierarchical, reactive, particularistic. This led to an erosion of the prefigurative and experimental character of the Syntagma Square occupation, as Viktoria self-critically points out:

> I mean, you are able to not take the drug of violence. There is a way not to play their [state actors'] game. It's very easy to become a pawn. Very

176   Paradoxes of Emancipation

> easy. At some point, we became pawns. All the people inside Syntagma Square talked about what to do about the violence. They were pawns, because when we stopped dealing with what was going on in the Voulē [Parliament] and began dealing with violence, we missed things. (Viktoria, personal communication, October 22, 2014)

Viktoria's analysis regarding the role violence had in forcing upon the square the state's rules of the "game" are intriguing: if violence is an exercise of domination and subordination (and therefore an exercise in producing inequalities), then the use of violence does indeed bring a game to the square that is antithetical to the radical imagination. While it is true that there are clearly unequal power relations at play between the violence of police forces (with professional gear and certain legal powers) and the protesters resisting it, the act of being violent breaks with the prefiguration of the radical imagination. Violence requires tactical consideration. Much as with the regressive signification of crisis I theorized in chapter 2, it limits the imagination to threat and risk, as it is guided by uncertainty and insecurity. For David Graeber (2012), understanding the state means understanding violence. In the same vein, by enforcing violence, the state is ordering social relations in accordance with its own principles.

On the one hand, this points to the limits of prefiguring the radical imagination in the face of state violence. Critical accounts in both Marxist (Dean 2016) and post-Marxist and autonomist political traditions (Kioupkiolis 2019) claim it is precisely the absence of strategy and the refusal of more centralized forms of organization that restricts the potentialities of direct democratic, and antiauthoritarian approaches to challenge and overcome (neoliberal) state-institutional arrangements. On the other hand, however, it would not be accurate to assume that the Syntagma Square occupation fully lost its radical imagination with the arrival of state repression. The experience of repression also rendered the commonality of vulnerability (to repression) as a source of solidarity (chapter 3). Through the occurrence of solidarity in response to police repression—metro workers defying orders to shut down the Syntagma Square metro station in order to allow people to flee police violence, or the elderly who, having experienced violence during the junta, take a beating from riot police in order to protect younger people—violence did not break the radical imagination in its entirety. Although police violence is a tactic of reinstating obedience through fear and physical harm, in many instances it backlashed and did the opposite. An interesting observation in this regard is what I refer to as "tear gas as bonding." When the police used tear gas in the square, many of my interlocutors usually left and went to the nearby cafés to rest, get some fresh air, literally, and wait until the fighting was over. At the cafés, they say they could pick out those who had come from the square because their faces and eyelids were white from the Maalox[10] and tear gas. Protesters would smile at each other in affect and get into conversations about what they had experienced earlier, furthering a strong sense of togetherness and community. It was a bonding experience—one that was intended to disperse a crowd, but ultimately also brought people together.

Solidarity was not only a reaction to violence—it was also an answer to violence through means other than violence. The many musical performances during violent battles and the ensuing "war dances," as my interlocutors refer to them, can be viewed as both a response (anti-politics) and alternative (alter-politics) to violence.[11] For Panagiotis, "Dance and music performances during police attacks were tactics, a way of expressing politics *differently*" (personal communication, October 6, 2014; emphasis added). For Katerina, it was a message of pride and commitment. "We don't swallow it, guys. We're here! . . . I believe they saved us, all of those who came to play, from a lot more violence" (personal communication, February 7, 2016). For Viktoria, the radical imagination shined through, even in the violent days, as protesters handed flowers and written notes to riot police guarding Parliament in an attempt to convince them that the occupation was a common struggle (personal communication, September 19, 2017). Talking about the violence of June 29, Katerina remarks how, because of this solidarity in Syntagma Square, even negative experiences left a somewhat positive aftertaste.

10. Maalox is an antacid used by protesters as an anti–tear gas and pepper spray remedy.

11. For a comprehensive account of the role of emotion and music in the 2011 Syntagma Square occupation, see Papapavlou (2015).

The beautiful and the good ones were [within] this clique of solidarity, which I hadn't lived before to such an extent. Even in this shitty incident there were also moving moments of people who helped. Even there. Inside shit, you will also find good [things]. . . . You understand? (Katerina, personal communication, February 7, 2016)

While it was difficult to retain the radical imagination in the face of repressive assaults, Katerina tells us it did not fade. What the aforementioned examples show is that the radical imagination may even have been strengthened due to the juxtaposition with crass state practices. This strengthens the argument that the contradistinction of the radical imagination against and in confrontation with state practices (anti-politics) is the very basis for the emergence of critiques and the political quality of subjectivation. Put differently, my interlocutors' self-described negativity of experience with the state, in contrast to the self-described positivity with the radical imagination of the square, conditioned the ways in which they critiqued the former in relation to their idealization of the latter. This led them to critiques of the state that are essentially demystifying.

Demystifying the State

My interlocutors had varying expectations as regards state repression. For those interlocutors who had previously experienced repression—such as Lukas, Kostas, or Vasilis—violence, negative framing in media reports, and the attempted hijacking of the occupation by political parties largely confirmed their expectations as valid. Lukas, for example, rather soberly announces, "That it would end through repression has been proven historically" (personal communication, February 23, 2016). Kostas shows how this expectation evokes established patterns of practices in response to police violence when he half-jokingly stipulates "violence? It is an umbrella. When it rains, you use it" (personal communication, February 17, 2016).

For those "new" protesters—such as Kyriaki, Katerina, or Maria—who describe themselves as apolitical prior their participation in the Syntagma Square occupation—the experience of discursive and bodily violence indeed was a novel and unexpected one. Kyriaki, for example, states, "When you followed the mass media, you would see a distorted picture of the events in Syntagma, where protesters were rioting and provoking violence, using drugs." Only when she lived through the violence did she realize the mismatch between how she experienced events, and how they were framed in the media. As for state repression, she tells me, "You know what, I didn't expect that violence. I'll tell you. I didn't expect it." But as she suffered the consequences of multiple tear gas attacks, Kyriaki came to conclude that "the police are there to break up the people, to hit, to create trouble where they shouldn't. Because they are also part of that regime. They too are employees of the state" (personal communication, October 19, 2014). The unexpectedness of police practices leads Kyriaki to essentially critique the state. Broadly speaking, critiques of the state were generally very similar, despite variation regarding normative expectations between "experienced" and "newly exposed" interlocutors. What follows, then, is that the commonality of vulnerability—that is, the shared normative negativity of experience with the state—plays an important role in the generation of critique and politicization. The conditions of possibility for the political quality of subjectivation following on from demystifying critiques of the state and the status quo ante are essentially grounded in the precarization and the subversion of the "livability of a common life" (Liebsch 2016, 85).

My interlocutors' critique of the state broadly stems from their perception that it is absent when it is needed, and brutally present when it is not. Broadly speaking, my interlocutors' critique has to do with party politics and representative democracy and, related to this, their perception of the Greek state as an authoritarian institutional arrangement. Their experience is not merely an unfortunate episode of state intervention that could have gone differently. Instead, by jumping from critiquing representative democracy to a critique of authoritarianism, what my interlocutors do is strip down the mask of the state—they demystify it, by pointing to the actualities of domination and subordination.

Unmasking Representative Democracy

Political parties were viewed negatively by all of my interlocutors, without exception. The aversion toward parties was not only reflected in the

180 Paradoxes of Emancipation

ambiguous role of SYRIZA during the Syntagma Square occupation, or in the "no party" precursor norm I elaborated on in chapter 2. It showed also in the thousands of people who, by facing the Parliament building daily, cursed both parties and representative democracy in their rejection of what they perceived as the lies, theft, betrayal, and injustices of institutionalized politics. As I illustrated in chapter 2, for those protesters in the upper part of square, disappointment and anger often remained at the performative level. Critiques were liberal in "spirit," trapped in discourses of unfulfilled promises of middle-class belonging and the pursuit of happiness through consumption. For the participants in the lower square, which includes all of my interlocutors, critiques were often more radical, shaking the very foundations of the justifications of representative democracy. "The popular assemblies of Syntagma," Michalis theorizes, "create a consciousness through which . . . we will realize finally . . . that with elections and representation nothing changes. Because if [they] could change things, they would not exist (group discussion, March 28, 2016). The critique Michalis presents is grounded in the juxtaposition between Parliament and the popular assembly. Panagiotis clarifies this further by adding, "There was a stark contrast between the assemblies below, and the Voulē above. Above is the Voulē where they plan the measures, below is a popular assembly in Syntagma Square where decisions are taken direct democratically" (personal communication, October 6, 2014). Indeed, this juxtaposition is a powerful one, considering the crude cynicism of the occupation situation as a whole: Parliament (nominally the representation of the people) is protected by the police (funded by the people) from the people, so it can pass legislation to corporatize the state and privatize that same people's assets against its will. Whereas in the popular assembly of Syntagma Square people decide for themselves, for my interlocutors it appears Parliament decides against them.

For the state of Greek parliamentary politics, at the time at least, there is much reason to draw on William Davies's (2014, 134–35) theorization that it does not signify "a Rousseauian state of how to represent the collective," but rather "a Schmittian one of how to *decide* on behalf of others." In this regard, Lukas remarks, "Representative democracy all over the world has become corporate democracy." For this reason, he concludes, "I don't believe in *this* democracy. That does not mean that I am totalitarian" (personal communication, February 6, 2017; emphasis added). As Wendy Brown (2005, 48) observes, in its neoliberal formation, the very term *democracy* does not denote a set of institutions and practices built upon freedom, autonomy, and popular sovereignty. Far from this, it signifies merely the reorganization of state-subject relations in accordance with a market rationality. "Indeed, democracy could even be understood as a code word for availability to this rationality," she concludes soberly. Lukas's disapproval of representative democracy, which he qualifies as "corporate," needs to be appreciated against this backdrop. He is explicit in not favoring an authoritarian institutional formation ("does not mean that I am totalitarian"). What is implicit in his rebuttal is quite the contrary: a call for more participatory, direct democratic practices, like those of the Syntagma Square occupation. Moving on by saying that democracy is "the most fucked-up word in the world. The 'new' is not yet born" (personal communication, February 6, 2017), Lukas shows us how the very term has become what Jean-Luc Nancy (2011, 58) calls "an exemplary case of the loss of the power to signify." As the term *democracy* has seemingly lost its capacity to problematize, Lukas gives us a glimpse of the aspiration but also of the limits of radically envisioning an alternative to representative democracy that goes even beyond the practices of the Syntagma Square occupation ("not been born yet").

Another theme of critique that evolved is the juxtaposition between representation by parties and self-government in Syntagma Square (chapter 3). Like many other interlocutors, Michalis bemoans a situation in which "SYRIZA really capitalized on the direct democratic approach. When you are a representative, you aren't a direct democrat. So there was exploitation" (group discussion, March 28, 2016). What he refers to is the ambiguity of SYRIZA: the party presented itself as a supporter of Syntagma Square's self-governed practices, while at the same time it was being accused by many occupiers of strategically influencing the assembly and groups of the square in its favor, allegedly to gain support for its parliamentary aspirations. This leads Michalis to frame SYRIZA's agenda as one of exploiting direct democracy for its own benefit. His critique needs to be seen against the backdrop of the presumptions of the occupation's precursor norms that I elaborated on in chapter 3. One of the norms was that the practices of the Syntagma Square occupation ought not to

182   Paradoxes of Emancipation

be driven by particularistic group interests; they need to be "selfless," as Thanos remarked in the previous chapter. But since SYRIZA is part of a state-institutional arrangement that is built on competition rather than solidarity, with the ultimate pursuit of domination (in Poulantzas's [2000] sense) at its heart, its actions cannot be selfless because its political survival and relevance is measured and evaluated by its electoral success. Just like corporations, parties' characteristic feature of maximization rests on the capitalization that Michalis criticizes: "A pervasive form of valuation that propels a consideration of return on investment and shapes our world accordingly" (Muniesa et al. 2017, 11). Here too, representative party politics stand in stark contrast to the solidarity-based decision-making practices of the Syntagma Square occupation. This is also reflected in comments where my interlocutors point to the divisive nature of parties[12]—an observation that is rendered meaningful precisely because competition by definition creates inequality and division.

For others, party competition has been reduced at best to a performative formality of Greek parliamentary politics. Pantelis's dissatisfaction with representative democracy stems from the increasing depoliticization of politics during neoliberal crisis management (chapter 2):

> The entire parliamentary game is being played by forces that voted for each memorandum. KKE didn't vote for it, because it has a consistent tactic. I agree with them up to a point. But nothing will convince me that this force, through its pyramid hierarchy, will bring about a real solution from below. They played a very bad game against the movements from below. (Pantelis, personal communication, March 28, 2016)

Pantelis's critique regarding the parties' across-the-board support for the memorandum assumes that the (metaphysical) values of parties become increasingly indeterminate due to their adherence to the macroeconomic consensus of austerity and neoliberal restructuration. In effect, this consensus depoliticizes Parliament, in that it transforms Parliament from a locus

---

12. "The parties have done a lot of bad. I don't know if this is only a Greek thing or if this true for other countries. Because they divide people" (Viktoria, personal communication, October 22, 2014).

of democratic decision-making into an apparatus that merely ensures the stability of that consensus. The political vanishes and is substituted with technocracy—that is, the mere implementation of policies. Even though Pantelis feels that the Communist Party of Greece (KKE), is an exception to this parliamentary potpourri, he clearly takes a stance against not only the party's framing of the Syntagma Square occupation but also its hierarchical organization, which stands in stark contrast to the self-organized and self-governed practices of Syntagma Square. Similarly, Katerina tells us that the "KKE does not express me," because in her eyes they follow a "'soldieresque,' a militaristic model" (personal communication, February 7, 2016).[13]

While all of the aforementioned critiques can be read against the extraordinary situation of crisis and the ensuing exceptional measures taken to manage it, interlocutors such as Lukas would still uphold them if they were going through ordinary times and if parliamentary democracy was functioning "normally."

> The political shaping from below doesn't mean that this has to have a parliamentary imprint. Because you realize that, when you take part in such processes [referring to the Syntagma Square occupation], the broad range of your choices is a lot bigger than the narrow range of the choices the system gives you. Yes, the latter [the system] leaves you with a lot of choices. But they are very particular! So the shaping from below opens up the broad range of choices of what you can do. (Lukas, personal communication, February 23, 2016)

In a nutshell, Lukas describes the radical imagination in contrast to the status quo through the example of democracy. Moving beyond crisis, his

---

13. My interlocutors' attribution of an esprit de corps to political parties is a recurring theme. Kyriaki offers another curious example as he makes that claim: "The people were more spontaneous in the square, especially those who are not in parties. Because, let me tell you what's going on, when you are in a party . . . things are a bit more firm. I mean, they will chant together. They will say, 'Stop,' and they will stop. 'Start again,' and they will start. They are like soldiers. I don't like these things. I want to chant whenever I want. . . . The people should express themselves more freely" (personal communication, October 19, 2014). This assumes that it is not each parties' politics per se that my interlocutors take issue with, but rather their hierarchical and often loyalty-based style of organization.

184   Paradoxes of Emancipation

account indicates that the above critiques are far from merely seeking to return to some mythical point in time prior to the crisis (as is arguably the case with protesters in the upper square; see chapter 2). They seek above all a radical departure from the parliamentary system as a whole. My interlocutors' analysis with regard to representative democracy, seen as merely upholding the status quo, as well as with regard to the hierarchical and reformative character of parties, suggest that their critiques are intrinsically systemic. In effect, my interlocutors demystify the state by unmasking its claim as to legitimate democratic institutional arrangements and procedures. This is precisely because of the ways representative democracy and parties present themselves to my interlocutors. The next section centers my interlocutors' critique of authority and representative democracy on a more historical footing. The endpoint of this line of critiquing is to perceive the state as an inherently authoritarian institutional arrangement.

Unmasking State Authority

The perception among participants in the Syntagma Square occupation of persisting authoritarianism in Greek (parliamentary) politics is symbolized by the best-known slogan of the occupation: "Bread, Education, Freedom, the junta did not end in '73." Referring to the student-led occupation of the Technical University of Athens (also known as the Polytechneio) in November 1973, which eventually led to the fall of the fascist Regime of the Colonels, the first three words of that chant evoke one of the most iconic examples of resistance in modern Greece. By reviving this chant and adding the phrase *the junta did not end in '73*, participants in the occupation reflected on the chant's current pertinence, and not just with regard to the consequences of austerity for the welfare state. The manifold understandings circulating in Syntagma Square as to whom "the junta" refers to today—ranging from the government, the state system, the Troika and its constitutive parts, to banks and credit agencies, or all of these together—points to a shared perception of authoritarianism.[14]

14. Thodoris observed during the Syntagma Square occupation: "One [protester] was shouting against the bankers, the other was shouting against the foreign conquerors,

So when Thanos claims that Greeks have "very little experience with democracy," (personal communication, February 3, 2016), this statement may appear peculiar against the backdrop of the fetishization of Greek antiquity as the cradle of (Western) democracy.[15] But as Stathis Gourgouris (1996, 6) has argued, Greece is "history's sole witness of the consequences of the colonization of the ideal." Ottoman rule, Bavarian monarchy, Nazi occupation, and US-sponsored military dictatorship, among other things, have rendered democracy in modern Greece a relatively recent phenomenon. The experience of Parliament voting for measures that protesters clearly did not want to see passed reevokes images of an authoritarian past. From the viewpoint of political science (Offe 2015), this perception materializes not least in the fact that Parliament's sovereignty (indicated by its power to check against the budget) has been clearly compromised ever since the first memorandum (chapter 1). What this implies is that, at least for Greece, the mandate of Parliament is changing, in that citizens delegate to it the power to decide for them, rather than represent them. The difference being that democracy in this mode assumes that citizens legitimate authority, rather than express the exercise of their will by way of representation. This is reflected when Andreas bemoans that "all they wanted was to implement the memorandum. So you realize that there is no power that will protect you" (personal communication, February 11, 2016). The contradistinction between this mode of democracy and the popular assembly of Syntagma Square is one that is perhaps best expressed by Tsianos's (2016) distinction between "authoritarian representation" and "real democracy." As democracy vanishes, what also vanishes is politics, turned into a Schmittian state of exception that is rendered by experts as merely technical, rational, realistic, reasonable, and dogmatically without alternative. Drawing on Nicos Poulantzas, Ian Bruff (2014) remarks this process is a political response to the (capitalist) crisis as an effort to "manage the fallout from their own development" (119). He describes

---

another was shouting against capital, another was shouting against traitors, and yet another one was shouting against the cop" (personal communication, October 17, 2014).

15. Anna Carastathis (2014), for example, convincingly argues that Hellenism is itself a form of Orientalism.

186 Paradoxes of Emancipation

this shift as "neoliberal authoritarianism," where subordinate groups are explicitly marginalized and excluded through the "constitutionally and legally engineered self-disempowerment of nominally democratic institutions, governments, and parliaments" (116). In this formation, it appears, there is indeed "no power that will protect you," as Andreas contemplates. Neither representation nor rights are capable of appropriately addressing the livability of a common life.

Therefore, Syntagma Square—with its symbolic value as the "square of the constitution"—literally signifies the occupation of this state of affairs in an attempt to repoliticize it in democratic terms. For Jacques Rancière (2011a, 79), this is the very basis of what makes politics thinkable.

> If power is allotted to the wisest or the strongest or the richest, then it is no longer politics we are talking about. . . . Yes, democracy does have a critical function: it is the wrench of equality jammed (objectively and subjectively) into the gears of domination.

In summary, my interlocutors' experiences during the Syntagma Square occupation with the violence of state repression, the absence of parliamentary representation proper, and the perceived gain-motivated calculations of parties rendered many expectations of my self-described apolitical interlocutors, such as Maria or Katerina, obsolete. Others, who had a self-described firm political identity, such as Lukas or Panagiotis, only saw their expectations confirmed and consolidated.[16] What follows, however, in either case, whether expectations are met or not, is an experience-based, demystifying critique of state-institutional arrangements that points to the actualities of their dominating and subordinating capacities. These experiences led my interlocutors' subjectivation processes to include a political quality, which they describe with as "political maturation."

---

16. "The very existence of the authoritarian phenomenon—I mean, its premises are a ruler and a ruled—recycles the authoritarian phenomenon under different guises" (Lukas, personal communication, February 23, 2016).

Political Maturation

For my interlocutors, the consequences of experiencing the state catalyzed in a process they termed *political maturation*. In my analysis, this process signifies politicization, or, to put it another way, a political quality of subjectivation.[17] Broadly speaking, there is variation with regard to the self-assigned "state" of politicization. There are those—like Lukas, Petros, or Viktoria—who describe themselves as having had a "firm political identity" prior to their participation in the Syntagma Square occupation. Others—such as Maria, Katerina, or Stamatis—claim to have been politicized only through their experiences in the square. As I argued in chapter 2, the condition of possibility for this process to unfold lies in the liminal nature of crisis, my interlocutors' progressive signification of crisis, and this signification's spatial manifestation in the lower part of the square occupation. In this regard, Rancière (1999, 137) remarks:

> The political community is a community of interruptions, fractures, irregular and local, through which egalitarian logic comes and divides the police community from itself. It is a community of worlds in community that are intervals of subjectification: intervals constructed between identities, between spaces and places. Political being-together is a being-between: between identities, between worlds.

Tacitly acknowledging the liminal conditions of political subjectivation, Rancière's remarks allow us to consider how those self-described politicized or apolitical interlocutors collectively influence each other's processes of subjectivation within the dialectic spatial reproduction of the Syntagma Square occupation. For the latter group of interlocutors, "political maturation" assumes a rite de passage (Turner 2008; van Gennep 2011) from, in their own words, a previously "apolitical," or "unaware" state of mind to becoming "political," "aware," or "politically aware." For the former group, it signifies a consolidation and deepening of their previously held theoretical expectations about state-institutional arrangements,

17. These terms will be used interchangeably.

188   Paradoxes of Emancipation

through experiencing the practice of both the square and the state. But it also includes the concession that their assumptions about the seemingly apolitical character of what they variously call "society," "the people," or "the masses" needed reevaluation. As Kostas acknowledges:

> I mean, *nobody expected that* . . . so many people . . . would assemble, or that basic political premises would be so central. Generally, we didn't expect all that results from a wrong impression that we have about society. I mean, that they just sit around and are relaxed. That they are not interested in anything. And that we are somebody [important]. . . . It turned out this was totally wrong. I mean, this was almost my opinion, but Syntagma for me showed that: that society, whenever it decides, can be in the streets, and can have a meaningful dialogue about politics. (Kostas, personal communication, February 17, 2016; emphasis added)

Inherent to signifying political maturation as politicization is the liberal notion of autonomous personal growth and self-improvement: in this case through the accumulation of experiences and openness to those experiences—a theme I will critically scrutinize as reproductive of neoliberalism in the following chapter. How does the process of politicization come about?

> [The Syntagma Square occupation] was driven by something apolitical, like a type of protest because the money in our wallets diminished. But it acquired political characteristics. So through a *negative* framework of political maturity in the beginning, political maturity came. Because when you are inside the process . . . you mature. Except when you have decided not to do that ever. (Lukas, personal communication, February 13, 2016; emphasis added)

Lukas's viewpoint resonates among many of my self-described politicized interlocutors: at the beginning, the Syntagma Square occupation was a reaction to the economic uncertainties people had to cope with. As their protest initially, especially in the upper square, merely sought the restoration of the pre-crisis status quo with regard to economic certainty, it cannot be deemed political. Presenting Thanos with this narrative, he skeptically replies:

Look. I am not so sure. I will not agree with this easily. [The Syntagma Square occupation] reinforced some political processes inside our minds. It may have strengthened them. But I think that this happens through various events in life. I wouldn't say entirely "apolitical." I would say "with their own philosophy." I myself, for example, I don't want to belong to a party or to a particular political stream, but I don't consider myself apolitical. I have political opinions. But if I consider that now we need a particular kind of politics that I don't think we will need in ten years, or that I didn't think the same way in the previous five to ten years, this too is a political opinion. That I can change, according to the needs of society, what I consider to be "the good" for society, this too is a political opinion. (Thanos, personal communication, February 16, 2016)

The conceptual implications of this interaction are puzzling. First, this is because they illustrate the contest of signification regarding meanings of "the political." Lukas's narrative presumes that the political and the economic are separate spheres, where the latter is considered inherently apolitical. This relates to the discourse theory of Ernesto Laclau and Chantal Mouffe (2001, 127–45), in that it presumes the primacy of "the political" over "the economic" for processes of change and the (re)production of meaning. But as the construction of the political subject is contingent upon, and structured within, the realm of politics—specifically liberal democracy—it also relates to Thanos's position regarding self-change according to "the needs of society," as he puts it. What these contesting acts of signification illustrate is that politics is "far from being 'everything'" (Nancy 2002, 21). That is to say, that instead of assuming the supremacy of the political, it may be worthwhile to pay attention to the ways in which subjects decide to politicize some spheres instead of others. This is not to dispute that everything may very well have political implications. However, as Sergei Prozorev (2014) argues, in the end, it is only the subject herself who decides what is to become political and what remains, for the time being, apolitical.

For Lukas, those "inside the process" eventually become political, starting through a "negative framework of political maturity." In a later conversation I asked Lukas to further qualify this statement. He added that "sometimes we reproduce ourselves against something. We reinvent

190   Paradoxes of Emancipation

ourselves against something. It's out of a process of necessity" (personal communication, February 5, 2017). Theorizing from this consideration, the condition of possibility for the formation of political subjectivity lies in the normative negativity of experience as to the livability of a common life. Political subjectivation begins with being against and in confrontation with the (governmental) practices that render the livability of a common life precarious.[18] In this antipolitical stance, the political quality of subjectivation can emerge (Liebsch 2016). The verb *can* here is an important one because, as Lukas informs us and as Prozorev (2014) theorizes, it is the subject who decides about signifying this quality. This is reflected whenever my interlocutors refer to the "openness" it requires toward the processes and practices of the Syntagma Square occupation. Openness is notoriously difficult to observe, let alone operationalize. However, the fact that those interlocutors who had a hesitant stance toward the Syntagma Square occupation (such as Panagiotis),[19] and others who participated far less actively due to work constraints (such as Kyriaki),[20] describe their experience in the occupation as one that only marginally affected them may indeed be indicative of the importance of openness for political subjectivation. "If you are open," Lukas remarks, "this can evolve into political maturation. If you simply let it pull you along, you will stay at the level of an intense experience, without political content" (personal communication, February 23, 2016).

Therefore, perhaps what openness means with regard to politicization is really the will to participate in the practices of the square. Or to put it another way, the political quality of subjectivation materializes in the ways in which the political is (re)conceived in practice. This relates to my

18. Similarly, Thanos remarks, "I have a theory that only when the people are seriously overstrained, will they become more mature" (personal communication, February 3, 2016).

19. "But as for me, I don't know. I am the same and I was conscious. I didn't realise anything new. OK? OK, as always, I saw some people being more conscious and others being less conscious" (Panagiotis, personal communication, October 19, 2014).

20. "I'm telling you that it didn't influence my consciousness, because it didn't, from my point of view, bring forward anything that was radical or that changed the way I thought about some things. But maybe that happened for some people who, until then, hadn't had any involvement, any contact with demonstrations" (Kyriaki, personal communication, October 6, 2014).

Challenging the Dystopian   191

previous consideration in the introduction of this book: in trying to understand processes of political subjectivation, what matters is to understand the subject not so much as the foundation of political (or other) practices, but rather of tracing its formation in these practices. In this regard, Thodoris theorizes the importance of practice for both self-described previously politicized participants and for apolitical participants in the occupation.

> Well you know, political maturity is this: let's go back to when you are a kid. And you start believing in some political ideologies. You are attracted by political ideologies and then you start observing their lifestyle. . . . A moment like Syntagma is a moment where you see that ideology is not a performance. You see that a political stance is not a performance. It's actually *actions* that have to be taken and *consequences* that will arise from these actions. That action gives you certain maturity. You understand that what you say actually results in something. So you have to be careful what you say. (Thodoris, personal communication, October 14, 2014; emphasis added)

In speaking about "actions," Thodoris acknowledges the importance of practices for politicization, especially the many forms of change-directed discussions ("what you say") that I have framed in the previous chapter under the term *Zymōsē* (chapter 3). What is more, he takes into account the consequences of such practices. Politicization here can be seen as a process stemming from both the practices of the radical imagination of the Syntagma Square occupation ("actions") and the experience of state repression ("consequences"). This juxtaposition is important as it contrasts the prefigurative, egalitarian, and antiauthoritarian practice of the occupation with the strategic, subordinating repression on the part of the state in ways that allow for the emergence of demystifying critiques. These, then, can serve as meaningful guidelines for subjectivity. Thodoris adds that this process has similar consequences for those participants of the occupation whom he views as apolitical.

> Also, it was a moment of political maturity for people who didn't have any political background. So it was a moment of maturity for the apolitical ones who hadn't had any contact with political activities. That was a kind of opportunity, where they could gain some experience. So it was

192   Paradoxes of Emancipation

> a moment of maturity for everyone involved. Apart from the idiots with the flags.[21] (Thodoris, personal communication, October 14, 2014)

Politicization, then, does not stem from abstract theoretical knowledge alone. Subjects need to be able not only to "know" and express their desires and frustrations but also to be regarded—by being heard, listened to, and taken seriously, as happened in the discussions and assemblies in the square through Zymōsē, or through more affective categories such as "belonging" or "being among like-minded people" (chapter 3). Or by being ignored, harmed, ridiculed, and humiliated, as occurred in the ways the state interacted with subjects. The political, then, materializes in practice by voicing, being listened to, by disrupting, and destroying. In this sense, political subjectivation is a process that occurs between subjects and cannot occur through what Michel Foucault (1982) refers to as self-subjectivation. This view resonates with those interlocutors, such as Maria or Katerina, who describe themselves as having been apolitical prior to their participation in the Syntagma Square occupation. Katerina remarks:

> You know, before I wasn't anywhere ideologically. Now I am more "searched". . . . I mean, back then I was a little naive, let me put it that way. Before I was like, "All people value each other and nobody is an enemy and we all love each other and peace," and so on. Then, and if you ask me still now, I have a lot of these characteristics. But if somebody attacks me, I won't tell him, "Come and fuck me up." No! I will resist. I will use violence then. So this of course became very obvious in Syntagma, right? When the cops attacked us and there was this continuous violence. (Katerina, personal communication, February 11, 2017)

Related to this, just a few days earlier, when Katerina and I went on an ethnographic walk through the square, she shared with me the following about her experience of participating:

---

21. In derogatory terms, Thodoris seems to refer to protesters of the upper square. Although he does not spell it out, it could be argued here that it may precisely be the lack of any meaningful practices and forums of discussion in the upper square (chapter 2) that led Thodoris to exclude them from being able to become politicized.

> As an experience it was redemptive. . . . I mean, "What's this thing I live? Why do I live it? What is the democracy that they say that I have? What role do politicians play in this? The cop?" All that, it was a lesson that made me question many basic things. That's why Syntagma Square was very important to me. (Katerina, personal communication, February 7, 2017)

Highlighting the normative negativity of experiences of state repression, Katerina's example illustrates that the political quality of subjectivation cannot be reduced to a positive identity. Using a term with spiritual connotations (*redemptive*), Katerina indicates how the political quality of subjectivation emerges in the act of distancing oneself from that identity. What ensues from this experience are the diverse demystifying critiques she attributes to state actors and state-institutional arrangements. "In the end," Petros summarizes, "regardless of the content, the action produces politics de facto. Then it produces an identity, an ideology" (personal communication, February 9, 2017).

Where Do We Go from Here?

This chapter has explored the ways in which my interlocutors experienced state repression in the Syntagma Square occupation. The experiences my interlocutors underwent with the state during the occupation produced critiques that catalyzed into the emergence of meaningful guidelines as politicized subjectivity. If the state is an exercise in naturalizing authority, then the Syntagma Square occupation is a practice of demystifying that exercise. That is precisely because my interlocutors' critiques of the state shift toward a concern with the actualities of domination and subordination. Against the backdrop of my interlocutors' experience with, and practice of, the radical imagination, state repression produced an almost Manichean juxtaposition between the equality and self-governance of the Syntagma Square occupation and the subordination and authority of the Greek state. Through this, my interlocutors repoliticize the elites' anti-crisis discourses—that is, that which is proclaimed as necessary, that what is deemed to have no alternative (chapter 2). In so doing, they challenge the depoliticization that occurs in and through the neoliberalizing Greek polity (chapter 1). At the same time, through the negativity of their experiences and through practicing the radical imagination, they undergo a politicization of the self that leads to "a search for possibilities of another living or even another life that is not doomed to reproduce the sameness of a basically unaltered identity" (Liebsch 2016, 76).

These experiences and critiques influenced the ways in which my interlocutors faced up to the eventual degeneration of the occupation. As a liminal space, "betwixt and between" structural states (Turner 2008, 95), the occupation was never built to last. Occupiers were very aware of that.

> I don't think that there is a place in the world where people thought that the square would last forever, that we would stay there for four years in the square with the tents. . . . We stayed there as long as we could, and we endured. With the repression and the violence that there was there. What matters is that during the time we were there we managed to get to know one other, to connect with one other, to act, to create groups, to sow these seeds that I told you about. And these seeds blossomed. Some blossomed. And some others will later. (Katerina, personal communication, October 19, 2014)

With continuous attempts by the police and the municipality to evacuate Syntagma Square, and a general sense of fatigue among protesters,[22] the question of how to continue grew in pertinence. Discussions in the square increasingly dealt with where and how to continue and what the occupation of Syntagma Square stood for. There were a few advocates of continuing the fight and holding on to the square, in the hopes of building a revolutionary momentum that would force at least the government to step down. But the main possible courses under discussion as to the future of the movement were two others. "The first was . . . to demand

---

22. "In August there was a sharp decline, because we got tired. Psychologically and physically. And there was no longer strength to keep it up. Plus, there was an incredible attack by the city. And they raided everything. One night, they took it all down" (Katerina, personal communication, February 7, 2016).

Challenging the Dystopian   195

from the state to become more state. And the other, in my opinion more productive, was 'alright, we will do it. We don't need you. We will do it ourselves'" (Kostas, personal communication, February 17, 2016). For many of my interlocutors, the rise of support for SYRIZA, from 4.6 percent in the 2009 elections to 26.9 percent in the June 2012 election (Simiti 2014, 15), was testimony to that first way that Kostas refers to. In this sense, the Syntagma Square occupation did not succeed in contributing to a departure from institutionalized politics and representation altogether. Disappointed, some of my interlocutors come to the conclusion that there is no "societal maturity for taking decisions on our own. There is a lot of immaturity among ordinary people" (Thanos, personal communication, February 3, 2016). In practice, with the end of the Syntagma Square occupation, ambiguities between the radical imagination and the turn to representation and the state ensued for some. Thanos, for example, voted for SYRIZA along with the "ordinary people" he refers to. But these contradictions aside, all my interlocutors except for Kyriaki[23] and Thodoris[24] continue their work in the spirit of the second course that Kostas outlines in the aforementioned quote. After the Syntagma Square occupation, they sustained their activism in various groups established during or after the occupation as well as in neighborhood assemblies that were either reinforced by those who had participated in the occupation or were newly formed as a result of the experience of occupying the square. In short, the radical imagination and extraordinary spatiality of the Syntagma Square occupation has been transferred into my interlocutors' everyday lives. The following chapter explores what remains of the Syntagma Square occupation experience many years on.

23. As a nursery school teacher, Kyriaki at times organizes events with children at such spaces as solidarity festivals. She knows the solidarity movements scene and often attends cultural events. She has also provided clothing for those living in refugee squats. But she has not been actively organized in any of these spaces.

24. Thodoris actually remained active in neighbourhood assemblies from the end of the occupation until 2015. Today his work remains political, but in the form of freelance journalism.

5

Paradoxes of Emancipation

Between Resistance and Reproduction

In the spring of 2016, the cooperative Café at the Academy of Plato held an event at their space to commemorate the fifth anniversary of the Syntagma Square occupation. Located next to the ancient Platonic academy, home to philosophical skepticism, the cooperative café is one of the most known solidarity spaces in Athens. Dating back to 2009, shortly before the crisis hit the Greek economy, the café was conceived of as "a way to reach out to society," in an effort to "disseminate" principles of "anti-consumerism, decentralization, non-violence, and collectiveness" (Kontodima 2016). As such, there could not have been a better venue to celebrate the radical imagination of the Syntagma Square occupation. The event was organized by one of my interlocutors, Katerina, and a screening of *The Unfinished Project,* a documentary about the occupation, was to be followed by a discussion in which experiences and opinions would be shared. I arrived early, together with Viktoria, and was baffled to see nearly half of my interlocutors present. Not everyone at the event knew each other, and there was a sense of reserve among those in the café that only faded as the screening began. It must have been the third time I had watched the documentary in such a setting. And having acquired a decent grasp of its content, I learned to pay more attention instead to how the audience was watching the film, at what points they laughed, wept, yelled, gasped, or groaned. This is to say that I paid closer attention to the "affective atmospheres" (Anderson 2009; see chapter 3); that is, how affect moves and circulates in space. In the beginning, I found it discomforting to observe people reliving the intimacy of experience. But then the sincerity of the audience's expressions allowed me to relate to what they must have lived through in the square in ways that rendered the experience almost common, much as in Sara Ahmed's (2004) theorizations on "collective feelings," and Lynne Segal's (2017) work on "collective joy" and "radical happiness." After the documentary came to an end, there was a contemplative silence that quickly gave way to something else entirely. Gone was the shyness of the beginning of the event, as people got into lively discussions somewhere between euphoria and nostalgia, sharing with each other how they had lived a common experience. They talked of the Cretan lyra player, all the tear gas they had "eaten," the cleaning of the square—milestones in the collective memory of the Syntagma Square occupation experience. It was a space for walking down memory lane as though no time had passed since the occupation, as if these people had never been out of touch and their bonds were still in place. At the same time, this meeting was also a space for critical reflection as to what remains of the Syntagma Square occupation experience today. Lukas was eager to offer his analysis.

> One of the very positive things is that it became a common political custom that we can do things from below. . . . Collectives mushroomed and popular assemblies were in all of the neighborhoods—this shows today also through the solidarity with our fellow human beings who happened to become refugees. . . . We aren't talking about NGOs or the charity of the church. We are talking about self-organization and self-management. As far as the friends of direct democracy are concerned . . . we still have a long way to go. Because the questions [among] them are still whether they will transform themselves into a political organization based on the system. So here we need a lot of discussion. (Lukas, group discussion, March 28, 2016)

Lukas's analysis resonated well among participants. Indeed, the Syntagma Square occupation left a legacy of self-organized solidarity spaces and a politics from below that can be viewed as an alternative to parliamentarism and state-centered forms of decision-making. What is more, these spaces offer alternatives to philanthropy and what has been referred to as the

198   Paradoxes of Emancipation

"NGO-ization" of service provision (Alvarez 2009).[1] In this sense, Lukas frames the legacy of the Syntagma Square occupation as inherently alter-neoliberal. At the same time, his remarks on democracy essentially demystify statehood (chapter 4) in ways that live up to the Syntagma square's principle of self-governance (chapter 3). Overall, it appears as though the ethical benchmark against which Lukas judges the failures and successes of politics from below since the Syntagma Square occupation are the guiding principles of the alter-political and antipolitical qualities of the square. This supports the claim that my interlocutors, as ethical beings, aspire to orient their subjectivity in the spirit of the radical imagination of the Syntagma Square occupation.

As he moves on in his analysis, Lukas focuses more closely on the role of practices. In his words, "Our everyday practice determines our political project. And our political project determines our political approach. And because that space [referring to Syntagma Square] condensed all of society, it determined how every one of us behaves politically from 2011 onward" (group discussion, March 28, 2016). Translating Lukas's overall analysis to the core sensitizing concepts of this book, the guiding principles of everyday practices ("solidarity," "self-organization") determine the political project, which I define as the radical imagination of the Syntagma Square occupation. The political approach that determines the political project is prefiguration. Further, Lukas's assertion that the Syntagma Square occupation "determined how every one of us behaves politically from 2011 onward" supports my claim that the subject is not so much the foundation of (in this case political) practices, but rather is constituted through these practices.

In this chapter, therefore, I analyze and systematize what remains of the Syntagma Square occupation experience years on. I will pay particular

---

1. NGO-ization refers to the depoliticization-by-technocratization of discourses and practices by protest actors, and the simultaneous provision of services previously under the domain of state-institutional arrangements. The organizational principles of NGOs are more often than not grounded in New Public Management techniques of audit and evaluation. Consequently, critics have pointed to the fact that NGO-ization contributes to the deepening of neoliberal imaginaries (Alvarez 2009).

attention to the kinds of subjectivities and spatialities that emerged as a consequence of (the practices of) the occupation, until I concluded my study in the fall of 2018. Put differently, in order to better understand the long-term consequences of the Syntagma Square occupation as a moment of "waking up" (chapter 2), this chapter delves into how my interlocutors demarcate their subjectivity from how they view themselves to have been during the Syntagma Square occupation (chapters 3 and 4), as well as before, in the period of modernization (chapter 1).

Regarding subjectivities, it is argued here that my interlocutors orient their selves in line with the spirit of the Syntagma Square occupation. Or to put it another way, the guiding principles of the radical imagination of the occupation (chapter 3) and the demystifying critiques (chapter 4) with regard to state-institutional arrangements in particular, serve as meaningful guidelines for my interlocutors' subjectivity: collectivity, solidarity, self-organization, mutual respect, autonomy, and self-government all form the egalitarian and antiauthoritarian precepts that my interlocutors aspire to in their everyday practices. In this sense, these principles have translated into routinized technologies of the self (Foucault 2008).

As a matter of fact, almost all my interlocutors today are involved in the solidarity movement in one way or the other. Katerina and Thanos, for example, are active in a variety of organizations in the social and solidarity economy, including solidarity festivals, alternative currency initiatives, and psychosocial support spaces. Eleftheria is part of a cooperative cafeteria and grocery store that cooperates with small, local producers and Zapatista communities on the basis of fair trade and ecological produce. Panagiotis and Sotiris set up a collaborative maker space focusing on open design and fabrication. Stamatis and Petros are very actively involved in the refugee support movement and squats. Maria joined an open cultural space and an artist collective. Viktoria and Aggelos decided to move away from Athens and establish autonomous solidarity structures and eco-communities in outlying regions of Greece. Meanwhile, Lukas and Kostas continue their political work in anarchist collectives. In pragmatist terms, one way of reading the heightened engagement in the movements from below is as a consequence-in-action of the Syntagma Square occupation experience. This is supported by my interlocutors' own narration of developments.

Regarding spatialities, my interlocutors, in addition to various case studies (Arampatzi 2016; Giovanopoulos 2016; Siapera and Theodosiadis 2017; Stavrides 2015; Tsomou 2014a), point to the "mushrooming" of social and solidarity economy spaces in Greece after the Syntagma Square occupation. In this regard, and similarly to my theorizations on crisis in chapter 2, Angelos Varvarousis and Giorgis Kallis (2017) convincingly illustrate that the liminal conditions of Greece at the time benefited the proliferation of this development. Consequentially, I argue that the extraordinary spatiality of Syntagma Square has been transferred into my interlocutors' everyday activities in these movements. Anti-consumerist exchange bazaars, cooperative cafeterias, refugee squats, social solidarity clinics, among many other examples, signify prefigurative spatialities that are structured in the spirit of the Syntagma Square occupation. Just like the example of the attempt by the Café at the Academy of Plato to reach out beyond activists that was discussed earlier, I argue further that these prefigurative spatialities serve the critical function of public pedagogies. From a cultural studies viewpoint, they are a "response to an urgent need to critically analyze relations of power" around (intersectional) nodal points of class, gender, race, sexuality "and rational-bureaucratic (state) domination" (Coté et al. 2007, 317–18), as well as sites for creating and disseminating concrete, everyday alternatives to the status quo of neoliberal reproduction (Giroux 2004a, 2004b). As public pedagogies, and with the figure of thought of social dialectics in mind, these prefigurative spatialities also structure the subjectivities of those individuals and collectives who (re)produce them.

It is very tempting to read these new subjectivities and prefigurative spatialities as emancipatory success stories and paradigmatic examples of liberation from the shackles of neoliberal governmentality. But as Michel Foucault (1990, 95) famously remarks, "Where there is power, there is resistance, and yet, or rather consequently, this resistance is never in a position of exteriority in relation to power." Informed by pragmatic sociology of critique (Boltanski 2011; Boltanski and Chiapello 2017), the second part of this chapter pays close attention not only to the ways in which these subjectivities and spatialities (functionally) undermine the status quo of neoliberal (governmental) rationality, but also to the capacities in which they reproduce it. In *The New Spirit of Capitalism*, Luc Boltanski and Ève Chiapello (2017) convincingly argue that political and economic elites from above, as much as ordinary people from below, are not only allowed but also expected to mobilize the empowering resources inherent in their critical, reflexive, and productive capacities. As Simon Susen (2014a, 195) remarks, the "key ingredients of this 'new spirit'—such as 'initiative,' 'creativity,' 'imagination,' 'transparency,' 'commitment,' 'openness,' 'dialogue,' and 'team work'—provide capitalist forms of domination not only with systemic elasticity and adaptability, but also with an unprecedented degree of ideological legitimacy." Against this backdrop, I will shed light on the paradoxical relationship between emancipatory subjectivities and spatialities on the one hand, and neoliberal governmental rationality on the other. Specifically, I will investigate how, at times, the latently entrepreneurial and managerial character of these emergent subjectivities and spatialities, as well as the increasingly psychologized self-management of the subject, unwittingly feed into neoliberal imaginaries of statehood and personhood.

Prefiguring Emancipation

Emancipatory Subjectivities

> In Syntagma Square you have all of society's malaises. But it was a personal cleansing. Many things, then, I learned, I understood, I consolidated. And I think this is true for many of us and I think this is what we need to hold on to. (Aggelos, group discussion, March 28, 2016)

Reminiscent of the Aristotelian notion of catharsis, Aggelos's metaphor of "personal cleansing" points to the purifying character of his experience in the Syntagma Square occupation. Grounded in "the feeling that we are as we would like to be in our imagination" (Moreno, quoted in Kellerman 2006, 79), catharsis signifies a form of "education" based on a temporary revelation that helps us "to become virtuous in character" (Janko 1987, xviii). In this reading, participating in the Syntagma Square occupation is a learning experience of becoming, allowing meaningful guidelines as to subjectivity ("what we need to hold on to") to emerge. For Lukas, to be truly emancipatory and liberating, "it takes an inner catharsis. So we don't substitute one authoritarian phenomenon with another authoritarian phenomenon" (personal communication, February 23, 2016), underlining his striving for egalitarian and antiauthoritarian principles in his conduct. Like many other interlocutors, Lukas underlines in his theorizations the reflecting subject as the basis for the potentialities of self-realization and self-transformation. Maria provides another example:

> I started to understand what the banking system is. I started to understand what politics is. I started to understand what is going on in workplaces. I saw how the system wanted you to be, with the timetables, with how you have to live your life, how you have to present yourself so they accept you. Before, I got into this trip that didn't suit me. And all of that [referring to crisis and her experience in the Syntagma Square occupation] then made me understand and see who I truly am, and who I want to be, and who I want to be the people around me. All this started before, but there [in Syntagma Square] I started to see things differently. . . . I started to learn to live differently. With few things. But I wasn't put off, it was alright. It gave me a lot of strength and turned my mind around. I mean, I started to find meaning in other things. (Maria, personal communication, February 10, 2016)

Maria's self-reflection underlines Nikolas Rose's (1999) framing of subjectivities as ontological ("who I truly am") and ethical ("who I want to be") beings. Her participation in the Syntagma Square occupation forced upon Maria's ordinary conduct a reconsideration ("see things differently") in ways that juxtaposes her past self (during the period of modernization, see chapter 1) in negative terms, in contrast to her seemingly transformed (post-) occupation self. Bringing back to mind Viktor Turner's (1986) theorizations on subjectivity and experience, it is structurally unimportant whether the past is "real" or "mythical." What matters is whether meaningful guidelines emerge "from the existential encounter within a subjectivity of what we have derived from previous structures or units of experience in living relation with the new experience" (36). By emphasizing, almost apologetically ("But I wasn't put off, it was alright"), Maria's altered and alternative (that is, in relation to the ordinary and conventional) everyday practices, she also provides insights into the changing ways of signifying the meaning of these practices ("I started to find meaning in other things"). In an analogous manner, Maria also theorizes about this change by observing those around her.

> MARIA: My mother was a Trotskyist before. But she also got more
> into the capitalist system. She changed her mentality. She was a
> leftist, but she didn't have that lifestyle. Now, I see her and I am
> happy. Her mentality changed. She went, and she went with me
> to Syntagma [Square] to various events. She started dealing more
> with the commons. She began not to pay attention so much to the
> value of money and work. Because my mom used to be a workaholic. Her work was the most important thing. And now she sees
> other things.
> DIMITRIS: And you think this has to do with Syntagma?
> MARIA: Yes. It has to do with the change in people, from the crisis
> onwards. (Maria, personal communication, February 10, 2016)

As I argued in chapter 4, the precarization and subversion of the livability of a common life may result in acts of distancing, from both the self and status quo power relations, forming the conditions of possibility for the political quality of subjectivation. In the context of the liminal character of crises that I elaborated on in chapter 2, the political emerges as anti-politics—against and in confrontation with the practices of the existing orderings of power. Meanwhile, being exposed to the square's radical imagination—that is, its egalitarian and antiauthoritarian principles—and practicing it prefiguratively, allows what I refer to as unthought-of experiences to be generated. This quality of subjectivation emerges as alter-politics. In this regard, Katerina says that in the Syntagma Square occupation:

> My idea of collective action started to unfold. So whatever I thought
> regarding work from then onwards had to do with teams. I never thought
> about Katerina and my own company again. This disappeared. I had
> that before. In the beginning, I wanted to start a company for [planning]
> parties. And the collective [approach] arose because whatever we did [in
> the square occupation] was collective. We cooked collectively, . . . the

assembly was collective—everybody was there. The groups had assemblies. This whole part of assemblies and direct democracy and so on arose from there. Before, I had no idea about this model. (Katerina, personal communication, February 11, 2017)

Having had "no idea" about collective approaches to social organization, Katerina's experience of the occupation signifies precisely the unthought-of character of radically alternative imaginaries. In the spirit of Syntagma Square, the ways in which she henceforth went about issues relating to work was informed by collective, rather than individualist, conceptions of action. Katerina's experiences with collective practices, and her critical reflections on work lived on after the occupation.

So after that, I got into collaborative things. So the logic in which I treated work, how I perceive work, changed completely. The only thing I kept from before is this: That I want to be happy. I need to like what I do. I cannot do a job that doesn't give me pleasure. And this is why I can never imagine myself returning to jobs of the likes of [mobile phone providers]. That I can't think of. I would prefer to go hungry [laughing], to make less money, rather than getting into that kind of work. (Katerina, personal communication, February 11, 2017)

Katerina continues to aspire to the practices of the square. She disobeys the *illusio* (Bourdieu 2013) of the workplace as a locus for "capitalizable" (Muniesa et al. 2017) self-subjection. Instead, her self-conduct prefigures alternative approaches toward labor. "These kinds of rejections," Isabell Lorey (2015, 102) remarks, "are not a deliverance from all previous neoliberal entanglements, but rather the beginning of engagements and struggles to no longer be governed and no longer govern oneself in this way, at this price." Aggelos shows how far he is willing to go in this rejection of classical labor relations. While mentioning in passing that he makes "some money on the internet," he clarifies:

I live—we said that before and we laughed—like an autonomous nomad. Let's say, if I want to sleep somewhere, I go to Maria, I tell Penelope. . . . So through solidarity, I am OK. But it's not me. The thing

Paradoxes of Emancipation   205

is that everybody understands [laughing] that through solidarity structures, we can live and create and do things. . . . We all can. As long as one person trusts another. That one feels solidarity for the other. All of us. And I, if I can, whoever needs help, I will do it. (Aggelos, personal communication, January 27, 2016)

Clarifying the universal possibility ("we all can") of prefiguring alternatives, Aggelos highlights "trust" and "solidarity" as collective guiding principles of conduct—arguably emanating from the Syntagma Square occupation experience, and the role of affect in mediating them ("one feels solidarity for the other"). The "solidarity structures" he is referring to are prefigurative commons spaces—structured by and structuring alternative modes of doing and, to be more precise, doing together and for each other. For now, it is important to highlight that the principles of collectivity and solidarity, against the backdrop of the vulnerabilities created through crisis, also influence the ways in which my interlocutors continued their Syntagma Square occupation–born reconsiderations regarding consumption and consumerism. Maria tells me:

Seriously, we were broke. But we somehow got by! I mean . . . I was in need of clothes?—something I learned in the past years to buy, the previous years I never lacked any—I found clothes, through the exchange bazaars. Or we made our own. I didn't have shoes? I found shoes. I don't know. I didn't have furniture? They gifted me furniture. The ones you see here are a special offer. Incredible things. I don't know. And somehow you got by, without having [anything]. Through people and friends. (Maria, personal communication, February 10, 2016)

This example illustrates a radical departure from previous conceptions about commodities and consumption (chapter 1). Similar to Maria's earlier statement ("I started to find meaning in other things"), Katerina points out her changed attitude, or changed expectation rather, toward the role of consuming goods and services.

I have learned to be happy with nothing. We don't have any money, we all put together the money we have, buy two beers, and relax in the

206   Paradoxes of Emancipation

> park. You understand? Others want to go out to eat, to drink in cafés
> and restaurants. (Katerina, personal communication, February 7, 2016)

In a perhaps exaggerated manner, by demarcating those "others" as doing essentially similar things but in pricier ways, Katerina underlines her rejection of consumerist culture. Centering her statement on "we all" (the occurrence of being together), rather than on "don't have" (the absence of means for consumption), Katerina also indicates that it is practicing collectivity (and solidarity for that matter) that brings her happiness, more so than the experience of pleasure so inherent to consuming. This leads back to the assumptions about tracing subjectivity through practice, of which Viktoria offers a fruitful example.

> In Syntagma [referring to the occupation], I understood how important
> it is for change to come from within us. From small, everyday practices.
> If they change, for me, there's nothing else it takes to create a world that
> is sustainable and in unison with nature. . . . The power that humans
> have if they put solidarity and love first: This! . . . The parties have
> done a lot of damage . . . because they divide people. If we can tear
> ourselves away from that thing and unite and change our everyday practices, things will change without people noticing and without violence.
> I believe in a nonviolent revolution. (Viktoria, personal communication, October 22, 2014)

Though speaking of revolution, Viktoria's emphasis on the importance of everyday practices "without people noticing," may at first render her understanding of change essentially as reformist. But in line with my assumptions in chapter 3, prefigurative practices potentially transcend the dichotomy between reform versus revolution (Harding 2015), as well as means and ends, through both the antipolitical and alter-political capacities of the radical imagination. In the same vein, her nonviolent approach to change underlines the departure from the subordinating and dominating qualities of state-institutional arrangements more generally, and parties in particular. To be more precise, as an ethical being, Viktoria juxtaposes the divisive and authoritarian nature of parties against what to her seem to be pivotal moral principles of conduct: "solidarity" and "love." Cornell West

Paradoxes of Emancipation   207

points out that as opposed to the individual and inward underpinnings of "pleasure" in commodified contexts, "love, care, kindness, service, solidarity, the struggle for justice" are all "nonmarket-values" which "provide the possibility of bringing people together" (quoted in Dent 1992, 1). Against this backdrop, Viktoria's emphasis on "unite" can be signified as striving for the creation of quite literally "comm-unity"—the prefiguration of commons spaces. In line with the considerations in chapter 2, in particular regarding dialectics, subjectivities structure spatialities in practice in ways that reproduce the radical imagination, leading to the generation of various such commons spaces.

Prefigurative Commons Spaces

> The appropriation of public space though didn't only concern Syntagma Square [referring to the occupation]. It then spread to other situations. In festivals where they don't need to get a permit from the municipality, like in Metaxourgeio,[2] and other actions in the everyday. . . . And these are initiatives "from below." This was a thing that was achieved after 2011. De facto. It didn't need some sort of political maturity to do that. The very process brought this about. And it is one of the important achievements. (Lukas, personal communication, February 23, 2016)

In line with socio-spatial dialectics (Soja 1998), subjectivities structure and are structured by spatialities, and vice versa. Indeed, many of my interlocutors were keen to answer my questions regarding "what remains" of the Syntagma Square occupation by pointing out how political collectives and various groups and activities, broadly subsumed under the banner of the "solidarity economy" (Laville 2010), have made their way into the mainstream of society. In a similar vein, scholars have called attention to the "metastatic character" (Stavrides 2015, 13) of such initiatives and their

---

2. Metaxourgeio ("silk factory") is a central Athenian neighborhood, known for artistic and cultural events as well as street festivals. In the past few years it has gained a hip reputation due to gentrification processes and an increase of art spaces, trendy restaurants, and cafés (Trimikliniotis et al. 2015).

role in furthering practices guided by solidarity and collectivity (Rakopoulos 2017; Zafiropoulou and Papachristopoulos 2016) and their links to the reappropriation of public space (Hadjimichalis 2013; Leontidou 2012; Stavrides 2016).

Because my interlocutors' conduct is based on collectivity, solidarity, self-organization, self-governance, and mutual respect, they produce "commons" spaces alongside the same principles. Lukas underlines this claim by pointing out how "the very process brought this about." These commons spaces are collectively "owned" and seek to cater for the well-being of every member of the community (Kioupkiolis and Karyotis 2015). The examples are many: from social healthcare structures providing free medical services for people without access to public health facilities; to social economy cooperatives, organizing microeconomies without middlemen or money in order to heighten solidarity and strengthen social bonds; to alter-cultural initiatives and the organization of free events; to open information technologies, promoting open-source hardware and software and freedom of information; to neighborhood assemblies, tackling a wide range of local issues. Essentially grounded in practices of social reproduction, commons have been described as the great "Other" of the market (Caffentzis 2013; Caffentzis and Federici 2014), requiring a community based on equal access to the means of (re)production as well as egalitarian decision-making. Similarly, Andrew Cumbers (2015, 63) summarizes commons in this articulation as "collective spaces created 'outside' of the workings of capital where different social relations and norms, based upon reciprocity, trust and care—rather than individualism, competition and self-interest—can be nourished."

In this sense, commons may radically depart from the practices assumed to be normative and necessary in the neoliberal imagination. However, as I theorized in chapter 2 with regard to the upper part of the Syntagma Square occupation, the moral character and (ethical) guiding principles of the very practices that constitute spaces can take quite different forms. This is why it seems more adequate to render Cumbers's conceptualization of commons as an empirical possibility rather than an ontological inevitability. Nonetheless, the takeaway here is that commons are spatially produced through practices. In producing prefigurative commons spaces, my interlocutors transfer the extraordinary spatiality of the Syntagma Square occupation into their quotidian activities. By doing so, they reproduce these spatialities in the spirit of the Syntagma Square occupation. The following section exemplifies some of these prefigurative commons spaces in order to show how their (organizational) practices and structural logics reproduce the radical imagination of the Syntagma Square occupation.

City Plaza

As the Balkan route was effectively closed down in March 2016, through the implementation of the European Union–Turkey deal on the migration crisis, sixty thousand refugees found themselves stranded in Greece under desolate living conditions. Partially in response, a collective effort by refugees and Greek activists decided to accelerate their plan to occupy the three-star City Plaza Hotel in central Athens. Abandoned since 2010, the hotel was transformed from what was originally a mere space of commodified lodging into "a space of safety and dignity" (Best Hotel in Europe 2019). In Lefebvrian terms, the conceived space of a hotel was transformed into something else entirely—appropriated in use. Although the occupation ended in 2019 due to both continued threats by the conservative New Democracy government to evacuate the hotel, and political differences between squatters as to how to proceed,[3] in its over three years of operation, City Plaza hosted over 2,500 refugees in a self-organized and direct democratic fashion. Petros, who took part in the hotel occupation, explains:

> In City Plaza I was there from the very beginning. We didn't have the squares in mind consciously. And the people who are in City Plaza are people who are more, what we call, "organized on the Left". . . . The corpus was leftists. The squares gave a tendency to people to be able to have an active role in the ways in which they confront politics. So [the squares] gave them a way to deal with politics in a way more direct and

3. Further information regarding the decision to end the occupation of City Plaza Hotel can be found at https://best-hotel-in-europe.eu/.

material way. People could, for example, produce politics in Syntagma Square through the assembly. They could talk to hundreds of people and tell them what they believed. This hadn't existed until then. Exactly then, these people felt the need to continue this fight. This is why, as we said, they organized in various places. [Some with] the solidarity movement, some with unions, some with neighborhood assemblies—many things, political things. These are all forms and attempts at politics. Plaza is also a new form of politics. (Petros, personal communication, February 9, 2017)

It is interesting to note that Petros did not have the Syntagma square occupation "in mind consciously" when he engaged in the squatting of City Plaza. At a later point in our conversation, however, he did acknowledge that "the latter wouldn't exist, if it wasn't for the former," without necessary implying a causal relation between the two. Instead, Petros's account raises questions as to whether his experiences in the Syntagma Square occupation contributed to the internalization of disruptive space-making practices as normalized political acts, which he carried on to the occupation of City Plaza. What is more, Petros acknowledges the continuation of the Syntagma Square occupation through other venues, and highlights City Plaza as a "new form of politics," implicitly hinting at the theorizations in chapter 2 regarding the previously unthought-of.

In a conversation with Petros and two of his fellow squatters, Magdalini and Thanasis, we talked about the core motivations for taking over the hotel as well as the guiding principles of the practices of City Plaza that led them to view it as a "new" kind of politics. Beginning with anti-politics, the squatting was "a direct reaction to the border closure and the defamation of the solidarity movement by the media and the state, who started treating [the movement] as a scapegoat for everything" (Magdalini, personal communication, December 11, 2016). Building on the demystifying critiques of the status quo that I elaborated on in the previous chapter, Petros acknowledges that City Plaza existed "in a context of exploitation and domination" and therefore "cannot be a paradise." Against this backdrop, "City Plaza is not the solution, but an answer" (personal communication, December 11, 2016). Taking as a starting point the question "What is more important? The right to private property or the right to dignified living?" the occupiers reflect upon the issue of "legality versus justice" and conclude that what matters is "making cracks"[4] in status quo relations by doing things "here and now" (personal communication, December 11, 2016).

So since its inception, the practices of producing City Plaza as a radically alternative spatiality[5] were informed by autonomy from both state[6] and market practices. This also shows in the fact that City Plaza Hotel ran through donations. Arguably, precisely because of the guiding principle of autonomy from the state, City Plaza neither accepted EU subsidies nor any kind of international aid. This refusal highlights a distancing from the marketization of help and other forms of philanthropy and charitable acts (Dean 2015), as participants at City Plaza instead advocate the guiding principles of "solidarity," "self-organization," and "dignity" (Best Hotel in Europe 2019). For Petros, the City Plaza occupation was

> an attempt to live better. Because we believed and still believe that you can have a better life through a collective, with others who are in a similar position trying to live your life in a better way. We believe in this and we fought for this through Plaza—as a form [of organization]. We already believed in this possibility in the back of our minds. It just took its material form later and turned into Plaza. (Petros, personal communication, February 9, 2017)

Grounded in the commonality of vulnerability ("similar position"), the hotel occupation's collective approach to overcoming these vulnerabilities was not merely a way of getting by in dire times. It is based on the belief that living together is living "better." In so doing, the occupation of City

4. What comes to mind here is the book *Crack Capitalism* by sociologist John Holloway. Here, Holloway (2010, 17) points out that moves to make cracks "begin with a No"; that is, the anti-politics of dignity, required to widen cracks further.

5. In Petros's own words, the City Plaza occupation is "proof that there are alternatives and they can work" (personal communication, December 11, 2016).

6. "The state will always be the state. We just want to push it as far as it goes" (Petros, personal communication, December 11, 2016).

Plaza radically departs from the neoliberal tenet of "governance through enterprise," which "construes the individual as an entrepreneur of his own life, who relates to others as competitors and his own being as a form of human capital" (McNay 2009, 63). Important to this belief is the capacity to radically imagine alternatives ("we already believed in this possibility in the back of our minds") and practice them prefiguratively ("through Plaza—as a form"). In short, doing so makes possible the radical imagination and generation of processes of change, which by definition can create different social realities.

Asking Petros how his experience of taking part in the City Plaza occupation influenced him, he stated, "It changed me very, very much, the space. The people influence me and I influence them. We learn from each other" (personal communication, December 11, 2016). His answer is similar to those of many others among my interlocutors, describing their experiences in the Syntagma Square occupation. First, Petros's example highlights the benefits of a spatial approach for grasping the dialectics of transformative experiences. Second, it substantiates the claims that the extraordinary spatiality of the Syntagma Square occupation—and with it its radical imagination—has been transferred into my interlocutors' everyday lives.

In this way, the City Plaza occupation served the function of a public pedagogy ("we learn from each other"); that is, a site of informal learning and education (Giroux 2004a, 2004b; Sandlin et al. 2011). By transferring the extraordinary spatiality of Syntagma Square elsewhere, my interlocutors play a part in dialectically producing everyday prefigurative commons spaces that allow other participants to undergo similar kinds of transformative experiences with the radical imagination. In this sense, the end of the City Plaza occupation does not mean the end of its radical imagination. Underlining the prefigurative character of the radical imagination, Thanasis tells us that City Plaza was an "experiment in political and social emancipation for us all" (personal communication, December 11, 2016). Arguably, as prefigurative commons spaces spread "metastatically" (Stavrides 2015, 13) they diffuse radical alternatives to those regnant pedagogies "whose aim is to produce competitive, self-interested individuals vying for their own material and ideological gain" (Giroux 2004b,

497). Regarding antiracism, which is inherently grounded in an antiauthoritarian and egalitarian ethic, the City Plaza occupation was case in point. The hotel is located in the Viktoria Square area, and nearby Aghios Panteleimonas, a part of Athens with a "high concentration of migrants, which . . . had become a stronghold for the gangs of Golden Dawn and was thus off limits for social movements" (Cappuccini 2018, xii). It was chosen by the squatters precisely because of its contested location. Thanasis informed me that local residents, at first hesitant and suspicious, "over time became important supporters of the project" (personal communication, December 11, 2016). This underlines the ways in which prefigurative spatialities can serve the purpose of public pedagogies.

From Time Banks to Cooperatives and Beyond

Public pedagogy is a crucial function of the initiative that Andreas is involved in as well. Together with others, he has established an integrated cooperative network of time banks, anti-consumerist exchange bazaars, solidarity festivals, and an alternative school of ecological farming, among other things. Subsumed under the social and solidarity economy sector (e.g., Malamidis 2020) the cooperative is to cover basic needs, rather than maximizing profit and satisfying consumerism. It further seeks to produce and circulate ecological goods with "minimal energy footprints," and to strive for "monetary autonomy" within the network through the launch of an alternative currency system. At the same time, the cooperative's practices are understood as "creative forms of resistance through self-organization and self-management," as well as cooperation and autonomy (Oloklērōmenos Synetairismos Athēnōn n.d.). According to Andreas, through the cooperative "we want to create a holistic way of life beyond capitalism, authoritarianism and patriarchy." As a public pedagogy, the cooperative's foremost goal is "educating," in order to "change people's mentality" away from "capitalist ways" (personal communication, June 5, 2016). In a conversation between Andreas and two fellow campaigners, Stavros and Vasiliki, at the Fourth Festival of Solidarity Economy in Athens, they emphasized the importance of building trust as the basis for such an endeavor. Vasiliki highlights how organizational practices can

214   Paradoxes of Emancipation

contribute to this end: "Assemblies, not voting. Voting is not the fairest way to settle things" (personal communication, June 5, 2016). The assemblies are open to everybody who wants to participate. In this sense, the egalitarian and antiauthoritarian groundings of self-governance and self-organization further trust among participants in ways that are strikingly similar to those of the radical imagination of the Syntagma Square occupation (on "trust," see chapter 3). Highlighting the importance of "changing mentalities," the members of the cooperative recognize the "need to educate ourselves to change," as Vasiliki puts it (personal communication, June 5, 2016). In this light, and by pooling a wide variety of initiatives under one umbrella guided by an antiauthoritarian and egalitarian ethic, the cooperative is likewise functioning as a public pedagogy in the spirit of the Syntagma Square occupation.

The Time Bank of Syntagma Square (TBSS) is an important component of the cooperative. Katerina and Thanos, together with dozens of others, cofounded this first Greek time bank during the 2011 occupation of the square. Conceptually, time banks are based on the reciprocal exchange of services that use time as currency—always valued at an hour's worth of any person's labor. On its website, TBSS states:

> We, the people who live, work and produce on this soil, Greeks and immigrants together, take our lives into our own hands, decide for ourselves equally, based on direct democratic procedures. The road is difficult, and it is essential for us to be interested in alternative ways of economic organization. Economy is not numbers and indicators, but the organization of our homes, our employment and our lives. (Trapeza Chronou Athēnas 2018)

The self-description underlines precisely the egalitarian and antiauthoritarian precepts of the Syntagma Square occupation, based on self-governance ("decide for ourselves," "direct democratic") and self-organization ("take our lives into our own hands"). Through this, alternatives to the economy are radically imagined. Most interestingly, TBSS's understanding of the economy is also a radical departure from neoliberal conceptions. By strongly underlining that the economy is "not numbers and indicators," it counters precisely the logic of numbers I elaborated on in chapter 1 as well as the creeping economization (by which neoliberalism is ultimately defined) of what were previously social and political domains. In this sense, TBSS quite literally chooses to favor political economy over economics, and arguably reconceives it around the radical imagination of Syntagma. As a public pedagogy, the time bank also spreads its radical imagination to people who otherwise would not have considered taking part. With regard to her mother, Katerina explains:

> My mother has become very conservative. Despite her thinking, she participates in the time bank. . . . She exchanges, fixes balconies, gardens. . . . She received psychotherapy. She comes along to many events, to the festival [for solidarity and collaborative economy]. She passes by. Sure, people say many good things about me and she is very proud. "My kid does something," you know. But her mentality has also changed. (Katerina, personal communication, February 7, 2016)

What all these prefigurative commons spaces have in common is that they either actively work against, or subvert and trick, state-institutional arrangements. In this regard, anarchist theorist Saul Newman (2007, 8) argues that "radical politics—if it emerges from and creates spaces that are beyond the reach of the state—can serve to highlight the limits of state power."

Between Anti-Politics and Getting By

As a matter of fact, many of these spaces operate at the margins of the state (Das and Poole 2004). They are sometimes formally legal, but work against the state (which brings us again to the question posed by Foucault, whether rights given by authority can ever be truly emancipatory).[7]

---

7. As a legal entity, Social Cooperative Enterprises (KoinSEp) were introduced by the Ministry of Labour (law 4019/2011 on "social economy and social entrepreneurship" formulated by the social democratic PASOK government, and superseded by law 4430/2016 on the "social and solidarity economy" by SYRIZA). Arguably this effort to normalize and legalize radical spaces came at the cost of partly entrepreneurializing and economizing their practice.

216   Paradoxes of Emancipation

Or they are formally illegal, but tolerated.[8] This state of affairs suggests that these spaces demystify state-institutional arrangements in ways that are similar to those I elaborated on in the previous chapter. In so doing, the ways in which subjectivities and spatialities relate to state-institutional arrangements are changing as well. Reiterating the importance of the Syntagma Square occupation for this development, Viktoria claims that

> many people, who until then used demonstrations as a reaction, stopped it. Because they say, "there is no reason to go out to try to tell some worthless people what needs to change and get beaten and tear-gassed. *I will just bypass the system.* I will build autonomous units and support structures on my own, without having to protest." From then on, the protests ended. You will find it difficult to find people to go protest. And that may seem like it's bad for Greek society, but it isn't. Because if you look at it from the inside, it's just that the way of reaction has changed. And that's a good thing. (Katerina, personal communication, October 22, 2014; emphasis added)

By dismissing those forms of protest that seek the expression of demands and grievances, Viktoria underlines that change will not come through state-institutional arrangements of representation. On the contrary, she assumes that protesting them will only lead to violent forms of domination and subordination. Instead, she calls for alternative practices of contestation that further the radical imagination of the Syntagma Square occupation ("autonomous units and support structures"). "Reactions" have not changed only through prefigurative commons spatialities. Apart from the more formal initiatives, a whole set of subversive practices has unfolded that have variously been called "quiet encroachment of the ordinary" (Bayat 2009), "weapons of the weak" (Scott 1985), the "art of trickery" (Ismail 2006, building on de Certeau [2002]), "misbehavior" (Ackroyd and Thompson 1999), "sabotage" (Mitchell 2011), or "misdoings" as a form of cracking capitalism (Holloway 2010), among other terms. In Athens, these practices play out

---

8. According to Monia Cappuccini (2018, xxii), although it remained formally illegal, the SYRIZA government gave City Plaza Hotel an official permit at the time, allowing it to take part in government-run camps.

particularly at the level of neighborhoods. Thodoris was among those advocating direct action in the neighborhoods and became active as soon as the Syntagma Square occupation was about to come to an end.

> Instead of demanding things from the state, [people] took them themselves. They broke open the junction boxes and reconnected power. The same with water. They also set up defense [measures] to protect their houses from DEI [Public Power Corporation] technicians trying to reverse that. There were people supporting each other: "Call us if they want to cut your phone line, or electricity line." (Thodoris, personal communication, August 29, 2016)

Instead of demanding representation, people take matters into their own hands in order "to acquire the basic necessities of their lives (land for shelter, urban collective consumption or urban services, informal work, business opportunities, and public space) in a quiet and unassuming illegal fashion" (Bayat 2009, 45). Other than power reconnections, "anti-Charatsi"[9] practices also include subversive methods of payment, such as

> limiting the bill payment to the amount corresponding to electricity consumption—in this way disregarding the amount related to the *Charatsi*—to be paid at banks' cashpoints (where the electricity user decides on the total amount to be paid) or at specific DEI company payment offices where the directors, in solidarity with the movement, were willing to accept partial payments. (Alexandri and Chatzi 2016, 204)

This highlights again the question of legality versus justice that Petros raised earlier. Here, demystifying the state to expose the actualities of

---

9. Due to "urgent national reasons that forge the need to minimise the public deficit" (Law 4021/2011, quoted in Alexandri and Chatzi 2016, 200), between 2011 and 2014 the Greek government imposed taxation on the consumption of electrical power (known as the Emergent Special Tax on Electrical Power Supplied to Built Spaces). The tax became popularly known as the Charatsi. Etymologically, the word can be traced to Arabic. In Islamic Law, the *Kharāj* is an individual tax on agricultural land. The fact that, during the Ottoman Empire, non-Muslims were required to pay this tax to the sultan, is telling of how the Charatsi is popularly perceived in Greece.

218   Paradoxes of Emancipation

inequality—that is, domination and subordination—seems to justify acts of sabotage:

> A state will never be one that will benefit "the many." It will suppress. I mean: It will be a state. But when you see that you win something by corrupting state mechanisms, surely you value that and try to gain something more going forward. This is true for every societal need and provision. (Petros, personal communication, February 9, 2017)

It is out of necessity that acts of sabotage quietly encroach upon the orders of the status quo. And as Petros moves forward in his narration, what becomes abundantly clear is that even such mundane acts, grounded in the anti-politics resulting from the commonality of vulnerability as to the livability of a common life, make possible the prefiguration of alternative radical imaginaries.

> PETROS: We don't expect everything from the state. We won't always say, "Do it, do it, do it!" while we wait. We will try to do things on our own that we regard as needed.
>
> DIMITRIS: And why do you do that? Because you think the state won't do it anyways?
>
> PETROS: No. We do it because we think there is a direct need for them to exist. We do it to show that [these things] can happen even without middlemen. They can be done because the people believe that and want to do that. So we believe in active participation, self-organization and the possibilities for subjects to take matters into their own hands. And meanwhile we regard this process as a process of conflict with which the subject fulfills itself and plays an active role in its everyday life. It can also have characteristics of resistance against the ways in which power and governments, let's say, impact their future and their rights. (Petros, personal communication, February 9, 2017)

Petros illustrates how material necessities can ground the ideational and, in turn, prefigure new material realities in the form of counterhegemonic practices. This relates not least to Lukas's consideration that oftentimes "necessity becomes political belief" (personal communication, February

6, 2017). Here, commons spaces prefigure counterhegemonic institutions that also substitute many of those services that ordinarily fall under the state's domain.

> From the time banks and alternative currencies, from the refugee movements, to the social clinics. You know all that. They cover the entire social domain. We have seen movements for recycling. . . . And this is what I see—the new things. (Pantelis, group discussion, March 28, 2016)

While these spaces indeed signify the novel and alternative—prefigured in the spirit of the Syntagma Square occupation—closer scrutiny raises an important question: What does it mean that these spaces "cover the entire social domain" against a yardstick of neoliberal restructuring in Greece? Apart from the question of whether prefigurative commons spaces are ways of getting by or acts of deliberate resistance,[10] how do they relate to the neoliberal imagination of devolving previously state-held functions of welfare provision down to the individual?

Reproducing Power

Although these spaces resist neoliberalism, they also unwittingly reproduce facets of the neoliberal imaginary. In order to scrutinize the ways in which my interlocutors' practices and, in turn, the prefigurative spatialities, reproduce neoliberalism, I will use neoliberal principles and ideas as heuristic devices to make these reproductive consequences visible. This is because "any critical analysis of neoliberalism . . . must also draw on an interpretation . . . of neoliberal ways of thinking, measuring, evaluating, criticizing, judging and knowing" (Davies 2014, 12). This will be the task of this second part of this chapter. Building on my elaborations in chapter

---

10. Such subversive acts may not necessarily be considered resistance in an informed political sense. Rather than building on people's intention, Salwa Ismail (2006, xxii) informs us, drawing on Sherry Ortner (1995), that it is not so much intentions that constitute resistance. Instead, "intentions evolve through practice. As such, the meanings ascribed to an act, rather than being fixed, are of a dynamic nature."

220 Paradoxes of Emancipation

1 regarding neoliberalism as the disenchantment of politics by economics, I will first focus on the role of critique in neoliberalism. I will then take a closer look at key practices of neoliberalism: managerialism and entrepreneurialism. Finally, I will delineate the increasingly psychologized management of the self, in order to shed light on the paradoxical logics of emancipation in my interlocutors' practices between resistance and unwitting reproduction. This allows careful attention to be paid to the ways in which everyday forms of neoliberalism are deeply rooted in ordinary conduct.

The Role of Critique in Neoliberalism

The role of critique in neoliberalism constitutes a key concept in the oeuvre of Luc Boltanski and Ève Chiapello (Boltanski 2011; Boltanski and Chiapello 2017). Their pragmatic sociology broadly claims that critique is a driving force for societal change in that it permits actors to shape social relations in accordance with their search for principles that are defensible for both their practical worth and normative validity.

In his *On Critique: A Sociology of Emancipation*, Boltanski (2011) distinguishes between two different modes of critique that he refers to as "registers." The "practical register" is "marked in particular by a low level of reflexivity and a certain tolerance for differences" (83). This register is illustrated when, for example, we become aware of societal pains, but find ways of coping and getting by, as these pains are not yet unbearably excruciating. On the other hand, there is the "metapragmatic register," where reflexivity is deepened in ways that shifts our attention from tolerating what is happening "to the question of how it is appropriate to *characterize* what is happening" (67). This relates to chapter 4, especially with regard to acts of distancing from a given order, grounded in the commonality of vulnerability as to the livability of a common life. In Boltanskian terms, it is in the metapragmatic register that the forces of confirmation and justification find their articulation: our ability to confirm and justify the legitimacy of our practices is central to our capacity to take part in the reproduction of normatively regulated orders. Here, Boltanski sees the possibility for "hermeneutic contradictions" between the world (everything that is the case) and reality (everything that is constructed), that allows us to question "the apparent givenness of objectivity by facing up to the genuine arbitrariness of all forms of normativity" (Susen 2014b, 19). Through hermeneutic contradictions, the authority of critique can be confirmed only by criticizing the authority of confirmation, as much as the authority of confirmation can be criticized only by confirming the authority of critique. As Susen (2014a, 187) remarks, "The necessity of critique presupposes the critique of necessity, without which there is no emancipatory transformation of reality."

The crux of the matter is that critique, arguably since the birth of liberal democratic polities (and certainly since the Taylorist factory), has been utterly professionalized, incorporated into the routines of social life. The widespread presence of processes of critique—of reflection, evaluation, judgment, benchmarking, and so on—makes it possible to attribute an unprecedented degree of legitimacy to those practices that are reproductive of the status quo. In this new spirit of capitalism, Boltanski and Chiapello (2017, 29) remind us that "the price paid by critique for being listened to, at least in part, is to see some of the values it had mobilized to oppose the form taken by the accumulation process being placed at the service of accumulation." Susen (2014a, 189) summarizes their work in this regard:

> The more a social system succeeds in giving a voice to critique without running the risk of being undermined, the more critique becomes an affirmative force contributing to, rather than a negative counterforce moving away from, the reproduction of social domination. The *Zeitgeist* that lies at the centre of the new spirit of capitalism is based on the idea of "dominating by change", thereby changing the very spirit of domination. It is because change is supposed to constitute "a source of energy" that the political forces cannot dominate without releasing the relentless dynamism of the productive forces. As a consequence, change is not only tolerated but even encouraged by the systems of managerial domination, at least to the extent that it does not jeopardize the fundamental normative parameters and implicit rules of the game.

Capitalism has historically been an outstandingly creative form of social organization in that it manages to draw imagination into its orbit, only to then co-opt it. The idea of change and creativity, historically raised by those dissatisfied with social relations largely based on the pursuit of profit, has been integrated into capitalism through practices of "creative economy," "creative cities," or "creative classes" (Haiven 2014, 10). Franco Berardi (2015, 167) aptly adds that "cognitive workers have been lured into the trap of creativity: their expectations are submitted to the productivity blackmail because they are obliged to identify their soul . . . with their work." There are myriad examples from literature to film to organizations that are splendidly imaginative but rarely ever shake the ontological foundations of social relations.

The key task for scrutinizing the reproductive capacities of critique, then, consists in deciphering the multiple codes and contents of its most ordinary forms. Or, to put it differently, the task is to make visible the "invisibilized" ways in which neoliberalism manages to incorporate processes of resistance and critique for the purpose of its own reproduction. With regard to my interlocutors' practices, throughout the coding of my data, these forms suggested at times the managerial and entrepreneurial methods in their everyday conduct, in their solidarity work within prefigurative commons spaces, as well as in the increasingly psychologized and latently economized management of their selves.

Managerialism and the Logic of Numbers

Asked about the challenges he and his comrades were dealing with at City Plaza Hotel, Petros mostly referred to finding ways of collectively organizing the everyday life of the four hundred residents living in the squatted hotel simultaneously: "We are looking into 'best practices' . . . different organizational models, and want to evaluate them, trying to find the most functional one" (personal communication, December 11, 2016). While he was clear about the collective nature of this undertaking, the language Petros uses to conceive of organization is reminiscent of, if not derived from, the formalized modeling of neoclassical economics (Chernomas and Hudson 2017), particularly techniques of managerialism. Managerialism seeks to maximize efficiency and reduce uncertainty via administration and organization through systemized and commensurable benchmarks, norms, formulas, and logics (Eagleton-Pierce 2016; Kutay 2014). To speak of "best practices," "models," "evaluation," and "function" is to economize social phenomena in utilitarian terms in ways that replace intrinsic values to extrinsic valuation (Davies 2014). For Pierre Dardot and Christian Laval (2017, 253), the reach of managerialism today has to do with the fact that it succeeded in presenting "itself as a universal cure for all the ills of society, reduced to issues of organization to be resolved by techniques systematically pursuing efficiency." Arguably, it is precisely because of managerialism's intrinsic quantitative potential—that is, its seeming neutrality by virtue of the authority, reduced ambiguity, and affective appeal of the logic of numbers (chapter 1)—that its underlying utilitarian assumptions can be easily "invisibilized." This (quasi)numerical capacity, then, can be read as analogous to Martin Heidegger's (1998, 235) observation that "calculation refuses to let anything appear except what is countable." By practicing managerialism, the search for ways of organizing prefigurative commons spaces is reduced to a technical procedure. What this reduction does, in effect, is to contribute to the (at least partial) reproduction of neoliberalism's very own epistemological logics of quantifiable efficiency-maximization. After being confronted with this analysis, Petros responded during a later conversation:

> I agree. . . . This powerful ideology [referring to neoliberalism], so the way in which power produces trends for the present and the future for subjects, is not only produced by the powerful, but essentially by others. I mean, the carrier of the dominant ideology is essentially those who are dominated. The "below." They reproduce [the ideology]. (Petros, personal communication, February 9, 2017)

Arguably, this is because of the naturalization of many of neoliberalism's principles. As Mark Fisher (2009, 16) remarks, an "ideological position can never be really successful until it is naturalized, and it cannot be naturalized while it is still thought of as a value rather than a fact." Accordingly, it is precisely because of neoliberalism's ruthless assault on the very category of value (in the ethical sense) that neoliberal principles become commonsensical. In the following chapter, I will formulate some considerations regarding an alter-neoliberal critique—that is, one that minimizes the reproduction of neoliberal principles, so as to eventually overcome them. For now, it is important to outline that once confronted,[11] many interlocutors agreed with the importance of making visible the ways in which critique reproduces neoliberalism.

Entrepreneurialism

(Quasi)numerical efficiency-maximization is not the only invisibilized way in which managerial techniques creep into ordinary conduct. It is noteworthy that while management for a long time prior to the 1970s was marked by the disciplining of Taylorist factories on both sides of the Iron Curtain (Streeck 2016), from the 1970s onward it has witnessed a cognitive turn drawing more on "insights of applied psychology than on the harsh rationalism of Taylorism or economics" (Davies 2011, 72). For Boltanski and Chiapello (2017), this shift is grounded in the events of May 1968 and what they call the "artistic critique"—that is, a demand for authenticity, flexibility, autonomy, and self-realization. Rather similar to Karl Marx's theory of alienation (e.g., Ollman 1976), this artistic critique initially caused a crisis in (French) capitalism, leading to the restructuring of capitalist practices in ways that widened autonomy, creativity, and self-realization in the workplace. By the 1990s, a "new normative vision of management emerged in the context of neoliberalism in which anything visibly hierarchical was substituted by workplaces where individuals felt empowered to nurture their own employability, particularly through a stress on exploring networks, projects, and flexibility" (Eagleton-Pierce 2016, 117). In this paradigm, individuals are not merely allowed but are expected to mobilize their empowering resources, which are integral to their critical capacities. As mentioned earlier, the appropriation of such initially liberating qualities as initiative, creativity, imagination, openness, teamwork, dialogue, commitment, or transparency provide neoliberalism

---

11. In the sense of the "community of inquiry" (Tavory and Timmermans 2014), I engaged some of my interlocutors with these contradictions in the second round of interviews to check the plausibility of my claims.

with elasticity, antifragility, and an unparalleled degree of ideological legitimacy (Susen 2014a).[12] This is where neoliberalism exploits the entrepreneurial qualities of the subject for the accumulation process. If managerialism refers to a set of formalized techniques of efficiency-maximization, entrepreneurialism refers to individual conduct under conditions of uncertainty that are characterized by its "'adaptability' and operating norm—constant change" (Dardot and Laval 2017, 119). Neoliberalism reconceives and exploits subjects' capacity to engage (*entreprendre*) and, in so doing, to learn (*apprendre*), for the purpose of utility-maximization. In entrepreneurship research, entrepreneurialism is marked by "an experimental attitude and by short-term projects" (Ylinenpää 2009, 1160). As Matthew Eagleton-Pierce (2016, 58) remarks, the particular appeal of entrepreneurialism "as a generalized ethic for governing both the self and different organizations became reflective of, and helped constitute, the mainstreaming of neoliberalism."

In this regard, empirical case studies, such as that of Trenholme Junghans's (2001, 384) on post-socialist Hungary, scrutinize precisely the ways in which neoliberal governmental rationalities aimed at liberating "entrepreneurial energies" and reorienting "behavioral and conceptual repertoires" in an effort to emphasize "the need for self-expression and self-actualization, and the need for conversion, or radical self-reform." In Greece, from the mid-2000s onward, neoliberal reform policies increasingly aimed at "boosting entrepreneurship" (Featherstone and Papadimitriou 2008, 144).[13] With the onset of the crisis, however, entrepreneurial activity in Greece plummeted. The 2016 Global Entrepreneurship Monitor, an organization measuring popular perceptions of entrepreneurial opportunities globally, found Greece had the lowest score in the sample

12. Blair Taylor (2013, 730) acknowledges that neoliberalism has increasingly adopted the language and themes of radical movements—"sustainability, authenticity, fairness, freedom." In his account, this is because those movements, especially the anti-globalization movement, succeeded, rather than failed, in having recuperated such themes into mainstream political and economic discourse.

13. "Then it was the party of the so-called 'Greek entrepreneurs' . . . that had to do with state business like roads, airports, hospitals, schools. Whatever the state was about to 'provide' for the people" (Lukas, personal communication, February 6, 2017).

(Global Entrepreneurship Monitor 2017). The European Commission, perhaps in response, established an operation program called Competitiveness, Entrepreneurship and Innovation in an effort to counter this trend. The managing authority for the program in Greece states that one of its goals is "to enhance the competitiveness and extroversion of enterprises, to facilitate the transition to quality entrepreneurship through innovation" (EPAnEK 2014).

Reflecting on her changing self since the Syntagma Square occupation, Katerina refers precisely to the extroverted, self-actualizing, and empowering qualities that neoliberalism attributes to, and cherishes in, entrepreneurial conduct:

> So yeah, through this process I think I have become a lot better. And this leadership thing that I had, I kept. Because I consider that being a leader isn't necessarily bad. The question is how you inspire those around you to be leaders. Can you have a team where everybody is a leader or . . . to have the confidence to be a leader? I think leadership has to do with confidence. Many people don't speak up because they don't have confidence to do so. Can I help them? Inspire them? Give them tools to make them more confident? (Katerina, personal communication, February 11, 2017)

Katerina's account of leadership overlaps with much of the entrepreneurial self-help literature.[14] In this regard, self-help guru Peter Handal, for example, claims that "what really matters is that leaders are able to create enthusiasm, empower their people, instill confidence and be inspiring to the people around them" (quoted in Moran 2013). At the same time, Katerina not only disregards the hierarchical presumption implicit in "leadership" that stands contrary to the antiauthoritarian and egalitarian ethic of the Syntagma Square occupation; by speaking of tools and individualizing confidence, Katerina's statement reproduces paternalistic notions of

---

14. Simon Sinek's (2009) bestselling book *Start with Why: How Great Leaders Inspire Everyone to Take Action*, or Richard Goosen and R. Paul Steven's (2013) *Entrepreneurial Leadership: Finding Your Calling, Making a Difference* are examples of the co-optation of creativity for the purpose of profit maximization.

empowering others, while placing responsibility for becoming confident and a leader firmly on the self (rather than on structural constraints). This feeds into the neoliberal imaginary that all it takes is willpower and hard work and we can all achieve what we dream of. "We could all be entrepreneurially successful," Rose (1999, 117) remarks, "we could all learn to be self-realizing, if we learned the skills of self-presentation, self-direction and self-management."

Arguably, however, it is not despite but precisely because of the currently grim economic realities in Greece that entrepreneurial activity is having a resurgence. Anthropologist Daniel Knight (2013, 117) found that people draw on entrepreneurial practices as "livelihood strategies" in an effort to "accommodate circumstances of chronic uncertainty." This is precisely because entrepreneurial subjectivity is "a prescription for those who are least able to live up to its ideals" (Fleming 2017, 99). Maria, who trained in graphic design and had to face unemployment and considerable economic hardship as the crisis hit her financial situation, is a case in point:

> Regarding work, I don't wait for a multinational [company], or for the public sector to recruit me so that I can work. I take my work into my own hands. I started as I told you. Now I work from home. I will now make my own group. I will have my own work. This. On all levels I try to do this. (Maria, personal communication, February 10, 2016)

Instead of hoping to find work in a regular employment relationship that may be covered by social insurance, Maria's take on encountering the crisis is entrepreneurial: taking the risk of self-employment, she individualizes the responsibilities of work ("into my own hands") as an active, productive, entrepreneurial subject. Her conduct is not so much defined by the Schumpeterian (2017, 93) conception of the entrepreneur: a heroic and creative man[15] (of the likes of Steve Jobs or Bill Gates) guided by "the will

---

15. To speak of entrepreneurs as men here is to underline Joseph Schumpeter's own view of humans as men. But it also seeks to signal the overlapping between neoliberal virtues such as competitiveness, success, and conquest with descriptions of toxic masculinity

228   Paradoxes of Emancipation

to conquer: the impulse to fight, to prove oneself superior to others, to succeed for the sake, not of the fruits of success, but of success itself." Rather, Maria's case is much more in line with the tradition of Mises-influenced Austrian economist Israel Kirzner (1973). Here, the entrepreneur may start *"without any means whatsoever"* (Kirzner 1973, 40), as long as they are in a state of alertness to opportunity. In light of the precarious realities of life in Greece, we may reasonably assume that this alertness relates more to threat, rather than opportunity. This is to say that the entrepreneurial subject is not so much driven by maximization, but, much in line with the Pareto improvement in neoclassical economics (e.g., Schlaudt 2018), "by a minimum rationality that impels it to assign means to the end of improving a situation" (Dardot and Laval 2017, 107).

Contrary to the prefigurative approach I discussed in chapter 3, the Kirznerian entrepreneur draws up an action plan, selects goals, and allocates resources thus constructing ends-means patterns in accordance with their own aspirations and desires. Because entrepreneurship here is assumed to be a trait already immanent to human "nature,"[16] the division between profit maximization and noncapitalist activity becomes blurred. In effect, this allows capitalist activity to be regarded as a natural part of ordinary human conduct.

The subfield of social entrepreneurship is paradigmatic for the expanded purview of Kirznerian entrepreneurialism, in that it fuses together social values with theories of the firm (see Coase 1937) and New Public Management (Hood 1991). Here, market-derived tools and methodologies are advanced to answer nonmarket questions.

> A business plan . . . I find very important . . . in order to organize your work, it helps a lot so it is more clear to you what you want to do, how you want to do it. . . . The SWOT analysis [Strengths, Weaknesses, Opportunities, Threats] is the first [thing you do]. . . . So all these tools

---

that "demands efficiency, competition, and emotional distance that separates them from one another" (Lindsey 2015, 310).

16. In the words of Ludwig von Mises (1998, 235), "In any real and living economy every actor is always an entrepreneur."

are totally "marketist." But, if you look at their substance some of them you can use for doing what you want to do without losing—now listen—your character. Because you remember what we said the other day: Don't become the same shit as them. But as a tool, they aren't evil. (Katerina, personal communication, February 11, 2017)

SWOT analyses are tools modeled in the field of business strategy and marketing (Hill and Westbrook 1997; Jackson et al. 2003). As such, and similar to the managerialism-derived techniques observed with Petros, SWOT analyses are likewise designed for efficiency maximization in competitive environments. Katerina's examples illustrates the ways in which managerialism and entrepreneurialism can significantly overlap: while Katerina claims the subject should be allowed to make use of these "marketist" tools if her conduct is guided by ethical principles ("without losing your character"), there are three interrelated pertinent dangers of fusing market-derived or market-based logics with social questions. First, managerial and entrepreneurial techniques subtly and almost invisibly foster and strengthen a Benthamite ethos via utility maximization. Second, the underlying logic of social entrepreneurship as a form of conduct that draws on market-derived or market-based tools to solve problems caused by markets in the first place ends up addressing the symptoms of inequality, rather than root causes (Dey and Steyaert 2012). And third, treating social questions as something that can be solved with tools and techniques from management, business strategy, and economics leads to a transformation of our very understanding and perceptions of solidarity and the social (Soudias 2021a). In line with my previous considerations regarding neoliberalism in chapter 1, social entrepreneurship disenchants the social through economics in ways that make it quantifiable—that is, measurable, intelligible, manageable, and commensurable, using neoliberal tools and techniques of evaluation. But this happens only at the cost of rendering invisible the inherent qualities, the value-rational (in a Weberian sense), of what the social entails. In effect, entrepreneurial conduct (and social entrepreneurship in particular), fused with managerial techniques, strengthens rather than overcomes the reproduction of neoliberal principles and imaginaries.

230   Paradoxes of Emancipation

Economized Practice

As a subjectifying (governmental) rationality, the neoliberalization of spheres of the social, the political, the cultural, etc., ultimately leaves traces on practices.

> So, this is the value of the square:. . . . For me it's that it changed me as a human being, that's the important thing. That means I saw progress in how I think, how I function, how I collaborate with the ones around me. This was my very own self-improvement. . . . There was a contribution from the square. But at a cost, for me. Because, I was there, and I can tell you that things around me got fucked. That means, my house didn't see me, my family didn't see me, my friends who weren't there didn't see me. But I wanted to be there. I changed inside of me—as a human being. (Katerina, personal communication, October 19, 2014)

An unsympathetic reading of Katerina's account renders it through its utilitarian underpinnings. Grounded in the processual logics of self-improvement, her analysis of the "value" of the Syntagma Square occupation is checked against "cost," thus rendering an experience in economized terms. Arguably, making these subtle logics visible is important because, as Oliver Schlaudt (2018) shows, what signifies the creeping economization of practice is not so much whether it "is" utility-maximizing, but rather whether we act "as if" we were maximizing utility. The danger of these considerations is the reduction of practices to mere "choice" or "preference" (in a neoclassical sense).

> At the end of the day, you see how your everyday practices and what you choose to support—what brands you buy and how you choose to live—that is what counts. And this can change many things. And if you say, "I don't like those guys in power" or "I don't like the companies who come and take my wealth"—see how far you are supporting them. (Viktoria, personal communication, October 22, 2014)

Viktoria's account begins in critical reflection, in that it builds upon questioning the foundations of her conduct as reproducing status quo power relations ("see how far you are supporting them"). In that sense, her critique can be read in Boltanskian terms as metapragmatic. But if we recall her previous considerations (chapter 4), that by changing everyday practices things will transform without "anybody noticing," Viktoria does not fully take into account the dominating and subordinating actualities of the status quo—that "being against" always occurs within the field of power. However tacitly, her take is one where "social critique is increasingly replaced by self-critique" (Salecl, quoted in Scharff 2015, 117). Here, it seems as though practices are conceived of as highly individualized choices of, say, consumption ("what brands you buy") and lifestyle ("how you choose to live"). Katerina provides a more blatant example.

> We came to the point where this crisis is an opportunity through which we all reflect on how we will live. No, I don't need three mobile phones and two cars. I don't need to drink Coca-Cola. I can drink Green Cola. Even what we eat, how we think, all this way of thinking about how we live our lives . . . the crisis was an opportunity to change that. (Katerina, personal communication, October 19, 2014)

Katerina affords us with a wonderful example of reconsidering and radically changing previous practices of consumption, grounded in what in chapter 2 I dubbed the progressive signification of crisis ("crisis was an opportunity to change that"). At the same time, however, her example of buying Green Cola instead of Coca-Cola illustrates what Philip Mirowski (2014, 144–45) refers to as "buycotting."

> Instead of seeming to bypass the market altogether, . . . everyday participants are enticed to believe that it is possible to mitigate some of the worst aspects of market organization by paying an "ethical premium" for particular commodities and helping to make the world become a better place. Previous generations had sought to punish firms that were perceived to violate ethical norms by boycotting them. . . . In the current neoliberal era, people have been weaned off the notion that concerted political abdication from market behavior can ever succeed in its objectives, and instead have been seduced into believing that the market itself

232   Paradoxes of Emancipation

can offer sufficient choice in expression of political programs along the entire spectrum.

The emphasis on alternative products and consumer activism reinforces capitalist processes of accumulation by creating new niche markets while "promoting the illusion of the powerful consumer operating within the inherently democratic market" (Taylor 2013, 735). In this understanding, the subject is reduced to a bundle of preferences and choices. Relatedly, Thomas Frank and Matt Weiland (1997, 15) observe that the "cultural crisis of our time cannot be understood without reference to the fact that certain modes of cultural dissidence that arose in the sixties are today indistinguishable from management theory."

Psychologization

What is striking in the aforementioned examples, then, is how my interlocutors think about their subjectivity through what is essentially a Cartesian split—where the mind is the master of the unruly body. In neoliberalism, "the managerial self, who manages both her subjectivity and the outer world, reproduces the Cartesian trope of the subordination of (risky) body to (rational) mind" (Moore and Robinson 2015, 2784). In doing so, the subject establishes a critical distance to themselves that allows them to work on it, to "function" and "self-improve," in a "constant mode of becoming" (Scharff 2015, 112).

> If you look at the negative, and get away from the anger that the negative creates in you—which is human—and integrate it into your lived experience, the way of maturation is unending. You always look for [something] finite, without accomplishing it. This is what development means. (Lukas, personal communication, February 23, 2016)

If not entrepreneurial, Lukas's take on personal "development" is firmly grounded in the escalatory growth logics of modernization (Rosa 2013) and the perpetuation of becoming ("maturation is unending"). At the same time, by rationalizing affectivities and turning them into a resource of self-improvement ("get away" from "the negative" and "integrate it"), Lukas indicates the utter psychologization and utilitarianization (reminiscent of Beckerian human capital) of the most intimate, the most personal aspects of subjectivity. As Nickolas Rose (1999) and William Davies (2015a) have argued in different ways, and overlapping with the turn to applied psychology in the workplace outlined earlier, subjects tend to formulate, understand, and respond to achievements and frustrations, to temptations and aspirations in increasingly psychologized ways.

> Contemporary human beings, that is to say, inhabit a network of assemblages which presuppose, fabricate and stabilise particular versions of the self, understood in terms that are psychological in that they refer to a "psy-shaped space" within us, even though their relation to the complex and contradictory domain of authorized psychological knowledge is one of bricolage, translation and hybridization. It is this subjectified environment that provides the ethical repertoires for those who are only "professionals" of themselves—experts of their own existence. Such repertoires—couched in the languages of trauma, of stress, of attitude, of intelligence, of self-esteem, of fulfilment and self-realization, . . . and accompanied by little maxims and techniques of self-conduct—make everyday actions possible and judgeable. (Rose 1999, 265)

Throughout this book, my interlocutors' references to "mentality," "opening" one's "mind," having a "closed mind," or being among the "like-minded," all make reference to the psyche as the driver of action and transformation. According to this logic, change, struggle, conflict all come from "within us."

> LUKAS: You need to know very well who your opponent is. And who your enemy is. I will tell you something Churchill said—who is one of the most systemic bastards that this planet has produced: "The opponent is opposite you. The enemy is sometimes next to you."[17] And for me, in developing this thought further, the oppo-

17. Lukas is likely referring to Winston Churchill's quote, "The opposition occupies the benches in front of you, but the enemy sits behind you."

234   Paradoxes of Emancipation

> nent is opposite, and the enemy is sometimes behind us and next
> to us. And mainly *inside of us*. And a thing that is an enduring
> challenge is to kill the cop and the fascist inside of us.
>
> DIMITRIS: We have also a fascist?
>
> LUKAS: He is more hidden. This may sound a bit hippie or alternative,
> but I believe that the most massive change doesn't occur without
> the change of individuality. And individualities change a lot quicker
> for the better when massive events occur, such as Syntagma Square
> of 2011. (Lukas, personal communication, February 23, 2016)

Although Lukas acknowledges the importance of the Syntagma Square occupation for the unfolding of "massive" transformations, he views this transformation through an assemblage of individuals, rather than through a collective experience. It seems as though his centering of individuality and change from "within" makes Lukas tacitly uncomfortable and apologetic ("hippie or alternative"). This may well be because his analysis overlaps with the spiritualized, self-centered approaches to change in (postmodern) New Age movements (e.g., Huss 2014). In this sense, Lukas provides a dauntingly paralyzing fusion between a fully autonomous subject and a self-sovereign subject: "An intuited Kantian transcendental ego that is generative of all knowable reality" (Bookchin 1995, 11), and a privatized, self-empowering, self-developing subject who acknowledges the limitlessness of development. To conflate these seemingly paradoxical characteristics, Lukas encourages self-control and self-management in order to develop the self in accordance with a set of ethical criteria. But as Andrea Muehlebach (2012) suggests, although "the ethical" may be widely perceived as a counterpoint to neoliberal principles and attitudes, it never entirely escapes them.

In this regard, Phoebe Moore and Andrew Robinson's (2015, 2784) work on the quantified self convincingly argues that the entrepreneurial subject fertilizes the Cartesian split for neoliberalism by "insisting on processual, system-level thinking. It continues to subordinate such thinking to the project," as defined by the managing self. Managerialism may not find its dominant expression in my interlocutors' activities in the prefigurative commons spaces (although I have outlined that this is indeed the case at times). However, it is worth considering how far managerial techniques have become an expression of the "therapeutic culture" (Foster 2016) of psychologized self-perception—in the sense of habitualized modes of thought and action within the self—in order to navigate through the stressful and daunting terrain of uncertainty. Katerina provides an exemplary case. After her latently authoritarian conduct met with disapproval among fellow occupiers in Syntagma Square, Katerina tries to "improve" that characteristic about herself.

> The tools [learnt from the Syntagma Square occupation] afterwards of course helped a lot. Because after, the element of generally improving as a human overtook me. That what I did was violent, I was exercising violence on the group. I needed to realize that what I did was violent and try to correct it: through workshops we did on violent communication, various workshops on self-improvement. (Katerina, personal communication, February 11, 2017)

Among the workshops[18] were a variety of "social movement trainings" that integrated "various aspects of security, including psycho-social, digital and physical security" in order to strengthen "resilience." They also included "methods" that allow activists to "avoid burnout and stay in it for the long haul." They are grounded in a "regenerative" approach, which "goes beyond sustainability to explore how we can organize in ways that actually renew or revitalize our own resources and those of our groups." Such an approach, the workshop series promises, "can help us stay inspired, nourished, and more creative in our tactical approach." This underlines the utter psychologization of human activity and the subject, the Cartesian mind-body split, and the related reduction of the body to a bundle of resources that need to be cared for in order to be effectively employed. Self-management, particularly atomized self-care of the body and the psyche, needs to be seen against the crisis of actual care. With state-sponsored social and health service provision in Greece at (or rather, beyond) breaking point, self-management becomes an act of radical self-preservation.

18. For reasons of confidentiality, I decided to anonymize the workshop series.

Better than the State?

The emergence of prefigurative commons spaces in Greece can be seen as the need to establish sites of self-preservation. This is to say that spaces such as solidarity clinics were established not necessarily out of political convictions, at least initially, but rather due to the need to get by in times of utter hardship, crisis, and the lack of state-based welfare provision. Yet, as I showed in chapter 4, the inability to satisfy needs can translate into political demands and politicized subjectivity. Indeed, most prefigurative commons spaces created in the aftermath of the Syntagma Square occupation are grounded in the spirit of the square. At the same time, self-organization, self-responsibility, and autonomy from the state are unwittingly close to the Hayekian ideal of "spontaneous order." For Friedrich Hayek (2005, 20), such an order "forms of itself" and is made possible not by state-institutional arrangements that order society, "but precisely in their absence, whence order develops spontaneously and becomes established, over time, as culture or expected patterns of behavior" (Bamyeh 2009, 23). Blair Taylor (2013), perhaps in an overtly harsh analysis, claims there is considerable ideological resonance between neoliberal ideas and what he calls "neoanarchism," especially with regard to voluntary association and the dismissal of the regulatory role of the state. As argued in chapter 1, neoliberalism requires wholesale intervention, regimentation, and control despite the illusion of free markets that is mobilized in public discourse. It is also true that, as opposed to spontaneous orders, the prefigurative commons spaces my interlocutors' practice are guided by solidarity, rather than competition. But we need to ask: what are the consequences of, say, autonomy, self-organization, and self-responsibility against the backdrop of the vision of neoliberal governmental rationality?

For anarchist theorist Murray Bookchin (1995, 12), "autonomy" connotes individual-centric self-sovereignty. It rests on "a self-managing ego, independent of any clientage or reliance on others for its maintenance." As opposed to "freedom," autonomy does not necessarily interweave the individual with the collective and is more reminiscent of "personal liberty." Autonomy, in Bookchin's reading, then, is merely the absence of coercion from the individual. Against the backdrop of Hayekian spontaneous orders, autonomy, together with the self-centered notions of self-organization and self-responsibility, may well reproduce neoliberal imaginaries of selfhood and (social) organization. What is more, taking for granted—for the sake of argument—the internalization of the sovereign state in our imagination for ordering social relations (see Hansen and Stepputat 2001), solidarity clinics, refugee squats, food banks, etc., may well contribute to an imagining of the state in which it is no longer responsible for social and healthcare provision, thus unwittingly playing into the ideal of neoliberal statehood. In this reading, Petros's mantra of "we do what the state does, but better" (personal communication, December 11, 2016) is unwittingly complicit in the project of neoliberalization, in that the individual has to henceforth embark on a journey of totalized self-responsibility by substituting individual action for what were previously collectivized domains of the state. Counterfactually, within the context of the actualities of neoliberal restructuring, the cultural endpoint of this opaque process of negotiating welfare provision may be that a neoliberal imagining of state-institutional arrangements and services, especially welfare, becomes commonsensical (Jensen and Tyler 2015). A culture of unemployment insurance or health insurance will be morphed into "entitlements" for unemployment or health "benefits"—something we need to "deserve" but should never seek to claim regardless. Something that we no longer expect to be either a legal right, or universally provided. Something that is coated with shame—a stigma for not trying hard enough on one's own; for needing "aid" (rather than solidarity) from others.

What this example illustrates is that imaginings of statehood that shift toward neoliberal ideas and ideals may well, in turn, strengthen conceptions of the entrepreneurial subject far beyond abstraction. Prefigurative commons spaces are an answer to precarity and shrinking state-service provision. Yet their existence alone does not overcome the "life and death climate" that neoliberals nurture in order to "govern the work ethic and social order more generally" (Fleming 2017, 100).[19] Critics

19. This also relates to Lauren Berlant's (2011, 16) notion of "cruel optimism," where subjects desire and aspire to the very "modes of life that threaten their well-being."

claim such precarious conditions limit prefigurative practices in direct democratic and antiauthoritarian traditions, pointing to their difficulty in counterhegemonically challenging neoliberalism, and in developing strategies of not just resistance, but revolutionary transformation (e.g., Kioupkiolis 2021).

At the intersection between processes of neoliberalization of everyday life and the economic and social solidarity movement, morally ambiguous situations are emerging. Participants in the solidarity movement engender new interdependencies that function in ways that are detrimental to their guiding ethical and moral principles, just as they unintentionally reproduce the neoliberal principles they oppose. In participating in the solidarity movement, my interlocutors are on the threshold of becoming custodians for the welfare of others, and in this responsibility they actively struggle with the systems of patronage and hierarchy against which they define themselves. Challenging the state but also unwittingly supporting it, insisting on orders but also bending them, being providers but also recipients of care, these are questions my interlocutors face in their everyday practices. These paradoxical findings and considerations are perhaps best summarized in Petros's thoughts on the matter:

> In the final analysis I don't believe that—how should I put it?—we can in an abstract way come to challenge [power] without getting our hands dirty. You understand? The basic question is: How do you challenge a confrontational ideology that you consider to be opposed to you? That affects you? And the next [question] is—if it doesn't exist everything becomes pointless—how to implement that? (Petros, personal communication, February 9, 2017)

6

Toward an Alter-Neoliberal Critique

> Free your mind of the idea of deserving, the idea of earning, and
> you will begin to be able to think.
> —Ursula K. Le Guin, *The Dispossessed*

This chapter addresses the potentialities for overcoming the paradoxes of emancipation emanating from the findings of this book. On the one hand, my interlocutors aspire their conduct to be guided by the spirit of the Syntagma Square occupation. Building on the dialectic considerations in chapter 2 as to the structuring and structured relationship between subjectivities and spatialities, my interlocutors transfer the extraordinary spatiality of the Syntagma Square occupation—and with it its radical imagination—into their quotidian activities in the prefigurative commons spaces. In this sense, these spaces serve the critical function of public pedagogies—that is, everyday sites of learning and experiencing alternatives to the status quo of neoliberal (governmental) rationality.

On the other hand, while my interlocutors' conduct oftentimes explicitly seeks to defy the state, the system, capitalism, or neoliberalism (all in-vivo codes), their drawing on managerial techniques, their latently entrepreneurial practices, and the increasing psychologization and management of their selves leads to a critique that, at times, begins inwardly, where social critique is replaced with self-critique.

In this sense, the findings of the book are utterly paradoxical, in that my interlocutors' views of individual change, and some of their practices in the solidarity movements, radically challenge but also unwittingly stabilize the orderings of the status quo. Subjectivities, then, are manifold and paradoxical, rather than clean-cut and consistent. Patrick Love (1997,

385) notes that whereas a contradiction refers to a process that is logically incongruous or inconsistent, or even denies itself, a paradox refers to a process that is "seemingly self-contradictory but in reality expresses a truth."

So, what is to be to done in light of the paradoxes of emancipation? Because this book is guided by hopes and desires similar to those of my interlocutors, in this final chapter I seek to formulate some initial theorizations toward an alter-neoliberal critique. How do the experiences and practices of my interlocutors—in their journey from modernizing Greece to crisis, to the Syntagma Square occupation, and then to the solidarity movements—allow us to formulate a foundationally alternative normative critique of neoliberalism that minimizes its reproduction? And what would be core criteria upon which such a critique could rest? To put it another way, how, and according to which principles, is it possible to distinguish between emancipatory processes of transformation and immanent critiques that reproduce and foster the domination of neoliberal rationalities?

To address these questions, I first follow Michel Foucault's claim that an individual "does not begin with liberty but with the limit" (quoted in Bernauer and Mahon 2005, 151). Basing this argument on the ways in which practices and movements of emancipation—sexual liberation, enlightenment in the human sciences, penitentiary reforms—eventually become normalized, Foucault observes how even the brightest of human possibilities have become impoverished eventually. As Luc Boltanski and Ève Chiapello (2017) convincingly argue, this is because neoliberalism has managed to co-opt the artistic critique of alienation for the purpose of integrating it into the accumulation process. If Boltanski (2011) is correct to assume that every mode of confirmation generates its own mode of justification, then, for critique to foundationally transform social relations, the mode of confirmation must never succeed in determining the mode of justification. For if it does, we are left with an immanent critique that reproduces (facets of) the status quo: merely regulating and correcting. As such, any emancipatory critique ought to minimize the reproduction of neoliberal orderings, as no emancipatory process in the here and now can completely rise above the logic of domination. In the words of Simon Susen (2014a, 190), this is due to the fact that "behind every discursive process of justification lurks the affirmative suspicion of confirmation. On this account, every empowering practice reminds us, simultaneously, of the solid fragility of the justified and of the fragile solidity of the confirmed." As public pedagogies, prefigurative commons spaces ought to be conscious of, and explicit about, this relationship.

Second, in order to imagine a critique that is foundationally alternative to the orderings of neoliberal governmental rationality, what is required is not merely an acceptation of the factual character of these orderings—that is, the fact that they are constructed. It is also necessary to confront the fact that they are normative—that is, that they are value-laden. In synthesis, an alter-neoliberal critique must make these values and the constructed character of neoliberalism visible, so as to be able to first defamiliarize, and eventually overcome, them. In this sense, the principles of the radical imagination that guide my interlocutors' conduct (alter-politics), as well as their efforts to demystify neoliberal and statist values to the bare bones of the actualities of domination and subordination (anti-politics), already form the foundation of an alter-neoliberal critique.

These considerations ought to be viewed as the conditions of possibility for the formation of an alter-neoliberal critique. Building on this, I suggest the emancipatory and transformative quality of such a critique rests on the following dimensions, all of which are theoretical considerations grounded in the findings of this book.

Public Pedagogies

The first criterion I would like to suggest is making explicit the public-pedagogical character of prefigurative commons spaces. Not only do they proliferate radical imaginations in practice, they also repoliticize and redemocratize what had previously been deemed to have no alternative: the necessary, the efficient, the rational. That this continues to be pertinent is reflected in this observation by eminent Marxist theorist Raymond Williams (1965, 339) more than forty years ago:

> The relative absence of democracy in other large areas of our lives is especially relevant. The situation can be held as it is, not only because

> democracy has been limited at the national level to the process of elect-
> ing a court, but also because our social organization elsewhere is con-
> tinually offering non-democratic patterns of decision. This is the real
> power of institutions, that they actively teach particular ways of feeling,
> and it is at once evident that we have not nearly enough institutions
> which practically teach democracy.

Williams's words are as relevant as ever, underlining the importance of prefiguring spaces that make possible the practice of democracy and therefore serve the function of public pedagogies. By doing so, the spaces remain "'infectious,' osmotic and capable of extending egalitarian values and practices outside their boundaries" (Stavrides 2015, 13). In this case, biologistic metaphors such as *infection* or *contagion* may indeed be helpful to underline the disseminating and "spilling" character of public pedago-gies. In *Discipline and Punish*, Foucault (1995, 198) provides an example with regard to a plague from the viewpoint of government. He considers the plague to be "a form, at once real and imaginary, of disorder that had as its medical and political correlative discipline. Behind the disciplinary mechanisms can be read the haunting memory of 'contagions,' of plague, of rebellions, crimes." The plague is required to define the norm of what is healthy. From the viewpoint of the requirements of an alter-neoliberal cri-tique, the contagious qualities of public pedagogies need to be inversed; they need to be mobilized precisely because they spill over, spread, cast doubt onto norms, and make cracks in the walls of neoliberal rationalities and its orderings of power.

Against Economization

Neoliberalism rests on positivism, in that although it is socially con-structed, it presents its underlying market logics as natural. Through the proliferation of its intrinsic methods and tools of audit, measurement, and valuation neoliberalism reproduces its normative assumption. A positivist critique of neoliberalism will therefore find it difficult to "denaturalize" neoliberalism—that is, to shake its ontological foundation. George Stein-metz (2005) has convincingly illustrated that positivism deeply penetrates our habits of thought and action. This is why an intuitive turn to orthodox Marxism as source of critique needs to be treated with caution. Yes, Marxist theorizations are indispensable for the study of class relations and inequality, but they first need to be stripped off their "positivistic and naturalistic overtones" (Thompson 1982, 659).

Therefore, for normative critical activity to be radically alter-neoliberal, it cannot rest on positivist assumptions. It must be based on alternative ontological and epistemological presumptions. Throughout this book, I decided to draw on pragmatist and post-structuralist thought as a promising starting point for an alter-neoliberal critique. The abductive research approach outlined in the introduction of this book, for example, is an attempt to "depositivize" the construction of knowledge in order to allow for a foundationally alternative critique to neoliberalism, because to discover, in pragmatist thought, requires an antifoundational approach to inquiry. Similarly, the work by Claude Lefort (1986), Cornelius Castoriadis (1998), or Paul Ricoeur (2008), with regard to the constitution of the world as temporary and creatively negotiated and produced sociohistorical imaginaries, may well offer an intriguing theoretical "bricolage" (Lévi-Strauss 1966) that departs from the cold and calculating utilitarianism of neoliberalism. Importantly, drawing on epistemologies of the South (Santos 2016) is a way of incorporating anticolonial (and decolonizing) forms of knowing that stand in stark contrast to the hegemonic forms of Western knowledge production upon which neoliberal reasoning rests.

Apart from these more epistemological issues, there is a set of empirical questions that need closer attention in this regard: Does the visibilization of the constructed nature of the world at all allow an internalization of its norms? Did neoliberalism succeed above all because it presented its constructed agenda as natural and true? Is that something an alter-neoliberal critique should draw on, in light of neoliberalism's success? Or will such an approach betray the very principles on which an alter-neoliberal critique ought to rest? In this sense, these questions are for or against Gayatri Chakravorty Spivak's (2012) felicitous phrase, *affirmative sabotage*. Conceptually, affirmative sabotage turns a binary into a subtle dialectic: in suggesting that affirmation can include a critical capacity, and vice versa, it pushes against and beyond the dichotomy of affirmative

244 Paradoxes of Emancipation

versus critical culture, and suggests that instruments of dominant discourses can be modified so as to become techniques for its transgression.

If neoliberalism is the disenchantment of politics by economics, then any critique of neoliberalism must question its underlying utilitarian precepts. Neoliberalism seeks to reconcile the relationship between price and value, in the hope of constructing objective, commensurable metrics for the purpose of colonizing every sphere of life through the logic of maximizing profit, utility, and efficiency. Utilitarianism views people's aspirations as fixed, and external to action. Jeremy Bentham's (1876) Greatest Happiness Principle, for example, axiomatically considers that action is taken to obtain positive future sensations. Utilitarianism does not view expectations and aspirations as derived from, or changing through, experience. Rather, human conduct is merely an expression of universally valid principles derived from logical deductions or anthropological presumptions (Beckert 2016). On an individual level, there needs to be an awareness of the fact that utilitarian logics are deeply engrained in our habits of thought and action. Therefore, the strategies and tools we make use of in order to organize activities need to be put under careful scrutiny. Market-derived tools of management, business strategy, or marketing have oligopolized, if not monopolized, the ways in which organization is structured. Drawing on such tools only reproduces neoliberal rationalities via economization, valuation, measurement, and calculation, in that they offer market-based solutions for every sphere of life. "The terminal dystopia of Benthamism," William Davies (2015a, 261) observes, "is of a social world that has been rendered totally objective, to the point where the distinction between the objective and the subjective is overcome." Therefore, we need to embrace what neoclassical economists, behavioral economists, and neoliberal political elites would deem to be "irrational": we need to not behave in a utility-maximizing fashion. We need to not treat relations as if they were cost-benefit analyses, as if they were binary decisions based on pros and cons. Instead, I suggest noneconomic questions can only be tackled in accordance with the ethical precepts of the guiding principles of our conduct. The notion of radical imagination is a case in point, as it departs significantly from the utilitarian approaches on which much neoliberal reasoning rests.

If utilitarian logics replace intrinsic values with extrinsic valuation (i.e., measurement), any critique of neoliberalism also needs to address explicitly the role of quantification for the existence and continuation of neoliberalism. This is not least because "the spectrum of the possible is much larger than the range of probability" (Berardi 2015, 224). Quantification does not construct neutral, let alone independent facts. Numbers are always political, constructed to further a narrative or agenda, yet neoliberalism conveniently denies that economized logics are political at all. Karl Marx (1887, 25) presciently described in this respect how economic debate had become "no longer a question [of] whether this theorem or that was true, but whether it was useful to capital or harmful, expedient or inexpedient, politically dangerous or not." Similarly, Phoebe Moore and Andrew Robinson (2015, 2784), building on Jean Baudrillard (1983), convincingly argue that the relationship between question and answer in quantitative reasoning is cyclical: "The system receives answers which affirm it because the questions are less a free choice than a 'test' or because they present false choices which lead back to the system." As (anti)intellectual dominance, quantification is not the quest of truths, but the pursuit of power. In this regard, Foucault (2009) has shown that the quantitative and positivist (disciplinary) technology of statistics made it possible for governments (and corporations) to create a reality, which they could then control. Relatedly, Giles Deleuze and Felix Guattari (2005, 389) convincingly argue that quantification "has always served to gain mastery over matter, to control its variations and movements . . . to submit them to the spatiotemporal framework of the State." Neoliberalism relies on the determination of quantifiable standards, only so as to account for what counts for one.

Arguably, as long as neoliberalism is a hegemonic reality, any critique that builds on quantitative logics is destined to be immanent, for it reproduces at the very least neoliberalism's epistemological and ontological presumptions about the world. This is because quantification, as a logic of measure, assumes equivalence and comparable value across objects and subjects. In neoliberalism, this equivalence is constructed only to then perform evaluations of inequality (i.e., rankings, performance measures, etc.), the very driving force of the competitive accumulation process. While this process initially reduces the ambiguity and uncertainty of complex (social) relations to the (quasi-)numerical, the price paid for this seeming simplification is that everything nonutilitarian, everything metaphysical, or ethical, is simultaneously rendered invisible.[1]

An alter-neoliberal critique must reject the universal application of quantification to every sphere of life. I suggest, therefore, that any critique of neoliberalism must be qualitative and explicitly anti-positivist so as to be able to provide a radical alternative. It must move beyond the correlative and causalistic. In this regard, Deleuze and Guattari (2005) highlight the importance of the "nondenumerable"[2]—that is, that which cannot be quantified—relations, connections, flows, and becomings. For everyday life, this is to say that the self ought to substitute instrumental evaluations with qualitative, value-based judgments (in their ethical sense). The subject must not only question the underlying principles of the goals she ought to aspire to but also the quantified and inherently utilitarian logics of self-managing, self-tracking, or self-monitoring in order to achieve these goals. This is all the more pertinent against the backdrop of the increasing quantification of the self as a mode of subjectification (Lea 2016; Moore 2018; Till 2014).

Against Psychologization

This brings forth the role of the increasing (mostly behavioral-economical) psychologization of social relations and subjectivity: "An attempt to grasp the social world without departing from mathematical, individualist psychology" (Davies 2015a, 197). The tendency to psychologize reduces social problems to economized cognitive considerations, such as incentives and behavior, and essentially rests on the Cartesian mind-body

---

1. Philip Mirowski and Edward Nik-Khah (2017) rather aptly reflect this consideration in the title of their book *The Knowledge We Have Lost in Information*.

2. "What characterizes the nondenumerable is neither the set nor its elements; rather, it is the connection, the 'and' produced between elements, between sets, and which belongs to neither, which eludes them and constitutes a line of flight" (Deleuze and Guattari 2005, 470).

dualism. In this regard Foucault (2005) theorizes that the modern gaze entails a split between the observing subject (mind) and the captured, observed object (body). Here, the subject's psychologization against the backdrop of neoliberal governmentality leads to the management of the self: the cognitive management of the functional and functioning body in accordance with criteria of efficiency maximization. The notions of mindfulness, well-being, happiness economics, and positive psychology (see Hamilton et al. 2006; see also Sin and Lyubomirsky 2009) are case in point for the economization of self-care according to cognitive, quantifiable criteria. It is as though the subject competes against themselves in a constant effort to outpace themselves, to become a better version of themselves. Meanwhile, the social is medicalized to a prescription—reduced to a resource for gain maximization (see Kilgarriff-Foster and O'Cathain 2015). In consequence, the self-managing subject simultaneously observes themselves, while exploiting themselves. In this sense, the psychologization of the subject is a form of self-surveillance set against constructed categories that can rarely be achieved, very much in accordance with the processual and escalatory logics of capitalist modernity (Rosa et al. 2016).

An alter-neoliberal critique, therefore needs to depsychologize the subject. This is not to say that we should retreat to the realm of the mystical and arcane. New Age movements are case in point for the marriage between the ultrarationalist objectivism of happiness economics and the affective subjectivism of spirituality (Ehrenreich 2010; Huss 2014). Instead, depsychologizing the subject means resocializing the subject. This is equally true for the fields of politics and organization. Unhappiness and dissatisfaction need to lead to critique and radical contestation against structures of power, rather than to therapeutic treatment via psychotherapy, coaching, or resilience workshops. Stress needs to be seen as a political issue, rather than a medical one. Change needs not to come from within us, but from relations between us. In depsychologizing subjectivity by resocializing it, the isolating loneliness of individualism can be overcome through the togetherness of collectivism. An alter-neoliberal critique, therefore, seeks to find the reasons for grievances not in psychologized individual behaviors, attitudes, or moods, but instead in intersectional social relations of inequality.

248 Paradoxes of Emancipation

Against Productivity

Because neoliberal capitalism "must constitute itself subjectively . . . develop the desires and habits necessary for it to perpetuate itself" (Read 2010, 114), an alter-neoliberal critique also needs to question internalized logics of productivity. The question seems to be, however, how far we go in that questioning. When my interlocutors talk about the importance of "creating something," "being productive," or the "need" to "do something," is it not worth questioning whether the intrinsic logics of productive activity—the seemingly naturalized urge to achieve and progress—are not in and of themselves conducive to the productivity paradigm of capitalist modernity? If so, I suggest we might consider thinking about whether we instead ought to refuse: to be disloyal, to be noncollegial, to not synergize; that is, to try and be uncooperative with anything productive. This resonates with Stefano Harney and Fred Moten's (2013) work on the undercommons—a realm that is not that of critique and rebellion, but of refusal. For them, refusal creates dissonance and, more importantly, allows dissonance to continue. At the same time, they refuse to recognize the logic of refusal as inactivity. Taking this line of thought even further, the realm of the undercommons requires us to refuse what was first refused to us "and in this refusal reshape desire, reorient hope, reimagine possibility and do so separate from the fantasies nestled into rights and respectability" (Halberstam 2013, 12). Relatedly, Peter Fleming's (2013, 629) work on silence also makes a case against productivity:

> Silence might be suggestive of an emergent kind of sub-commons, no doubt transitory, but crucially collective. Its commonality is founded on the shared misgiving that the neoliberal project now gains sustenance from any kind of communicative participation between it and "the 99%". In its last dying stage of development, corporate hegemony even welcomes critical discourse into its language game, as long as it abides by prefixed rules.

Silence gives voice to the invisible. It refuses to acknowledge. The notion of refusal and silence in light of productivity and engagement also counterpoints the more subtle and tacit ways in which we reproduce competition. If to beat the system is to overcome it, then there is only winning or losing, thus reproducing its "language game," as Fleming would have it. To be against, then, is to antagonize. But this always happens, Michel de Certeau (2002) argues, on power's home turf. If we play, we obey. If we compete, if we try to win, it will be in a game dictated by power, one that by virtue of sheer resources will be nearly impossible to win. So a case against productivity is one where we need to free ourselves from the idea of winning. We need to refuse not only the rules, but the logics of motion and activity upon which these rules rest. For even to bypass the system is merely to hope to go unnoticed.

These parameters form the conditions of possibility for radically imagining alternative futures. Yes, performing an alter-neoliberal critique will inevitably reproduce the actualities of power, but must exist to challenge and hopefully overcome them. In Søren Kierkegaard's (1985, 37) words, the paradox of this line of thought is "to want to discover something that thought itself cannot think." In theorizing a first set of parameters for an alter-neoliberal critique, I hope they will be taken on by others for their further development. And because my interlocutors seem to have struggled with this challenge and the paradoxes of emancipation so much longer than I, it only seems just to give them the last word:

> I believe in something that has not been born yet. Which is a collective narrative and at the same time has not yet been narrated in the collective history. It's going to be something new, totally new. . . . It will have something to do with the past but not as much as we think. So direct democracy, self-organization, etc., everything will be part of it, but it won't be the main factor I think. It's something that we can't describe because what is happening [referring to austerity in Greece] is indescribable. (Lukas, personal communication, February 6, 2017)

Epilogue

This book has sought to make sense of the relationship between transformative experience in the 2011 occupation of Syntagma Square and subjectivity within the context of neoliberalization in Greece. Participants often describe their experience as inherently transformative, as a "magical" one that changed them for the better. Following participants' own narrative accounts by way of a pragmatist research approach, this book examined the following guiding questions: Why do participants in the Syntagma Square occupation emphasize the transformative character of the experience? What do participants aspire to and what do they demarcate their selves from against the backdrop of crisis and neoliberalization? And what remains of their participation experience with regard to subjectivity? This epilogue summarizes the central answers to these questions and sketches out an outlook for the future of the radical imagination in Greece and beyond in light of the country's consecutive crises since I concluded my study in 2018.

Central Findings

The Syntagma Square occupation should be seen as both a structural consequence of and an anti-structural answer to the crisis in Greece. For my interlocutors, the experience of taking part in the Syntagma Square occupation was a moment of "waking up"—a transformative experience of being against the orderings of power (anti-politics) and for something else entirely (alter-politics). As such, throughout this book I have delineated the ways in which the occupation signifies a spatially manifested response to austerity and the societal everyday vis-à-vis the period of neoliberal modernization prior to the crisis as well as a radical imagination that the future could be different; that it could be better.

To tackle the second guiding question is to understand what my interlocutors are "waking up" from exactly. In trying to make sense of processes of subject formation through the Syntagma Square occupation, this book claims that the subject is not the foundation of political practice. Rather, the formation of subjectivity ought to be traced in practices. As such, this book has paid particular attention to the ways in which my interlocutors do practices, in order to abstract the underlying ethical guiding principles of their conduct. Here, my interlocutors' narrations are intersectionally positioned: as they move through time and space, they resignify their experiences, their practices, and ultimately their selves.

These changes are embedded in the wider situation of neoliberal governmental rationality in Greece. The introduction of neoliberalism in Greece occurred long before the financial crisis. The inquiry of this book therefore begins in the period of neoliberal modernization in Greece in the early 1990s. The goal of modernization is to reregulate (rather than deregulate) relations between the market, the state, and the subject in ways that allow everything to be evaluated as if it is a market, in an effort to increase national competitiveness. In the push to do this, neoliberalism seeks to mold and subject individuals to its (governmental) rationalities through the cultivation of conditions of uncertainty (via privatization and reregulation), and the perpetuation of (existential) threat in the guise of opportunity, risk-taking, and self-realization. Neoliberalism promises through this subjection a refuge from perpetual economic insecurity and uncertainty. At the same time, the symbiosis of competition and uncertainty is neoliberalism's driving ideational and material force. With respect to subjectivity, neoliberalism has a parasitical connection with uncertainty because it exploits the subject's fears and anxieties for furthering the accumulation process. Neoliberals provide individuals with managerial, entrepreneurial, and psychological tools and quasi-ethical discourses[1] on

1. I say quasi-ethical because neoliberalism seeks to eradicate the category of ethical value itself by replacing it through presumably neutral valuation and utility maximization. Refusing ethical considerations, however, is an ethical position in itself.

self-optimization, so that they can navigate through uncertainty and brace themselves for competition.

The ways in which my interlocutors narrate their personal experiences and lives during the modernization period (prior to the financial crisis) are marked by a sense of unease and negativity. Disparaging the societal everyday as "empty," "without spirit," or even "rotten," my interlocutors demarcate how they perceive they are now from how they perceive they were back then, regardless of how submissively they were following the parameters set by neoliberal modernization. Through this demarcation, my interlocutors allude to changes in their subjectivity that indicate a tacit refusal to subject themselves to the neoliberal norms of personhood, especially with regard to individualism, self-interest, competitiveness, and consumerism.

Central to understanding this demarcation and essential for tackling the first guiding question on transformative experience is the liminal nature of crisis. Crises are situations in which the latently cyclical reproduction of the status quo can unravel: individuals are shocked out of their habitual acceptance of taken-for-granted norms and into a more critical stance. Here, doxic assumptions are raised to the level of discourse, where they can be contested and radically reimagined. Political elites therefore attempt to reduce crisis to an anticritical Schmittian state of exception that is radically extraordinary, but does not allow for alternative judgments and critiques. They do so hoping that subjects will adhere to a regressive signification of crisis, which shuts down the imagination from what is possible to what is necessary, guided by the violent threat of uncertainty, rather than the hopes of radical potentiality. Ultimately, this serves to safeguard the continuing existence of neoliberalism.

The ways in which elites managed the crisis, however, involved suspending the rules of the market and, by extension, competition's very conditions of possibility. My interlocutors show that neoliberalism's *illusio* becomes untenable and the hegemony of the capitalist imaginary is put into doubt. Subjects are now able to question the anti-crisis narrative and organize and resist governmental rationalities. In this progressive signification, subjects radically imagine and prefigure alternatives to the status quo and its future, in ways that seek to conceive of social organization beyond capitalism.

Both significations of crisis found their spatial manifestations in Syntagma Square. The upper part of the square was marked by a regressive signification of crisis—where what is possible is reduced to what is necessary. The lower part—where all of my interlocutors participated—was meanwhile marked by a progressive signification of crisis. Here, the spatially manifested, progressive signification of crisis conditioned the possibility for the emergence of the radical imagination. This is because the progressive signification structures the out-of-the-ordinary use of Syntagma Square and the simultaneous construction of space as a situation in which doxic assumptions become visible. The visibility of the previous taken-for-grantedness relative to the realities of practicing the out-of-the-ordinary constructs Syntagma Square as a liminal spatiality: a temporary reversal of, or even an expulsion from, the social order, a transitional time in which norms, rules, and cultural templates of what is conventional, appropriate, and justified can be collectively (re)negotiated. This process allows the generation of what I call the *unthought-of*: an experience that transcends normative expectations and allows what was previously tacitly internalized to be reevaluated.

On a conceptual level, the radical imagination is characterized by a certain balance between anti-politics and alter-politics. Anti-politics signifies a reaction against, or rejection of, the practices and discourses associated with the orders of power. Alter-politics provides alternatives to these orders. The radical nature of the radical imagination lies precisely in that it differs fundamentally from the experience of the status quo, both ontologically and epistemologically.

On an empirical level, the economic consequences of the financial crisis, the technocratic and authoritarian ways in which political elites went about managing these consequences, and the violent strategies the police employed to repress the occupation and eventually evacuate Syntagma Square led to the precarization and subversion of the livability of a common life. For my interlocutors, these experiences resulted in acts of distancing, against and in confrontation with the practices of the

254   Paradoxes of Emancipation

existing orderings of power. Against the backdrop of my interlocutors' experiences with (and prefigurative practice of) the square's egalitarian and antiauthoritarian ethic, the violence and precarization of the status quo created an almost Manichean contradistinction between the equality and self-governance of the Syntagma Square occupation, and the subordination and authority of the Greek state. In broad terms, the Syntagma Square occupation serves as an ethical benchmark against which my interlocutors compare their past selves—particularly during the period of modernization before the crisis—with their self-proclaimed transformed (post-)Syntagma Square occupation selves. This means they judge their selves as ontological beings ("who I truly am") and ethical beings ("who I want to be").

Regarding the question of what remains of the Syntagma Square occupation experience many years later, the most pertinent finding is that the principles of the radical imagination of the occupation have translated into technologies of the self around which my interlocutors' orient their everyday conduct. These principles are grounded in collectivity, equality, mutual respect, autonomy and self-governance, self-organization, and solidarity, and form a set of meaningful guidelines around which subjects, as ethical beings, orient themselves. Therefore, my interlocutors are careful to frame their actions in juxtaposition with conventional patterns of, for example, work, consumption, or authority. Additionally, the ways in which they conceive of the organization of state services, for example, or party politics, or the police, essentially continues to demystify state-institutional arrangements so as to reveal the actualities of domination of subordination.

Building on the dialectic considerations as to the structuring and structured relationship between subjectivities and spatialities, I have shown how my interlocutors transfer the extraordinary spatiality of the Syntagma Square occupation into their quotidian activities in the refugee solidarity movement, and the social and solidarity economy. Often referred to by the Greek words for "the space" (o Chōros), refugee squats, time banks, solidarity clinics, etc., are all structured in the spirit of the Syntagma Square occupation. By taking part in the reproduction of these spaces—that is, by being active and practicing in these initiatives—individuals structure these spaces and, as they do so, are also structured by them. In this sense, these spaces serve the critical function of public pedagogies: everyday sites of informal and experimental learning and experiencing radical alternatives to the status quo of neoliberal (governmental) rationality. This is to say that, in such spaces, we can observe processes of subject formation that are isomorphic (or at the very least similar) to those in the Syntagma Square occupation, albeit on a smaller scale.

While my interlocutors' conduct oftentimes explicitly seeks to defy the state, the system, capitalism or neoliberalism (all in-vivo codes), they sometimes unwittingly contribute to their reproduction. This is firstly because neoliberalism incorporates critique into its disciplinary apparatus. My interlocutors' latently entrepreneurial conduct, their drawing on managerial techniques of problem-solving, and the increasing psychologization and management of their selves all lead to a critique that, at times, begins inwardly, where social critique is replaced with self-critique. As I have shown throughout this book, this is because neoliberalism first cultivates conditions of uncertainty, and then manages to coopt much of the creativity and critique of alienation used to understand and navigate this uncertainty for the purpose of furthering the accumulation process. Second, the notion of unwitting reproduction has to do with the fact that subjectivities are not clear-cut, but paradoxical and discordant. When some of my interlocutors took part in the 2015 general elections in order to make possible the first-ever Coalition of the Radical Left (SYRIZA) government, as well as the subsequent *ochi* (no) referendum and general election, they were effectively betraying the antiauthoritarian and egalitarian critique of state-institutional arrangements that was at the heart of the Syntagma Square occupation. These instances of reproducing representative institutions illustrate how subjects make a rupture from the status quo but also continue to reproduce it, as they themselves are marked by continuity and change. Yes, as ethical beings, my interlocutors do indeed evaluate themselves against the moral standards of the radical imagination. But in their everyday, ethics become practical procedures of prohibition and judgment through which they come to understand and act upon their conduct, rather than being foundational and formalized moral codes of good and bad, right and wrong.

Building on the paradoxical empirical findings as to my interlocutors' conduct, as well as the emancipatory character of the radical imagination, in chapter 6, I suggested ways of addressing and minimizing the paradoxes of neoliberal reproduction by providing an initial theorization of what I call an alter-neoliberal critique. As a starting point, such a critique must begin with an understanding of how critique has been professionalized in neoliberalism, incorporated into the routines of social life. An alter-neoliberal critique therefore begins by critiquing the role of critique in neoliberalism. To be a radical alternative, an alter-neoliberal critique must be defatalizing and denaturalizing: an uncompromising assault on the very ontological and epistemological assumptions of neoliberalism. What are the principles and logics neoliberalism cannot coopt and manipulate? What is unintelligible to neoliberal rationalities? As such, it builds on the principles of the Syntagma Square occupation. This is because its antiauthoritarian and egalitarian ethic, building on principles of mutual respect, autonomy and self-governance, self-organization, and solidarity, is in large part antithetical to the competitive, self-interested, calculative, hierarchical, and subordinating qualities of neoliberal governmentality. The key task for scrutinizing the reproductive capacities of critique, then, consists in deciphering the invisibilized ways in which neoliberalism manages to incorporate resistance and critique into its own reproduction processes. Building on this, I suggest that the emancipatory and transformative quality of an alter-neoliberal critique rests at the very least upon the following dimensions, all of which are theoretical considerations grounded in the findings of this book. The first relates to explicating the public pedagogical potential of the radical imagination. Prefigurative commons spaces ought to be aware of, and explicit about, the educative and pedagogical capacities of their practices as a response to an urgent need to analyze critically and challenge relations of power in neoliberalism. The second dimension requires the deeconomization of conduct. An alter-neoliberal critique must ruthlessly challenge and minimize the reproduction of utilitarianism, positivism, and the logic of numbers and quantification. Third, the ways in which we think about ourselves as subjects needs to be depsychologized. We need to emancipate ourselves from the Cartesian self-understanding of rational mind and irrational body, where the former unendingly seeks to master and optimize the latter. Fourth, an alter-neoliberal critique must question the notion of productivity in capitalism in ways that should consider endorsing refusal and silence as viable alternatives to doing something, creating, being active, or being productive (in-vivo codes). These dimensions offer the beginning of a discussion about an alter-neoliberal critique.

Future Outlook

Radically imagining an alter-neoliberal future is as pertinent as ever. This is not least because the entwinement of austerity neoliberalism, environmental breakdown, the COVID-19 pandemic, and forced migration resulting from new and old wars appears to require from us the enactment of what is necessary: what must be done encloses the imagination of what could be possible.

Since I finalized my study in 2018, the politics of austerity neoliberalism in Greece continued at a steady pace. Although former prime minister Alexis Tsipras rather epically announced in the summer of 2018 that "the odyssey's over" (in Ithaca, no less), Greece's exit from the memoranda marks neither the end of the period of reduced sovereignty for the country, nor the end of the government's austerity measures. Greece's lenders continue to expect that the dismantling of the public sector, far-reaching privatization, deteriorating wage and employment stability, massive pension cuts, and an increased retirement age will all remain firmly in place, so as to ensure that neoliberalism in Greece is there to stay (Sotiris 2018).

The election of the first post-bailout government in July 2019, led under conservative prime minister Kyriakos Mitsotakis—a former investment banker and financial analyst—has only accelerated this development. On the one hand, the election of Kyriakos—son of former prime minister Konstantinos Mitsotakis, brother of former mayor of Athens and minister of foreign affairs Dora Bakoyannis, and uncle of current mayor of Athens Kostas Bakoyannis—mean a return to institutionalized politics being in the hands of one of the three big family dynasties (Karamanlis, Mitsotakis, Papandreou) that have split government amongst themselves throughout the majority of Greece's post–Junta political history. On the other hand,

Mitsotakis's pre–COVID-19 reform agenda turned post–COVID-19 recovery program, tritely branded as "Greece 2.0" (Hellenic Ministry of Finance 2021), is all too familiar. "Productivity-enhancing reforms" that "improve competitiveness and promote private investments" (740), meaning privatization and deregulation; the reduction of "administrative costs and rent-seeking activities by various groups" (715), meaning reducing social benefits; initiatives to privatize parts of higher education and "setting up an evaluation system" (658), meaning implementing quantitative performance measures to increase competition; or the "modernization and simplification of the labor law" (479), meaning scrapping the eight-hour workday and overtime payments—all signify the unimaginative continuation of the neoliberal modernization paradigm. Unsurprisingly, analyses show that the European Union–sponsored recovery plan may lead to short-term economic growth, yet the €31 billion program's absence of funds for social programs, health, and education indicates the continuation and perpetuation of inequalities (Rodousakis and Soklis 2021, 24).

Perhaps the most substantial change in policy since Mitsotakis took over power from Tsipras is the government's fierce anti-immigration agenda and the "law and order" approach to street politics. Elected on a platform of returning to a "new normality," Mitsotakis touches upon the imaginaries of the upper square with regard to returning to a mythical point prior to the crisis (that has never existed). Having promised to "cleanse" the radical neighborhood of Exarcheia, police forces have been continuously evicting self-organized squats in the neighborhood and beyond, detaining hundreds of people, including many refugees (Vasilaki 2019). Just like City Plaza, these squats were a response to the crisis of housing and care for refugees after the 2015 border crossing. Equally contentious is the abolition of the country's Academic Asylum law, baring the police from entering university campuses unless explicitly permitted by university administrators. Academic asylum was put in place in response to the decision of the military Junta to send a tank into the Athens Polytechneio in 1973—an attack that led to the death of twenty-three students and, eventually, the downfall of the military regime. The law was to warrant that such crimes were never to happen again and protesters have made ample use of the asylum by using it as a safe haven against police repression. The goal of the Mitsotakis government is arguably not just to repress radical movements but also to eliminate their role in exposing and challenging the injustices of domination from the historical memory, and how the country's history is to be remembered moving forward.

Repression against radical movements has amplified significantly through the economization and securitization of the COVID-19 pandemic as a matter of "national security" (Soudias 2020). While the pandemic certainly is a novel crisis phenomenon, the ways in which the Greek government has been signifying and managing it is conceptually analogous to the anti-crisis narrative of the financial crisis: correlating death rates, infection numbers, and available intensive care units with economic data, such as growth or unemployment rates, serves the function of constructing a quantitative reality, which reduces the pandemic's qualitative potentialities for radical transformation to quantitative management through the logic of numbers. Numerical audits serve the purpose of reducing the possibility of the political and ethical questioning of the pandemic from the outset, while justifying the necessity of extraordinary measures. Indeed, the lockdown measures in Greece were amongst the strictest in Europe, with a visibly heightened presence of police forces in the streets of Athens forcefully, and at times arbitrarily, implementing them. As the lockdown ended and people started enjoying assembling in public squares in Athens after months of isolation, police forces have raided these collective gatherings with tear gas and batons in the name of national security and public health, denouncing them, cynically, as antisocial behavior.

But we may also argue that the current government's agenda—from yet another round of poorly refashioned neoliberal reforms, to scapegoating and further criminalizing street politics and migrants, to accelerating the reach and force of the police—is indicative of its very own crisis of imagination. The "social necrophilia" (Gournari 2016) of austerity and the pandemic barred the kind of hope for a better future that capitalism desperately requires for people to partake in the accumulation process. Putting together some kind of vision that makes life worthwhile in a country where the ideas of market opportunity and fairness have come to mean very little for the majority of people, the Mitsotakis government and their intellectual supporters are building on positive psychology, well-being economics, and the tourist's gaze at Greece to substitute the broken promises of capitalism with a new political imaginary of happiness. As shown elsewhere in more detail (Soudias and Katsinas 2022), happiness in this imaginary arises not by questioning or overcoming the precarious qualities of state-market-subject relations, but by having a positive attitude in navigating them. Happiness is not a means to another end, like competition and hard work are a means to the end of "making it" to relative wealth (like in the American Dream). Happiness does not require making such promises, as it is inherently autotelic, an end in and of itself. In this Greek Dream, as Oxford professor Stathis Kalyvas (2020) calls his vision for the country, we can either choose to be happy with what Greece has to offer (and consequently be successful) or choose to be miserable (and suffer the consequences). Once again, structural critique is reduced self-critique. Yet the capitalist promises, and ethical groundings, that once were mobilized to justify inequality and competition appear to be gone.

In light of the experiences made and subjectivities formed through the Syntagma Square occupation, it is precisely capitalism's very own crisis of imagination that arguably opens up the potentiality for alternative visions of the future to emerge. Mitsotakis's neoliberal agenda and his administration's repressive and latently racist "law and order" strategies have been met with resistance. Various mobilizations in Exarcheia and other Athenian neighborhoods occurred in response throughout the pandemic and the country's draconic lockdowns, in which interlocutors such as Lukas and Vasilis have been actively involved. Playing on the government's COVID-19 public relations campaign Menoume Spiti (We Stay Home), people launched a digital platform called Menoume Mazi (We Stay Together, and later on renamed We Stay Active), in an effort to connect and coordinate direct solidarity actions pertaining to care and health. Amongst others, these included buying groceries for at-risk groups, sharing information on workers' rights during the pandemic, or the self-organized production of hygiene products using open-source technologies. On their website, Menoume Mazi declares that "we set up mutual aid networks in our neighborhoods, stand by those around us and resist those who use this crisis to discipline us, exclude us and make a profit" (Menoume Mazi n.d.). Meanwhile, collectives of the Far Left as well as the anarchist milieu established collection points for food and basic needs items in various neighborhoods in Athens for people in precarious conditions and in need of care.

On the one hand, recent studies have pointed out that the move away from protest events to decentralized solidarity initiatives in the past years can be seen as a response to the crisis of social reproduction and the need to institute infrastructures of care (Gutiérrez Sánchez 2022). These initiatives signify a feminization of movement practices (Kouki and Chatzidakis 2021), which considerably overlaps with, but also further radicalizes, the practices of the radical imagination of the Syntagma Square occupation. As Lucas presciently remarked, such "structures, and the legacy of the squats and initiatives of Syntagma Square in 2011, help to keep the fire lit going forward" (personal communication, February 23, 2016). In so doing, feminized solidarity structures serve the public pedagogical task of repoliticizing the conservative government's anti-crisis discourses, while providing an alternative to the emergent political imaginary of happiness in Greece.

On the other hand, we can observe the recent emergence of predominantly leftist cultural organizations and think tanks, such as the ENA Institute of Alternative Policies (established in 2017), méta/Centre for Postcapitalist Civilisation, and Eteron—Institute for Research and Social Change (both established in 2021). These organizations hint at a shift away from the prefigurative politics of street mobilizations and square occupations to the strategic building of counterhegemonic institutions.[2] While the notion of challenging neoliberal rationalities by undermining their epistemological hegemony in policymaking is indeed a welcome development, from the viewpoint of this book, the question is to what extent the transgressive turn to the think-tank model—which has been the driving force of the proliferation of neoliberal ideas—reproduces neoliberal rationalities in challenging them.

---

2. Indeed, this development overlaps with efforts of large philanthropic organizations, especially the William and Flora Hewlett Foundation, to fund the production and dissemination of a "new intellectual paradigm" that is to replaces neoliberalism (William and Flora Hewlett Foundation 2020).

Yet, at a time when capitalism is going through its very own crisis of imagination, alter-neoliberal critique and the radical imagination task us to negate the necessity of experience. What if the radical imagination of feminized movements from the outside of institutional politics, and the emergent counterhegemonic epistemological strategy of Left think tanks from the fringes of institutional politics, were to become allies? What if alter-neoliberal critique were to be the basis of such an alliance, thus safe-guarding the minimization of neoliberal reproduction? What may be the radical potentiality of this transgressive alliance of "affirmative sabotage" (Spivak 2012) if it were to explicate and proliferate the public pedagogical character of their politics on a firm alter-neoliberal grounding? Taking the radical imagination seriously is to envision and enact a future that today feels to some extent as inconceivable, so that tomorrow it does not.

Bibliography

Index

Bibliography

Abrahams, Roger D. 1986. "Ordinary and Extraordinary Experience." In *The Anthropology of Experience*, edited by Viktor W. Turner and Edward M. Bruner, 45–72. Urbana: Univ. of Illinois Press.

Abrams, Philip. 1988. "Notes on the Difficulty of Studying the State." *Journal of Historical Sociology* 1 (1): 58–89.

Ackroyd, Stephen, and Paul Thompson. 1999. *Organizational Misbehaviour.* Thousand Oaks, CA: SAGE Publications.

Adams, Tristam Vivian. 2016. *The Psychopath Factory: How Capitalism Organises Empathy.* London: Repeater Books.

Agamben, Giorgio. 1998. *Homo Sacer.* Stanford, CA: Stanford Univ. Press.

Ahmed, Sara. 2014. *The Cultural Politics of Emotion.* 2nd ed. Edinburgh: Edinburgh Univ. Press.

———. 2004. "Collective Feelings: Or, the Impressions Left by Others." *Theory, Culture & Society* 21 (2): 25–42.

Akarsu, Albina Sıla, and Nuray Sakallı. 2021. "The Associations among Self-Silencing, Ambivalent Sexism, and Perceived Devaluation of Women in Turkey." *Current Psychology.* doi.org/10.1007/s12144-021-02353-8.

al-'Azm, Sadik Jalal. 1981. "Orientalism and Orientalism in Reverse." *Khamsin* 8: 5–26.

Alexandri, Georgia, and Venetia Chatzi. 2016. "Athens: Switching the Power Off, Turning the Power On—Urban Crisis and Emergent Protest Practices." In *Energy, Power and Protest on the Urban Grid: Geographies of the Electric City*, edited by Andres Luque-Ayala and Jonathan Silver, 197–212. Abingdon, UK: Routledge.

Almond, Gabriel A. 1988. "The Return to the State." *American Political Science Review* 82 (3): 853–74.

Almond, Gabriel A., and Sidney Verba. 1963. *The Civic Culture: Political Attitudes and Democracy in Five Nations.* Princeton, NJ: Princeton Univ. Press.

Alvarez, Sonia E. 2009. "Beyond NGO-ization? Reflections from Latin America." *Development* 52 (2): 175–84.

Amnesty International. 2012. "Police Violence in Greece. Not Just 'Isolated Incidents.'" July 3, 2012. https://www.amnesty.org/en/documents/eur25/005/2012/en/.

———. 2011. "Tear Gas Fired as Greek Police Clash with Athens Protesters." June 29, 2011. https://www.amnesty.org/en/latest/news/2011/06/tear-gas-fired-greek-police-clash-athens-protesters/.

Anderson, Ben. 2009. "Affective Atmospheres." *Emotion, Space and Society* 2 (2): 77–81.

Anderson, Malcolm. 2011. *In Thrall to Political Change: Police and Gendarmerie in France*. Oxford: Oxford Univ. Press.

Anderson, Perry. 2012. "After the Event." *New Left Review* 73: 49–61.

Apoifis, Nicholas. 2016. "Fieldwork in a Furnace: Anarchists, Anti-Authoritarians and Militant Ethnography." *Qualitative Research* 17 (1): 1–17.

Arampatzi, Athina. 2016. "The Spatiality of Counter-Austerity Politics in Athens, Greece: Emergent 'Urban Solidarity Spaces.'" *Urban Studies* 54 (9): 2155–71.

Aretxaga, Begoña. 2005. *States of Terror: Begoña Aretxaga's Essays*. Reno, NV: Center for Basque Studies.

———. 2003. "Maddening States." *Annual Review of Anthropology* 32: 393–410.

Arghyrou, Michael G., and John D. Tsoukalas. 2011. "The Greek Debt Crisis: Likely Causes, Mechanics and Outcomes." *World Economy* 34 (2): 173–91.

Arthur, Chris. 2012. *Financial Literacy Education: Neoliberalism, the Consumer and the Citizen*. Rotterdam: Sense Publishers.

Arvanitaki, Katerina, and Maria Stratigaki. 1994. "Computerization in Greek Banking: The Gendering of Payment and Practices. In *Bringing Technology Home: Gender and Technology in a Changing Europe*, edited by Cynthia Cockburn and Ruža First-Dilić, 59–77. Buckingham: Open Univ. Press.

Aslam, Ali. 2017. "Salat-al-Juma: Organizing the Public in Tahrir Square." *Social Movement Studies* 16 (3): 297–308.

Astrinaki, Rania. 2009. "'(Un)hooding' a Rebellion: The December 2008 Events in Athens." *Social Text* 27 (4): 97–107.

Athanasiou, Athena. 2014. "Precarious Intensities: Gendered Bodies in the Streets and Squares of Greece." *Signs* 40 (1): 1–9.

Augé, Marc. 1995. *Non-Places: Introduction to an Anthropology of Supermodernity*. London: Verso.

Badiou, Alain. 2005. *Being and Event*. New York: Continuum.

———. 2003. "Beyond Formalisation: An Interview." *Angelaki* 8 (2): 111–36.

Bakola, Maria. 2017. "Crisis and Concomitant Forms of Collective Action: A Critique of the Greek Indignant Movement." PhD diss., Newcastle University.

Balibar, Étienne. 2015. *Violence and Civility: On the Limits of Political Philosophy*. New York: Columbia Univ. Press.

Bamyeh, Mohammed A. 2013. "Anarchist Method, Liberal Intention, Authoritarian Lesson: The Arab Spring between Three Enlightenments." *Constellations* 20 (2): 188–202.

———. 2009. *Anarchy as Order: The History and Future of Civic Humanity*. Lanham, MD: Rowman & Littlefield.

Barnes, Trevor J. 2002. "Reading the Texts of Theoretical Economic Geography: The Role of Physical and Biological Metaphors." In *Postmodernism: Critical Concepts*, edited by Victor E. Taylor and Charles E. Winquist, 25–44. Abingdon, UK: Routledge.

Baudrillard, Jean. 1983. *In the Shadow of the Silent Majorities . . . or the End of the Social and Other Essays*. New York: Semiotext(e)

Bauman, Zygmunt. 2008. *The Individualized Society*. 5th ed. Cambridge: Polity.

———. 2007. *Liquid Times: Living in an Age of Uncertainty*. Cambridge: Polity.

———. 1999. *In Search of Politics*. Cambridge: Polity.

Bayat, Asef. 2009. *Life as Politics: How Ordinary People Change the Middle East*. Cairo: American Univ. in Cairo Press.

Becker, Gary S. 1962. "Investment in Human Capital. A Theoretical Analysis." *Journal of Political Economy* 70 (5): 9–49.

Beckert, Jens. 2016. *Imagined Futures: Fictional Expectations and Capitalist Dynamics*. Cambridge, MA: Harvard Univ. Press.

Benjamin, Walter. 2008. *The Work of Art in the Age of Mechanical Reproduction*. 2nd ed. London: Penguin Books.

———. 1999. "Experience and Poverty." In *Walter Benjamin: Selected Writings*, edited by Marcus Bullock and Michael W. Jennings, vol. 2, 731–36. Cambridge, MA: Belknap Press of Harvard Univ. Press.

———. 1978. "Critique of Violence." In *Reflections: Essays, Aphorisms, Autobiographical Writings*, edited by Peter Demetz, 207–301. New York: Harcourt Brace Jovanovich.

Bentham, Jeremy. 1876. *An Introduction to the Principles of Morals and Legislation*. 2nd ed. Oxford: Clarendon Press.

Berardi, Franco. 2015. *Heroes: Mass Murder and Suicide*. London: Verso.

Berezin, Mabel. 2001. "Emotions and Political Identity: Mobilizing Affection for the Polity." In *Passionate Politics. Emotions and Social Movements*, edited by Jeff Goodwin, James M. Jasper and Francesca Polletta, 83–98. Chicago: Univ. of Chicago Press.

Berlant, Lauren. 2011. *Cruel Optimism*. Durham, NC: Duke Univ. Press.

Berlin, Isaiah. 1969. *Four Essays on Liberty*. Oxford: Oxford Univ. Press.

Bernauer, James W., and Michael Mahon. 2005. "Michel Foucault's Ethical Imagination." In *The Cambridge Companion to Foucault*, edited by Gary Gutting, 149–75. Cambridge: Cambridge Univ. Press.

The Best Hotel in Europe. 2019. "39 Months City Plaza: The End of an Era, the Beginning of a New One." https://best-hotel-in-europe.eu/.

Bhabha, Homi K. 2004. *The Location of Culture*. 2nd ed. Abingdon, UK: Routledge.

Boletsi, Maria. 2016. "From the Subject of the Crisis to the Subject in Crisis: Middle Voice on Greek Walls." *Journal of Greek Media & Culture* 2 (1): 3–28.

Boltanski, Luc. 2012. *Love and Justice as Competencies: Three Essays on the Sociology of Action*. Cambridge: Polity.

———. 2011. *On Critique: A Sociology of Emancipation*. 2nd ed. Cambridge: Polity.

Boltanski, Luc, and Ève Chiapello. 2017. *The New Spirit of Capitalism*. 2nd ed. London: Verso.

Bookchin, Murray. 1995. *Social Anarchism or Lifestyle Anarchism: The Unbridgeable Chasm*. Edinburgh: AK Press.

Bourdieu, Pierre. 2013. *Outline of a Theory of Practice*. 28th ed. Cambridge: Cambridge Univ. Press.

———. 2000. *Acts of Resistance: Against the Myths of Our Time*. Cambridge: Polity.

———. 1996. "Understanding." *Theory, Culture & Society* 13 (2): 17–37.

———. 1994. "Rethinking the State: Genesis and Structure of the Bureaucratic Field." *Sociological Theory* 12 (1): 1–18.

Bradley, Benjamin. 2005. *Psychology and Experience*. Cambridge: Cambridge Univ. Press.

Break the Blackout. 2011. "Updates from the Greek Squares and People's Assemblies." Mute, July 11, 2011. http://www.metamute.org/community/your-posts/updates-greek-squares-and-peoples-assemblies.

Brenner, Neil. 2004. *New State Spaces: Urban Governance and the Rescaling of Statehood*. Oxford: Oxford Univ. Press.

Breton, Émilie, Sandra Jeppesen, Anna Kruzingsky, and Rachel Sarrasin. 2012. "Prefigurative Self-Governance and Self-Organization: The Influence of Antiauthoritarian (Pro)Feminist, Radical Queer, and Antiracist Networks in Quebec." In *Organize! Building from the Local for Global Justice*, edited by Aziz Choudry, Jill Hanley, and Eric Shragge, 156–73. Oakland, CA: PM Press.

Brown, Wendy. 2015. *Undoing the Demos: Neoliberalism's Stealth Revolution.* New York: Zone Books.

———. 2005. *Edgework: Critical Essays on Knowledge and Politics.* Princeton, NJ: Princeton Univ. Press.

Bruff, Ian. 2014. "The Rise of Neoliberal Authoritarianism." *Rethinking Marxism: A Journal of Economics, Culture & Society* 26 (1): 113–29.

Bruff, Ian, and Kathryn Starnes. 2019. "Framing the Neoliberal Canon: Resisting the Market Myth via Literary Enquiry." *Globalizations* 16 (3): 245–59.

Butler, Judith. 1997. *The Psychic Life of Power: Theories in Subjection.* Stanford, CA: Stanford Univ. Press.

Butler, Judith, and Athena Athanasiou. 2013. *Dispossession: The Performative in the Political.* Cambridge: Polity.

Butt, Ronald. 1981. "Mrs Thatcher: The First Two Years." *Sunday Times*, May 3, 1981. http://www.margaretthatcher.org/document/104475.

Cacioppo, John T., and William Patrick. 2008. *Loneliness: Human Nature and the Need for Social Connection.* New York: W. W. Norton.

Caffentzis, George. 2013. *In Letters of Blood and Fire: Work, Machines, and the Crisis of Capitalism.* Oakland, CA: PM Press.

Caffentzis, George, and Silvia Federici. 2014. "Commons against and beyond Capitalism." *Community Development Journal* 49 (1): 92–105.

Callison, William, and Zachary Manfredi, eds. 2020. *Mutant Neoliberalism: Market Rule and Political Rupture.* New York: Fordham Univ. Press.

Calotychos, Vangelis. 2013. *The Balkan Prospect: Identity, Culture, and Politics in Greece after 1989.* London: Palgrave Macmillan.

Cappuccini, Monia. 2018. *Austerity & Democracy in Athens: Crisis and Community in Exarchia.* London: Palgrave Macmillan.

Carastathis, Anna. 2014. "Is Hellenism an Orientalism? Reflections on the Boundaries of 'Europe' in an Age of Austerity." *Critical Race and Whiteness Studies* 10 (1): 1–17.

Carroll, Anthony J. 1999. "Disenchantment, Rationality and the Modernity of Max Weber." *Forum Philosophicum* 16 (1): 117–37.

Castoriadis, Cornelius. 1998. *The Imaginary Institution of Society.* Cambridge: MIT Press.

Castro Varela, Maria, and Nikita Dhawan. 2006. "Spatializing Resistance, Resisting Spaces. On Utopias and Heterotopias." In *Nowhere Somewhere: Writing, Space and the Construction of Utopia*, edited by José Eduardo Reis and Jorge Bastos da Silva, 237–50. Porto: Editora da Universidade do Porto.

Charmaz, Kathy. 2006. *Constructing Grounded Theory: A Practical Guide Through Qualitative Analysis.* Thousand Oaks, CA: SAGE Publications.

Chatzidakis, Andreas. 2014. "Athens as a Failed City of Consumption." In *Crisis Scapes: Athens and Beyond*, edited by Jaya Klara Brekke, Dimitris Dalakoglou, Christos Filippidis, and Antonis Vradis, 33–41. Athens: Synthesi.

Chenoweth, Erica, and Maria J. Stephan. 2011. *Why Civil Resistance Works: The Strategic Logic of Nonviolent Conflict.* New York: Columbia Univ. Press.

Cherniss, Cary. 1972. "Personality and Ideology: A Personological Study of Women's Liberation." *Psychiatry* 35 (2): 109–25.

Chernomas, Robert, and Ian Hudson. 2017. *The Profit Doctrine: Economists of the Neoliberal Era.* London: Pluto Press.

Christensen, Ann-Dorte, and Sune Qvotrup Jensen. 2014. "Combining Hegemonic Masculinity and Intersectionality." *NORMA* 9 (1): 60–75.

Clarke, Adele. 2005. *Situational Analysis: Grounded Theory after the Postmodern Turn.* Thousand Oaks, CA: SAGE Publications.

Clarke, Chris. 2015. "Learning to Fail: Resilience and the Empty Promise of Financial Literacy Education." *Consumption Markets & Culture* 18 (3): 257–76.

Coase, R. H. 1937. "The Nature of the Firm." *Economica* 4 (16): 386–405.

Cornish, Flora, Jan Haaken, Liora Moskovitz, and Sharon Jackson. 2016. "Rethinking Prefigurative Politics: Introduction to the Special Thematic Section." *Journal of Social and Political Psychology* 4 (1): 114–27.

Coté, Mark, Richard Day, and Greig de Peuter. 2007. "Utopian Pedagogy: Creating Radical Alternatives in the Neoliberal Age." *Review of Education, Pedagogy, and Cultural Studies* 29 (4): 317–36.

Coville, Peter. 2018. "A 'Minister for Loneliness' Is a Sticking Plaster for the Ills of Neoliberalism." Open Democracy, January 22, 2018. https://www.open democracy.net/en/opendemocracyuk/minister-for-loneliness-is-sticking-plaster -for-ills-of-neoliberalism/.

Cremonesi, Laura, Orazio Irrera, Daniele Lorenzini, and Martina Tazzioli. 2016. "Introduction: Foucault and the Making of Subjects: Rethinking Autonomy between Subjection and Subjectivation." In *Foucault and the Making of Subjects*, edited by Laura Cremonesi, Orazio Irrera, Daniele Lorenzini and Martina Tazzioli, 1–9. New York: Rowman & Littlefield.

Crossley, Nick. 2003. "From Reproduction to Transformation. Social Movement Fields and the Radical Habitus." *Theory, Culture & Society* 20 (6): 43–68.

Cumbers, Andrew. 2015. "Constructing a Global Commons In, against and beyond the State." *Space and Polity* 19 (1): 62–75.

Dalakoglou, Dimitris. 2013. "The Movement and the 'Movement' of Syntagma Square." *Cultural Anthropology*, February 14, 2013. https://culanth.org/field sights/the-movement-and-the-movement-of-syntagma-square.

Dardot, Pierre, and Christian Laval. 2017. *The New Way of the World: On Neoliberal Society*. 2nd ed. London: Verso.

Das, Veena, and Deborah Poole. 2004. "State and Its Margins. Comparative Ethnographies." In *Anthropology in the Margins: Comparative Ethnographies*, edited by Veena Das and Deborah Poole, 3–33. Santa Fe, NM: James Currey.

Daskalaki, Maria, Marianna Fotaki, and Maria Simosi. 2021. "The Gendered Impact of the Financial Crisis: Struggles over Social Reproduction in Greece." *Environment and Planning A: Economy and Space* 53 (4): 741–62.

Davies, William. 2015a. *The Happiness Industry: How the Government and Big Business Sold Us Well-Being*. London: Verso.

———. 2015b. "The Return of Social Government: From 'Socialist Calculation' to 'Social Analytics.'" *European Journal of Social Theory* 18 (4): 1–20.

———. 2014. *The Limits of Neoliberalism: Authority, Sovereignty and the Logic of Competition*. Thousand Oaks, CA: SAGE Publications.

———. 2013. "When Is a Market Not a Market?: 'Exemption,' 'Externality' and 'Exception' in the Case of European State Aid Rules." *Theory, Culture & Society* 30 (2): 32–59.

———. 2011. "The Political Economy of Unhappiness." *New Left Review* 71: 65–80.

Davou, Bettina, and Nicolas Demertzis. 2013. "Feeling the Greek Financial Crisis." In *Emotions in Politics: The Affect Dimension in Political Tension*, edited by Nicolas Demertzis, 93–123. London: Palgrave Macmillan.

de Certeau, Michel. 2002. *The Practice of Everyday Life*. 2nd ed. Berkeley: Univ. of California Press.

de Waal, Cornelis. 2013. *Peirce: A Guide for the Perplexed*. London: Bloomsbury.

Dean, Jodi. 2016. *Crowds and Party*. London: Verso.

Dean, Jon. 2015. "Volunteering, the Market, and Neoliberalism." *People, Place and Policy* 9 (2): 139–48.

Dean, Mitchell. 1994. *Critical and Effective Histories: Foucault's Methods and Historical Sociology*. Abingdon, UK: Routledge.

Delalande, Nicolas. 2012. "The Greek State: Its Past and Future." *Books & Ideas*, March 20, 2012. https://booksandideas.net/The-Greek-State-Its-Past-and.html.

Deleuze, Gilles, and Felix Guattari. 2005. *A Thousand Plateaus: Capitalism and Schizophrenia*. 11th ed. Minneapolis: Univ. of Minnesota Press.

Dent, Gina. 1992. "Black Pleasure, Black Joy: An Introduction." In *Black Popular Culture: A Project by Michele Wallace*, edited by Gina Dent, 1–20. Seattle: Bay Press.

Deutscher Bundestag. 2010. "Plenarprotokoll 17/42." May 19, 2010. http://dipbt.bundestag.de/doc/btp/17/17042.pdf.

Dey, Pascal, and Chris Steyaert. 2012. "Social Entrepreneurship: Critique and the Radical Enactment of the Social." *Social Enterprise Journal* 8 (2): 90–107.

Dhaliwal, Puneet. 2012. "Public Squares and Resistance: The Politics of Space in the Indignados Movement." *Interface* 4 (1): 251–73.

Diamandouros, Nikiforos P. 2012. "Politics, Culture, and the State: Background to the Greek Crisis." In *Reforming Greece: Sisyphean Task or Herculean Challenge?*, edited by Othon Anastasakis and Dorian Singh, 9–18. Oxford: South East European Studies at Oxford.

———. 1994. "Cultural Dualism and Political Change in Postauthoritarian Greece." Estudios/Working papers, Instituto Juan March de Estudios e Investigaciones, Centro de Estudios Avanzados en Ciencias Sociales Madrid 50.

Dimitriou, Orsalia. 2014. "Four Acts in/for Syntagma." In *Remapping 'Crisis': A Guide to Athens*, edited by Myrto Tsilimpounidi and Alwyn Walsh, 70–86. Winchester: Zero Books.

Douzinas, Costas. 2013. *Philosophy and Resistance in the Crisis*. Cambridge: Polity.

Due Billing, Yvonne, and Mats Alvesson. 2000. "Questioning the Notion of Feminine Leadership: A Critical Perspective on the Gender Labelling of Leadership." *Gender, Work & Organization* 7 (3): 144–57.

Dwyer, Sonya Corbin, and Jennifer L. Buckle. 2009. "The Space Between: On Being an Insider-Outsider in Qualitative Research." *International Journal of Qualitative Methods* 8 (1): 54–63.

Dziadosz, Bartek. 2013. *The Trouble with Being Human These Days*. Leeds: Bauman Institute.

Eagleton-Pierce, Matthew. 2016. *Neoliberalism: The Key Concepts*. Abingdon, UK: Routledge.

Easton, David. 1981. "The Political System Besieged by the State." *Political Theory* 9 (3): 303–25.

Economou, Leonidas. 2014. "Political and Cultural Implications of the Suburban Transformation of Athens." In *Crisis Scapes: Athens and Beyond*, edited by Jaya Klara Brekke, Dimitris Dalakoglou, Christos Filippidis and Antonis Vradis, 13–17. Athens: Synthesi.

Ehrenreich, Barbara. 2010. *Smile or Die: How Positive Thinking Fooled America and the World*. 2nd ed. London: Granta.

Ehrenreich, Barbara, and Ehrenreich, John. 2013. "The Real Story Behind the Crash and Burn of America's Managerial Class." AlterNet, February 20, 2013. https://www.alternet.org/2013/02/barbara-and-john-ehrenreich-real-story -behind-crash-and-burn-americas-managerial-class/.

Elden, Stuart. 2004. *Understanding Henri Lefebvre: Theory and the Possible*. New York: Continuum.

EPAnEK. 2014. "Frequently Asked Questions." Operational Program for Competitiveness, Entrepreneurship and Innovation (EPAnEK) 2014–2020. http:// www.antagonistikotita.gr/epanek_en/events.asp?cs=17.

European Commission. 1990. "Industrial Policy in an Open and Competitive Environment: Guidelines for a Community Approach." November 16, 1990. http://aei.pitt.edu/5690/1/5690.pdf.

European Council. 1993. "The Copenhagen European Council." *Bulletin of the European Communities*, no.6/1993, June 21–22, 1993. http://aei.pitt.edu /1443/1/Copenhagen_june_1993.pdf.

Featherstone, Kevin. 2008. "Greece: A Suitable Accommodation?" In *The Euro at 10: Europeanization, Power, and Convergence*, edited by Kenneth Dyson, 165–81. Oxford: Oxford Univ. Press.

———. 2005. "Introduction: 'Modernisation' and the Structural Constraints of Greek Politics." *West European Politics* 28 (2): 223–41.

Featherstone, Kevin, and Dimitris Papadimitriou. 2008. *The Limits of Europeanization: Reform Capacity and Policy Conflict in Greece*. London: Palgrave Macmillan.

Feigenbaum, Anna, Fabian Frenzel, and Patrick McCurdy. 2013. *Protest Camps*. London: Zed Books.

Ferguson, James, and Akhil Gupta. 2002. "Spatializing States: Toward an Ethnography of Neoliberal Governmentality." *American Ethnologist* 29 (4): 981–1002.

Fisher, Mark. 2009. *Capitalist Realism: Is There No Alternative?* Winchester: Zero Books.

Flam, Helena, and Debra King, eds. 2005. *Emotions and Social Movements.* Abingdon, UK: Routledge.

Fleming, Peter. 2017. *The Death of Homo Economicus.* London: Pluto Press.

———. 2013. "Common as Silence." *Ephemera* 13 (3): 627–40.

Foster, Roger. 2016. "The Therapeutic Spirit of Neoliberalism." *Political Theory* 44 (1): 82–105.

Foucault, Michel. 2009. *Security, Territory, Population: Lectures at the Collège De France, 1977–78.* 2nd ed. London: Palgrave Macmillan.

———. 2008. *The Birth of Biopolitics: Lectures at the Collège De France 1978–1979.* New York: Picador.

———. 2006. *The Hermeneutics of the Subject: Lectures at the Collège de France, 1981–1982.* 1st ed. Lectures at the Collège de France. New York: Picador.

———. 2005. *The Order of Things: An Archaeology of the Human Sciences.* 5th ed. Abingdon, UK: Routledge.

———. 1997a. *Ethics: Subjectivity and Truth.* New York: New Press.

———. 1997b. "What is Critique?" In *The Politics of Truth,* edited by Sylvere Lotringer and Lysa Hochroth, 23–82. New York: Semiotext(e).

———. 1995. *Discipline and Punish: The Birth of the Prison.* 2nd ed. New York: Vintage Books.

———. 1991. "Governmentality." In *The Foucault Effect: Studies in Governmentality,* edited by Graham Burchell, Colin Gordon, and Peter Miller, 87–104. Chicago: Univ. of Chicago Press.

———. 1990. *The History of Sexuality.* Vol. 1. 2nd ed. New York: Vintage Books.

———. 1986. "Of Other Spaces." *Diacritics* 16 (1): 22–27.

———. 1982. "The Subject and Power." *Critical Inquiry* 8 (4): 777–95.

Frank, Thomas, and Matt Weiland, eds. 1997. *Commodify Your Dissent: Salvos from The Baffler.* New York: W. W. Norton.

Friedman, Milton. 1982. *Capitalism and Freedom.* 2nd ed. Chicago: Univ. of Chicago Press.

Fukuyama, Francis. 1992. *The End of History and the Last Man.* New York: Free Press.

Bibliography 275

Gamble, Andrew, and Anthony Wright, eds. 1999. *The New Social Democracy.* Malden, MA: Blackwell.

García-Lamarca, Melissa, and Maria Kaika. 2016. "'Mortgaged Lives': The Biopolitics of Debt and Housing Financialisation." *Transactions of the Institute of British Geographers* 41 (3): 313–27.

Garelli, Stéphane. 2006. *Top Class Competitors: How Nations, Firms, and Individuals Succeed in the New World of Competitiveness.* Chichester, UK: John Wiley & Sons.

Georgas, James. 1989. "Changing Family Values in Greece: From Collectivist to Individualist." *Journal of Cross-Cultural Psychology* 20 (1): 80–91.

Gerbaudo, Paolo. 2017. "The Indignant Citizen: Anti-Austerity Movements in Southern Europe and the Anti-Oligarchic Reclaiming of Citizenship." *Social Movement Studies* 16 (1): 36–50.

Gieryn, Thomas F. 2000. "A Space for Place in Sociology." *Annual Review of Sociology* 26: 463–93.

Giovanopoulos, Christos. 2016. "Mehr als Helfen und Organisieren: Wie die Solidaritätsnetze in Griechenland materielle Macht aufbauen" [More than Helping and Organizing: How Solidarity Networks in Greece Build Material Power]. *Luxemburg. Gesellschaftsanalyse und Linke Praxis* 2: 82–97.

———. 2011. "Oi plateies ōs zōntanos organismos: H epanakoinōnikopoiēsē tēs agoras" [The Squares as a Living Organism: The Re-Socialization of the Market]. In *Dēmokratia under Construction: Apo tous dromous stis plateies* [Democracy under Construction: From the Streets to the Squares], edited by Christos Giovanopoulos and Dimitris Mitropoulos, 40–60. Athens: A/Synechia.

Giovanopoulos, Christos, and Dimitris Mitropoulos, eds. 2011a. *Dēmokratia under Construction: Apo tous dromous stis plateies* [Democracy under Construction: From the Streets to the Squares]. Athens: A/Synechia.

———. 2011b. "Ntokoumenta" [Documents]. In *Dēmokratia under Construction: Apo tous dromous stis plateies* [Democracy under Construction: From the Streets to the Squares], edited by Christos Giovanopoulos and Dimitris Mitropoulos, 327–44. Athens: A/Synechia.

———. 2011c. "Syntomo Chroniko" [Brief Timeframe]. In *Dēmokratia under Construction: Apo tous dromous stis plateies* [Democracy under Construction: From the Streets to the Squares], edited by Christos Giovanopoulos and Dimitris Mitropoulos, 273–325. Athens: A/Synechia.

Giroux, Henry A. 2004a. "Cultural Studies, Public Pedagogy, and the Responsibility of Intellectuals." *Communication and Critical/Cultural Studies* 1 (1): 59–79.

———. 2004b. "Public Pedagogy and the Politics of Neo-Liberalism: Making the Political More Pedagogical." *Policy Futures in Education* 2 (3&4): 494–503.

Giugni, Marco. 2004. "Personal and Biographical Consequences." In *The Blackwell Companion to Social Movements*, edited by David A. Snow, Sarah A. Soule, and Hanspeter Kriesi, 489–509. Oxford: Blackwell.

Global Entrepreneurship Monitor. 2017. "GEM Global Report 2016/2017." Global Entrepreneurship Research Association, February 4, 2017. https://www.gemconsortium.org/report/49812.

Goodwin, Jeff, James M. Jasper, and Francesca Polletta. 2004. "Emotional Dimensions of Social Movements." In *The Blackwell Companion to Social Movements*, edited by David A. Snow, Sarah A. Soule, and Hanspeter Kriesi, 413–32. Oxford: Blackwell.

Goosen, Richard. J., and R. Paul Stevens. 2013. *Entrepreneurial Leadership: Finding Your Calling, Making a Difference*. Downers Grove, IL: InterVarsity Press.

Gordon, Colin. 1991. "Governmental Rationality: An Introduction." In *The Foucault Effect: Studies in Governmentality*, edited by Graham Burchell, Colin Gordon, and Peter Miller, 1–52. Chicago: Univ. of Chicago Press.

———. 1987. "The Soul of the Citizen: Max Weber and Michel Foucault on Rationality and Government." In *Max Weber, Rationality and Modernity*, edited by Sam Whimster and Scott Lash, 293–316. London: Allen and Unwin.

Gottdiener, Mark, and Ray Hutchinson. 2010. *The New Urban Sociology*. 4th ed. Boulder, CO: Westview Press.

Gournari, Panayota. 2016. "The Necropolitics of Austerity: Discursive Constructions and Material Consequences in the Greek Context." *Fast Capitalism* 13 (1): 39–48.

Gourgouris, Stathis. 1996. *Dream Nation: Enlightenment, Colonization and the Institution of Modern Greece*. Stanford, CA: Stanford Univ. Press.

Goutsos, Dionysis, and George Polymenas. 2014. "Identity as Space: Localism in the Greek Protests of Syntagma Square." *Journal of Language and Politics* 13 (4): 675–701.

Graeber, David. 2012. "Dead Zones of the Imagination: On Violence, Bureaucracy, and Interpretive Labor: The 2006 Malinowski Memorial Lecture." *HAU: Journal of Ethnographic Theory* 2 (2): 105–28.

———. 2009. *Direct Action: An Ethnography*. Edinburgh: AK Press.

———. 2002. "The New Anarchists." *New Left Review* 13: 61–73.

Gutiérrez Sánchez, Isabel. 2022. "Dwelling as Politics: An Emancipatory Praxis of/through Care and Space in Everyday Life." *Environment and Planning D: Society and Space* 40 (3). doi.org/10.1177/02637758221078597.

Hadjimichalis, Costis. 2013. "From Streets and Squares to Radical Political Emancipation? Resistance Lessons from Athens during the Crisis." *Human Geography* 6 (2): 116–36.

Hadjiyannis, Stylianos. 2016. "Democratization and the Greek State." In *Transitions from Dictatorship to Democracy. Comparative Studies of Spain, Portugal, and Greece*, 2nd ed., edited by Ronald H. Chilcote, Stylianos Hadjiyannis, Fred A. López III, Daniel Nataf, and Elizabeth Sammis, 131–88. Abingdon, UK: Routledge.

Hage, Ghassan. 2015. *Alter-Politics: Critical Anthropology and the Radical Imagination*. Melbourne: Melbourne Univ. Press.

Hager, Philip. 2011. "The Protests in Athens: Indignant Dramaturgies and Geographies in Syntagma Square." *Contemporary Theatre Review* 21 (4): 550–53.

Haig, Brian D. 2008. "An Abductive Perspective on Theory Construction." *Journal of Theory Construction & Testing* 12 (1): 7–10.

Haiven, Max. 2014. *Crises of Imagination, Crises of Power: Capitalism, Creativity and the Commons*. London: Zed Books.

Haiven, Max, and Alex Khasnabish. 2014. *The Radical Imagination: Social Movement Research in the Age of Austerity*. London: Zed Books.

Halberstam, Jack. 2013. "The Wild Beyond: With and For the Undercommons." In *The Undercommons: Fugitive Planning & Black Study*, edited by Stefano Harney and Fred Moten, 2–13. New York: Minor Compositions.

Halvorsen, Sam. 2015. "Taking Space: Moments of Rupture and Everyday Life in Occupy London: Taking Space: Occupy London." *Antipode* 47 (2): 401–17.

Hamilton, Nancy A., Heather Kitzman, and Stephanie Guyotte. 2006. "Enhancing Health and Emotion: Mindfulness as a Missing Link between Cognitive Therapy and Positive Psychology." *Journal of Cognitive Psychotherapy* 20 (2): 123–34.

Han, Byung-Chul. 2017. *Psychopolitics: Neoliberalism and New Technologies of Power*. London: Verso.

Hanafi, Sari. 2012. "The Arab Revolutions; the Emergence of a New Political Subjectivity." *Contemporary Arab Affairs* 5 (2): 198–213.

Hansen, Thomas Blom, and Finn Stepputat, eds. 2001. *States of Imagination: Ethnographic Explorations of the Postcolonial State*. Durham, NC: Duke Univ. Press.

Haraway, Donna J. 1991. *Simians, Cyborgs, and Women: The Reinvention of Nature*. Abingdon, UK: Routledge.

Harders, Cilja. 2015. "Provincializing and Localizing Core-Periphery Relations." *Middle East—Topics & Arguments* 5: 36–45.

Harding, Eloise. 2015. "Prefiguration versus the 'Reformist Drift' in the Camp for Climate Action." *Capitalism Nature Socialism* 26 (4): 141–57.

Harney, Stefano, and Fred Moten. 2013. *The Undercommons: Fugitive Planning & Black Study*. New York: Minor Compositions.

Harvey, David. 2014. *Seventeen Contradictions and the End of Capitalism*. Oxford: Oxford Univ. Press.

———. 2007. *A Brief History of Neoliberalism*. Oxford: Oxford Univ. Press.

Hatem, Mervat F. 2012. "The Arab Spring Meets the Occupy Wall Street Movement: Examples of Changing Definitions of Citizenship in a Global World." *Journal of Civil Society* 8 (4): 401–15.

Hayek, Friedrich A. 2005. *The Road to Serfdom*. 4th ed. London: Institute of Economic Affairs.

———. 1992. *The Fatal Conceit: The Errors of Socialism*. Edited by W. W. III Bartley. 5th ed. Vol. I. *The Collected Works of Friedrich August Hayek*. Abingdon, UK: Routledge.

Heidegger, Martin. 1998. *Pathmarks*. Cambridge: Cambridge Univ. Press.

Hellenic Ministry of Finance. 2021. *Greece 2.0: National Recovery and Resilience Plan*. https://greece20.gov.gr/wp-content/uploads/2021/07/NRRP_Greece_2_0_English.pdf.

Herbert, Steve. 1997. *Policing Space: Territoriality and the Los Angeles Police Department*. Minneapolis: Univ. of Minnesota Press.

Hill, Terry, and Roy Westbrook. 1997. "SWOT Analysis: It's Time for a Product Recall." *Long Range Planning* 30 (1): 46–52.

Holloway, John. 2010. *Crack Capitalism*. London: Pluto Press.

Hood, Christopher. 1991. "A Public Management for All Seasons?" *Public Administration* 69 (1): 3–19.

Hoskyns, Teresa. 2014. *The Empty Place: Democracy and Public Space*. Abingdon, UK: Routledge.

Hui, Wang. 2011. *The End of the Revolution: China and the Limits of Modernity.* 2nd ed. London: Verso.

Hume, Lynne L., and Nevill Drury. 2013. *The Varieties of Magical Experience: Indigenous, Medieval, and Modern Magic.* Santa Barbara, CA: Praeger.

Huss, Boaz. 2014. "Spirituality: The Emergence of a New Cultural Category and its Challenge to the Religious and the Secular." *Journal of Contemporary Religion* 29 (1): 47–60.

Illouz, Eva. 2012. *Why Love Hurts: A Social Explanation.* Cambridge: Polity.

Inglehart, Ronald, and Wayne E. Baker. 2000. "Modernization, Cultural Change, and the Persistence of Traditional Values." *American Sociological Review* 65 (1): 19–51.

Ioakimidis, Panagiotis C. 2011. "Krisē kai Ellēnikos Exairetismos" [Crisis and Greek Exceptionalism]. *Greek Political Review*, February 4, 2011. http://politicalreviewgr.blogspot.com/2011/02/greek-exceptionalism.html

Ioannides, Yiorgos. 2012. *"Ē politikē oikonomia tēs ellēnikēs politikēs apascholēsēs, 1995–2008. To eurōpaiko plaisio kai oi egxrōioi metaschēmatismoi"* [The Political Economy of Greek Employment Policy, 1995–2008: The European Context and National Transformations]. PhD diss., University of Crete.

Ismail, Salwa. 2006. *Political Life in Cairo's New Quarters: Encountering the Everyday State.* Minneapolis: Univ. of Minnesota Press.

Jackson, S. E., A. Joshi, and N. L. Erhardt. 2003. "Recent Research on Team and Organizational Diversity: SWOT Analysis and Implications." *Journal of Management* 29 (6): 801–30.

Janko, Richard. 1987. *Aristotle: Poetics.* Indianapolis: Hackett Publishing Company.

Jasper, James M. 2011. "Emotions and Social Movements: Twenty Years of Theory and Research." *Annual Review of Sociology* 37: 285–303.

———. 2007. "Cultural Approaches in the Sociology of Social Movements." In *Handbook of Social Movements across Disciplines*, edited by Bert Klandermans and Conny Roggeband, 59–109. New York: Springer.

Jensen, Tracey, and Imogen Tyler. 2015. "'Benefits Broods': The Cultural and Political Crafting of Anti-Welfare Commonsense." *Critical Social Policy* 35 (4): 1–22.

Junghans, Trenholme. 2001. "Marketing Selves: Constructing Civil Society and Selfhood in Post-Socialist Hungary." *Critique of Anthropology* 21 (4): 383–400.

Bibliography

Juris, Jeffrey S. 2013. "The 99% and the Production of Insurgent Subjectivity." *Cultural Anthropology*, February 14, 2013. https://culanth.org/fieldsights/the -99-and-the-production-of-insurgent-subjectivity.

Kaika, Maria. 2016. "The Alchemy of Water . . . or . . . How Fighting for the Urban Commons Can Prevent an Anthropological Catastrophe." Keynote lecture, International Conference on Urban Autonomy and the Collective City, Athens, Greece, July 2, 2016.

Kaika, Maria, and Lazaros Karaliotas. 2017. "Athens' Syntagma Square Reloaded: From Staging Disagreement Towards Instituting Democratic Spaces." In *City Unsilenced. Urban Resistance and Public Space in the Age of Shrinking Democracy*, edited by Jeffrey Hou and Sabine Knierbein, 121–32. Abingdon, UK: Routledge.

———. 2014. "Spatialising Politics: Antagonistic Imaginaries of Indignant Squares." In *The Post-Political and Its Discontents: Spaces of Depoliticisation, Spectres of Radical Politics*, edited by Japhy Wilson and Erik Swyngedouw, 244–60. Edinburgh: Edinburgh Univ. Press.

Kalyvas, Stathis. 2020. *To ellēniko oneiro: Mia syzētēsē me ton Kōsta Giannakidē gia to parelthon kai to mellon tēs Elladas* [The Greek Dream: A Discussion with Kostas Giannakidis about the Past and the Future of Greece]. Athens: Metaichmio.

Karaliotas, Lazaros. 2017. "Staging Equality in Greek Squares: Hybrid Spaces of Political Subjectification." *International Journal of Urban and Regional Research* 41 (1): 54–69.

Karamessini, Maria. 2008. "Still a Distinctive Southern European Employment Model?" *Industrial Relations Journal* 39 (6): 510–31.

Katsambekis, Giorgos. 2014. "The Multitudious Moment(s) of the People: Democratic Agency Disrupting Established Binarisms." In *Radical Democracy and Collective Movements Today: The Biopolitics of the Multitude versus the Hegemony of the People*, edited by Alexandros Kioupkiolis and Giorgos Katsambekis, 169–90. Farnham: Ashgate.

Kavoulakos, Karolos I. 2013. "Kinēmata kai dēmosioi chōroi stēn Athēna: chōroi eleutherias, chōroi dēmokratias" [Movements and Public Spaces in Athens: Spaces of Freedom, Spaces of Democracy, Spaces of Domination]. In *To kentro tēs Athēnas ōs politico diakybeuma* [The Center of Athens as Political Stakes], edited by Thomas Maloutas, Giorgos Kadylis, Michalis Petrou and Nicos Souliotis, 237–56. Athens: National Centre for Social Research.

Kellerman, Peter F. 2006. *Focus on Psychodrama: The Therapeutic Aspects of Psychodrama.* 2nd ed. Philadelphia: Jessica Kingsley Publishers.

Kierkegaard, Søren. 1985. *Philosophical Fragments: Johannes Climacus.* Princeton, NJ: Princeton Univ. Press.

Kilgarriff-Foster, Alexis, and Alicia O'Cathain. 2015. "Exploring the Components and Impact of Social Prescribing." *Journal of Public Mental Health* 14 (3): 127–34.

Kingfisher, Catherine, and Jeff Maskovsky. 2008. "Introduction: The Limits of Neoliberalism." *Critique of Anthropology* 28 (2): 115–26.

Kioupkiolis, Alexandros. 2019. *The Common and Counter-Hegemonic Politics: Re-Thinking Social Change.* Edinburgh: Edinburgh Univ. Press.

Kioupkiolis, Alexandros, and Theodoros Karyotis. 2015. "Self-Managing the Commons in Contemporary Greece." In *An Alternative Labour History. Worker Control and Workplace Democracy,* edited by Dario Azzellini, 298–328. London: Zed Books.

Kirzner, Israel. 1973. *Competition and Entrepreneurship.* Chicago: Univ. of Chicago Press.

Knight, Daniel Martyn. 2013. "Opportunism and Diversification: Entrepreneurship and Livelihood Strategies in Uncertain Times." *Ethnos* 80 (1): 117–44.

Koliopoulos, John S., and Thanos M. Veremis. 2010. *Modern Greece: A History since 1821.* Malden, MA: Wiley-Blackwell.

Konsolas, Ioannis. 1999. "The Competitive Advantage of Nations: The Case of Greece." PhD diss., London School of Economics and Political Science.

Kontodima, Panayota. 2016. "In Kolonos There's a Café without Employers or Employees." AthensLive, January 18, 2016. https://medium.com/athenslivegr /in-kolonos-there-s-a-caf%C3%A9-without-employers-or-employees-717f3b 6a6e01.

Kotronaki, Loukia, and Seraphim Seferiades. 2012. "Along the Pathways of Rage: The Space-Time of an Uprising." In *Violent Protest, Contentious Politics, and the Neoliberal State,* edited by Hank Johnston and Seraphim Seferiades, 157–70. Farnham: Ashgate.

Kouki, Hara, and Andreas Chatzidakis. 2021. "Implicit Feminist Solidarity(ies)? The Role of Gender in the Social Movements of the Greek Crisis." *Gender, Work & Organization* 28 (3): 878–97.

Kousis, Maria. 2015. "The Transnational Dimension of the Greek Protest Campaign against Troika Memoranda and Austerity Policies, 2010–2012." In

282   Bibliography

Spreading Protest: Social Movements in Times of Crisis, edited by Donnatella della Porta and Alice Mattoni, 137–69. Colchester: ECPR Press.

Kouvelakis, Stathis. 2011. "The Greek Cauldron." *New Left Review* 72: 17–32.

Krugman, Paul. 1994. "Competitiveness: A Dangerous Obsession." *Foreign Affairs*, March/April 1994, 28–44.

Kurik, Bob. 2016. "Emerging Subjectivity in Protest." In *The SAGE Handbook of Resistance*, edited by David Courpasson and Steven Vallas, 51–77. Thousand Oaks, CA: SAGE Publications.

Kutay, Acar. 2014. "Managerial Formations and Coupling among the State, the Market, and Civil Society: An Emerging Effect of Governance." *Critical Policy Studies* 8 (3): 247–65.

Laclau, Ernesto, and Chantal Mouffe. 2001. *Hegemony and Socialist Strategy: Towards a Radical Democratic Politics*. 2nd ed. London: Verso.

Ladi, Stella. 2005. "The Role of Experts in the Reform Process in Greece." *West European Politics* 28 (2): 279–96.

Lapavitsas, Costas, Annina Kaltenbrunner, Duncan Lindo, J. Michell, Juan Pablo Painceira, Eugenia Pires, Jeff Powell, Alexis Stenofors, and Nuno Teles. 2010. "Eurozone Crisis: Beggar Thyself and Thy Neighbour." *Journal of Balkan and Near Eastern Studies* 12 (4): 321–73.

Laskos, Christos, and Euclid Tsakalotos. 2013a. *Crucible of Resistance: Greece, the Eurozone and the World Economic Crisis*. London: Pluto Press.

―――. 2013b. "Greek Neo-Liberalism in Fat and Lean Times." *Pôle Sud* 38: 33–52.

Laville, Jean-Louis. 2010. "The Solidarity Economy: An International Movement." *Revista Crítica de Ciências Sociais* 2: 3–41.

Lea, David. R. 2016. *Neoliberalism, the Security State, and the Quantification of Reality*. Lanham, MD: Lexington Books.

Lefebvre, Henri. 2007. *The Production of Space*. 2nd ed. Oxford: Blackwell.

Lefort, Claude. 1986. *The Political Forms of Modern Society: Bureaucracy, Democracy, Totalitarianism*. Cambridge: MIT Press.

Lehmann, Sandra. 2016. "Political Subjectivation and Metaphysical Movement." In *Subjectivation in Political Theory and Contemporary Practices*, edited by Andreas Oberprantacher and Andrei Siclodi, 97–107. London: Palgrave Macmillan.

Lemke, Thomas. 2011. "Critique and Experience in Foucault." *Theory, Culture & Society* 28 (4): 26–48.

Leontidou, Lila. 2012. "Athens in the Mediterranean 'Movement of the Piazzas' Spontaneity in Material and Virtual Public Spaces." *City* 16 (3): 299–312.

Lerner, Daniel. 1958. *The Passing of Traditional Society: Modernizing the Middle East*. New York: Free Press.

Lévi-Strauss, Claude. 1962. *The Savage Mind*. Chicago: Univ. of Chicago Press.

Levinson, Justin D., and Kaipeng Peng. 2007. "Valuing Cultural Differences in Behavioral Economics." *ICFAI Journal of Behavioral Finance* 4 (1): 32–47.

Liebsch, Burkhard. 2016. "On Theories of Subjectivity and the Practices of Political Subjectivation: Responsiveness, Dissent, and the Precarious Livability of Human Life." In *Subjectivation in Political Theory and Contemporary Practices*, edited by Andreas Oberprantacher and Andrei Siclodi, 73–96. London: Palgrave Macmillan.

Lindsey, Linda L. 2015. *Gender Roles: A Sociological Perspective*. 6th ed. Abingdon, UK: Routledge.

Lockman, Zachary. 2010. *Contending Visions of the Middle East: The History and Politics of Orientalism*. Cambridge: Cambridge Univ. Press.

Loewenstein, Karl. 1944. "Report on the Research Panel on Comparative Government." *American Political Science Review* 38 (3): 540–48.

Lorey, Isabell. 2015. *State of Insecurity: Government of the Precarious*. London: Verso.

Love, Patrick. 1997. "Contradiction and Paradox: Attempting to Change the Culture of Sexual Orientation at a Small Catholic College." *Review of Higher Education* 20 (4): 381–98.

Lynn, Matt. 2011. *Bust: Greece, the Euro and the Sovereign Debt Crisis*. Hoboken, NJ: Bloomberg Press.

Lysonski, Steven, Srinivas Durvasula, and Yorgos Zotos. 2004. "The Metamorphosis of Greek Consumers' Sentiments toward Marketing and Consumerism." *Journal of Euromarketing* 13 (4): 5–29.

Makridakis, Giannis. 2015. "Anoichtē epistolē ston prōthypourgo Alexē Tsipra [Open Letter to Prime Minister Alexis Tsipras]." TVXS, February 7, 2015. http://tvxs.gr/news/egrapsan-eipan/anoixti-epistoli-ston-prothypoyrgo-aleksi-tsipra.

Malamidis, Haris. 2020. *Social Movements and Solidarity Structures in Crisis-Ridden Greece*. Amsterdam: Amsterdam Univ. Press.

Malpas, J. E. 1999. *Place and Experience: A Philosophical Topography*. Cambridge: Cambridge Univ. Press.

Mann, Michael. 2004. *Fascists*. Cambridge: Cambridge Univ. Press.

Markantonatou, Maria. 2015. "State Repression, Social Resistance and the Politicization of Public Space in Greece under Fiscal Adjustment." In *City of Crisis: The Multiple Contestation of Southern European Cities*, edited by Frank Eckhardt and Javier Ruiz Sánchez, 199–211. Bielefeld, Germany: Transcript.

Marom, Nathan. 2013. "Activising Space: The Spatial Politics of the 2011 Protest Movement in Israel." *Urban Studies* 50 (13): 1–16.

Martin, Deborah G., and Byron Miller. 2003. "Space and Contentious Politics." *Mobilization* 8 (2): 143–56.

Marx, Karl. 1887. *Capital: A Critique of Political Economy*. Vol. I. Moscow: Progress Publishers. https://www.marxists.org/archive/marx/works/download/pdf/Capital-Volume-I.pdf.

Mason, Paul. 2013. *Why It's Still Kicking Off Everywhere*. 2nd ed. London: Verso.

Massumi, Brian. 2002. *Parables for the Virtual: Movement, Affect, Sensation*. Durham, NC: Duke Univ. Press.

———. 1995. "The Autonomy of Affect." *Cultural Critique* 31: 83–109.

Mazower, Mark. 2001. *Inside Hitler's Greece: The Experience of Occupation, 1941–44*. 3rd ed. New Haven, CT: Yale Univ. Press.

McAdam, Doug. 1999. "The Biographical Impact of Activism." In *How Social Movements Matter*, edited by Marco Giugni, Doug McAdam and Charles Tilly, 117–46. Minneapolis: Univ. of Minnesota Press.

McClelland, David. C. 1961. *The Achieving Society*. Princeton, NJ: D. Van Nostrand Company.

McKay, Ian. 2005. *Rebels, Reds, Radicals: Rethinking Canada's Left History*. Toronto: Between the Lines.

McNay, Lois. 2009. "Self as Enterprise: Dilemmas of Control and Resistance in Foucault's *The Birth of Biopolitics*." *Theory, Culture & Society* 26 (6): 55–77.

McNeill, William H. 1968. "Dilemmas of Modernization." *Massachusetts Review* 9 (1): 133–46.

Melucci, Alberto. 1985. "The Symbolic Challenge of Contemporary Movements." *Social Research* 52 (4): 789–816.

Menoume Mazi. n.d. "Schetika" [About]. https://menoumemazi.org/about/.

Milchman, Alan, and Alan Rosenberg. 2009. "The *Final* Foucault: Government of Others and Government of the Self." In *A Foucault for the 21st Century: Governmentality, Biopolitics and Discipline in the New Millennium*, edited by Sam Binkley and Jorge Capetillo, 61–71. Cambridge: Cambridge Scholars Publishing.

Minogue, Kenneth. 1989. "Equality: A Response." *Royal Institute of Philosophy Supplement* 26: 99–108.

Mirowski, Philip. 2014. *Never Let a Serious Crisis Go to Waste: How Neoliberalism Survived the Financial Meltdown.* London: Verso.

———. 2011. *Science-Mart: Privatizing American Science.* Cambridge, MA: Harvard Univ. Press.

———. 2009. "Postface: Defining Neoliberalism." In *The Road from Mont Pelerin: The Making of the Neoliberal Thought Collective,* edited by Philip Mirowski and Dieter Plehwe, 417–55. Cambridge, MA: Harvard Univ. Press.

Mirowski, Philip, and Dieter Plehwe, eds. 2009. *The Road from Mont Pèlerin: The Making of the Neoliberal Thought Collective.* Cambridge, MA: Harvard Univ. Press.

Mirowski, Philip, and Edward Nik-Khah. 2017. *The Knowledge We Have Lost in Information: The History of Information in Modern Economics.* Oxford: Oxford Univ. Press.

Mitchell, Timothy. 2011. *Carbon Democracy: Political Power in the Age of Oil.* London: Verso.

———. 2002. *Rule of Experts: Egypt, Techno-Politics, Modernity.* Berkeley: Univ. of California Press.

———. 1991. "The Limits of the State: Beyond Statist Approaches and Their Critics." *American Political Science Review* 85 (1): 77–96.

Mitsopoulos, Michael, and Theodore Pelagidis. 2011. *Understanding the Crisis in Greece: From Boom to Bust.* London: Palgrave Macmillan.

Monbiot, George. 2016. "Neoliberalism Is Creating Loneliness: That's What's Wrenching Society Apart." *Guardian,* October 12, 2016. https://www.the guardian.com/commentisfree/2016/oct/12/neoliberalism-creating-loneliness -wrenching-society-apart.

Moore, Phoebe. 2018. "Tracking Affective Labour for Agility in the Quantified Workplace." *Body & Society* 24 (3): 39–67.

Moore, Phoebe, and Andrew Robinson. 2015. "The Quantified Self: What Counts in the Neoliberal Workplace." *New Media & Society* 18 (11): 2774–92.

Moran, Gwen. 2013. "5 Keys to Inspiring Leadership, No Matter Your Style." *NBC News,* June 17, 2013. https://www.nbcnews.com/id/wbna52234434.

Morris, Charles W. 1970. *The Pragmatic Movement in American Philosophy.* New York: George Braziller.

Mouzelis, Nicos. 1996. "The Concept of Modernization: Its Relevance for Greece." *Journal of Modern Greek Studies* 14 (2): 215–27.

Muehlebach, Andrea. 2012. *The Moral Neoliberal: Welfare and Citizenship in Italy*. Chicago: Univ. of Chicago Press.

Muniesa, Fabien, Liliana Doganova, Horacio Ortiz, Alvaro Pina-Stranger, Florence Paterson, Alaric Bourgoin, Vera Ehrenstein, Pierre-Andre Juven, David Pontille, Başak Saraç-Lesavre, and Guillaume Yon. 2017. *Capitalization: A Cultural Guide*. Paris: Presses des Mines.

Nancy, Jean-Luc. 2011. "Finite and Infinite Democracy." In *Democracy in What State?*, edited by Giorgio Agamben, Alain Badiou, David Bensaid, Wendy Brown, Jean-Luc Nancy, Jacques Rancière, Kristin Ross and Slavoj Žižek, 58–75. New York: Columbia Univ. Press.

———. 2002. "Is Everything Political? (A Brief Remark)." *CR: The New Centennial Review* 2 (3): 15–22.

Nedos, Vasilis. 2005. "To klouvio 'augo tou fidiou'" [The Rotten "Serpent's Egg"]. *TO BHMA*, September 11, 2005. http://www.tovima.gr/relatedarticles/article/?aid=168197&dt=11/09/2005.

Nettl, J. P. 1968. "The State as a Conceptual Variable." *World Politics* 20 (4): 559–92.

Newman, Saul. 2010. *The Politics of Postanarchism*. Edinburgh: Edinburgh Univ. Press.

———. 2007. "Anarchism, Poststructuralism and the Future of Radical Politics." *SubStance* 36 (2): 3–19.

Nutt, Roberta L. 1999. "Women's Gender Role Socialization, Gender Role Conflict, and Abuse: A Review of Predisposing Factors." In *What Causes Men's Violence Against Women?*, edited by Michele Harway and James M. O'Neil, 117–34. Thousand Oaks, CA: SAGE Publications.

Offe, Claus. 2015. *Europe Entrapped*. Cambridge: Polity.

Ollman, Bertell. 1976. *Alienation: Marx's Conception of Man in Capitalist Society*. 2nd ed. Cambridge: Cambridge Univ. Press.

Oloklērōmenos Synetairismos Athēnōn. n.d. "Arches" [Principles]. http://athens.coop.collective.land/index.php/arxes/.

Ortner, Sherry B. 1995. "Resistance and the Problem of Ethnographic Refusal." *Contemporary Studies in Society and History* 37 (1): 173–93.

Pagoulatos, George. 2005. "The Politics of Privatisation: Redrawing the Public–Private Boundary." *West European Politics* 28 (2): 358–80.

———. 2003. *Greece's New Political Economy: State, Finance, and Growth from Postwar to EMU*. London: Palgrave Macmillan.

————. 2000. "Economic Adjustment and Financial Reform: Greece's Europeanization and the Emergence of a Stabilization State." *South European Society and Politics* 5 (2): 191–216.

Panagiotopoulou, Roy. 2013. "Oi epikoinōniakes praktikes tou kinēmatos tōn Aganaktismenōn" [The Communicative Practices of the Movement of the Indignants]. In *H Krisē kai ta MME* [The Crisis and Mass Media], edited by Giorgos Pleios, 421–61. Athens: Papazizi.

Papadimitriou, Dimitris. 2005. "The Limits of Engineering Collective Escape: The 2000 Reform of the Greek Labour Market." *West European Politics* 28 (2): 381–401.

Papapavlou, Maria. 2015. Ē Empeiria tēs Plateias Syntagmatos: *Mousikē, synaisthēmata kai nea koinōnika kinēmata* [The Experience of Syntagma Square: Music, Emotions and New Social Movements]. Athens: Ekdoseis ton Synadelphon.

Pappas, Takis S. 2017. "Greece's Current Modernisation Failure, Greek History's Déjà Vu." In *Greece: Modernisation and Europe 20 Years On*, edited by Spyros Economides, 18–22. London: Hellenic Observatory, London School of Economics and Political Science.

Papataxiarchis, Evthymios. 2016. "Unwrapping solidarity? Society Reborn in Austerity." *Social Anthropology* 24 (2): 205–10.

Paulson, Justin. 2010. "The Uneven Development of Radical Imagination." *Affinities: A Journal of Radical Theory, Culture, and Action* 4 (2): 33–38.

Pearlman, Wendy. 2013. "Emotions and the Microfoundations of the Arab Uprisings." *Perspectives on Politics* 11 (2): 387–409.

Peck, Jamie. 2010a. *Constructions of Neoliberal Reason*. Oxford: Oxford Univ. Press.

————. 2010b. "Zombie Neoliberalism and the Ambidextrous State." *Theoretical Criminology* 14 (1): 104–10.

Peirce, Charles. S. 1931. "The First Rule of Reason." In *The Collected Papers, Vol. I: Principles of Philosophy*. http://www.textlog.de/4249.html.

Petrakis, Panagiotis. 2012. *The Greek Economy and the Crisis: Challenges and Responses*. Berlin: Springer.

Pile, Steve. 2008. "Where Is the Subject? Geographical Imaginations and Spatializing Subjectivity." *Subjectivity* 23 (1): 206–18.

Placas, Aimee Jessica. 2008. "The Emergence of Consumer Credit in Greece: An Ethnography of Indebtedness." PhD diss., Rice University.

Polletta, Francesca, and Katt Hoban. 2016. "Why Consensus? Prefiguration in Three Activist Eras." *Journal of Social and Political Psychology* 4 (1): 286–301.

Polanyi, Karl. 2001. *The Great Transformation: The Political and Economic Origins of Our Time.* 3rd ed. Boston: Beacon Press.

Porter, Michael. 1998. *On Competition.* Cambridge, MA: Harvard Business School Press.

Porter, Theodore M. 1995. *Trust in Numbers: The Pursuit of Objectivity in Science and Public Life.* Princeton, NJ: Princeton Univ. Press.

Poulantzas, Nicos. 2000. *State, Power, Socialism.* 2nd ed. London: Verso.

Pouliasi, Katerina, and Maykel Verkuyten. 2011. "Self-Evaluations, Psychological Well-Being, and Cultural Context: The Changing Greek Society." *Journal of Cross-Cultural Psychology* 42 (5): 875–90.

Prentoulis, Marina, and Lasse Thomassen. 2014. "Autonomy and Hegemony in the Squares: The 2011 Protests in Greece and Spain." In *Radical Democracy and Collective Movements Today: The Biopolitics of the Multitude versus the Hegemony of the People,* edited by Alexandros Kioupkiolis and Giorgos Katsambekis, 213–32. Farnham: Ashgate.

———. 2012. "Political Theory in the Square: Protest, Representation and Subjectification." *Contemporary Political Theory* 12 (3): 166–84.

Profitt, Norma Jean. 2001. "Survivors of Woman Abuse." *Journal of Progressive Human Services* 11 (2): 77–102.

Prozorev, Sergei. 2014. *Theory of the Political Subject: Void Universalism II.* Abingdon, UK: Routledge.

Psimitis, Michalis. 2011. "The Protest Cycle of Spring 2010 in Greece." *Social Movement Studies* 10 (2): 191–97.

Rahtz, Joshua. 2017. "The Soul of the Eurozone." *New Left Review* 104: 107–31.

Rakopoulos, Theodoros. 2017. "Solidarity Bridges: Alternative Food Economies in Urban Greece." *Greek Review of Social Research* 149 (2): 1–21.

———. 2016. "Solidarity: The Egalitarian Tensions of a Bridge-Concept." *Social Anthropology* 24 (2): 142–51.

Rammstedt, Otthein, ed. 1969. *Anarchismus: Grundtexte zur Theorie und Praxis der Gewalt* [Anarchism: Basic Texts on the Theory and Practice of Violence]. Cologne: Westdeutscher Verlag.

Rancière, Jacques. 2011a. "Democracies against Democracy." In *Democracy in What State?,* edited by Giorgio Agamben, Alain Badiou, David Bensaid, Wendy Brown, Jean-Luc Nancy, Jacques Rancière, Kristin Ross, and Slavoj Žižek, 76–81. New York: Columbia Univ. Press.

———— 2011b. "The Thinking of Dissensus: Politics and Aesthetics." In *Reading Rancière,* edited by Paul Bowman and Richard Stamp, 1–17. New York: Continuum.

————. 1999. *Disagreement: Politics and Philosophy.* Minneapolis: Univ. of Minnesota Press.

Read, Jason. 2010. "The Production of Subjectivity: From Transindividuality to the Commons." *New Formations: A Journal of Culture/Theory/Politics* 70: 113–31.

Rebughini, Paola. 2014. "Subject, Subjectivity, Subjectivation." *Sociopedia.isa,* 1–14. doi:10.1177/20568460022.

Reckwitz, Andreas. 2003. "Grundelemente einer Theorie sozialer Praktiken. Eine sozialtheoretische Perspektive" [Basic Elements of a Social Theory of Practice. A Social-Theoretical Perspective]. *Zeitschrift für Soziologie* 32 (4): 282–301.

————. 2002. "Toward a Theory of Social Practices: A Development in Culturalist Theorizing." *European Journal of Social Theory* 5 (2): 243–63.

Reid, Julian. 2012. "The Neoliberal Subject: Resilience and the Art of Living Dangerously." *Revista Pléyade* 10: 143–65.

Ricoeur, Paul. 2008. *From Text to Action: Essays in Hermeneutics, II.* 3rd ed. New York: Continuum.

Rodousakis, Nikolaos, and George Soklis. 2021. "The RRP Multiplier Effects on the Greek Economy." Paper presented at the 25th Forum for Macroeconomics and Macroeconomic Policies Conference: Macroeconomics of Socio-Ecological Transition, Berlin, Germany, October 29, 2021. https://soklis.com/2021/11/05/the-rrp-multiplier-effects-on-the-greek-economy/.

Roos, Jerome E., and Leonidas Oikonomakis. 2014. "They Don't Represent Us! The Global Resonance of the Real Democracy Movement from the Indignados to Occupy." In *Spreading Protest: Social Movements in Times of Crisis,* edited by Donnatella della Porta and Alice Mattoni, 117–36. Colchester: ECPR Press.

Rosa, Hartmut. 2013. *Social Acceleration: A New Theory of Modernity.* New York: Columbia Univ. Press.

Rosa, Hartmut, Klaus Dörre, and Stephan Lessenich. 2016. "Appropriation, Activation and Acceleration: The Escalatory Logics of Capitalist Modernity and the Crises of Dynamic Stabilization." *Theory, Culture & Society* 34 (1): 53–73.

Rose, Nikolas. 1999. *Governing the Soul: The Shaping of the Private Self.* 2nd ed. London: Free Association Books.

Rossdale, Chris. 2014. "Occupying Subjectivity: Being and Becoming Radical in the Twenty-First Century: Introduction." *Globalizations* 12 (1): 1–5.

Rostow, Walt W. 1990. *The Stages of Economic Growth: A Non-Communist Manifesto*. Cambridge: Cambridge Univ. Press.

Roudometof, Victor. 2012. "The Role of Orthodox Christianity in Greece's Contemporary Cultural Politics." In *Rethinking the Space for Religion: New Actors in Central and Southeast Europe on Religion, Authenticity and Belonging*, edited by Catharina Raudvere, Krzysztof Stala, and Trine Stauning Willert, 235–58. Lund: Nordic Academic Press.

Roussos, Konstantinos. 2014. "Opseis tēs syllogikēs drasēs kai diadikasies ypokeimenopoiēsēs: to symban tōn 'aganaktismenōn' tēs plateias Syntagmatos" [Aspects of Collective Action and Processes of Subjectivation: The Occurrence of the "Indignants" of Syntagma Square]. Master's thesis, Panteion Univ.

Sack, Robert D. 1993. "The Power of Place and Space." *Geographical Review* 83 (3): 326–29.

Said, Edward. 2003. *Orientalism*. 5th ed. London: Penguin Books.

Sandlin, Jennifer A., Michael P. O'Malley, and Jake Burdick. 2011. "Mapping the Complexity of Public Pedagogy Scholarship: 1894–2010." *Review of Educational Research* 81 (3): 338–75.

Santos, Boaventura de Sousa. 2016. *Epistemologies of the South: Justice against Epistemicide*. 2nd ed. Abingdon, UK: Routledge.

Scharff, Christina. 2015. "The Psychic Life of Neoliberalism: Mapping the Contours of Entrepreneurial Subjectivity." *Theory, Culture & Society* 33 (6): 107–22.

Scheer, Monique. 2012. "Are Emotions a Kind of Practice? (And Is That What Makes Them Have a History?) A Bourdieuian Approach to Understanding Emotion." *History and Theory* 51 (2): 193–220.

Scheff, Thomas J. 1994. *Bloody Revenge: Emotions, Nationalism, and War*. Boulder, CO: Westview Press.

Schlaudt, Oliver. 2018. *Die politischen Zahlen: Über Quantifizierung im Neoliberalismus* [The Political Numbers: On Quantification in Neoliberalism]. Frankfurt: Vittorio Klostermann.

Schmitt, Carl. 2007. *The Concept of the Political*. 2nd ed. Chicago: Univ. of Chicago Press.

Schumann, Christoph, and Dimitris Soudias. 2013. "Präsenz und Raum in der Arabischen Revolte: Ägypten im Jahr 2011" [Presence and Space in the Arab

Revolt: Egypt in the Year 2011]. In *Präsenz und implizites Wissen: Zur Interdependenz zweier Schlüsselbegriffe der Kultur- und Sozialwissenschaften* [Presence and Tacit Knowledge: Two Key Terms in Cultural Studies and Social Science], edited by Christoph Ernst and Heike Paul, 297–315. Bielefeld, Germany: Transcript.

Schumpeter, Joseph A. 2017. *The Theory of Economic Development: An Inquiry into Profits, Capital, Credit, Interest, and the Business Cycle*. 2nd ed. Abingdon, UK: Routledge.

Scott, James C. 1985. *Weapons of the Weak: Everyday Forms of Peasant Resistance*. New Haven, CT: Yale Univ. Press.

Scott, Joan W. 1991. "The Evidence of Experience." *Critical Inquiry* 17 (4): 773–97.

Seferiades, Seraphim. 2003. "The European Employment Strategy against a Greek Benchmark: A Critique." *European Journal of Industrial Relations* 9 (2): 189–203.

Segal, Lynne. 2017. *Radical Happiness: Moments of Collective Joy*. London: Verso.

Shantz, Jeff. 2009. *Living Anarchy: Theory and Practice in Anarchist Movements*. Washington, DC: Academia Press.

Sherman, Rachel. 2017. *Uneasy Street: The Anxieties of Affluence*. Princeton, NJ: Princeton Univ. Press.

Shriver, Thomas E., Amy Chasteen Miller, and Sherry Cable. 2003. "Women's Work: Women's Involvement in the Gulf War Illness Movement." *Sociological Quarterly* 44 (4): 639–58.

Siapera, Eugenia, and Michael Theodosiadis. 2017. "(Digital) Activism at the Interstices: Anarchist and Self-Organizing Movements in Greece." *tripleC* 15 (2): 505–23.

Simiti, Marilena. 2014. "Rage and Protest: The Case of the Greek Indignant Movement." *Hellenic Observatory Papers on Greece and Southeast Europe* 82.

Simitis, Costas. 2017. "Assessing the Present While Mapping the Future: Reflections on the European Crisis and the Way Ahead." In *Greece: Modernisation and Europe 20 Years On*, edited by Spyros Economides, 10–17. London: Hellenic Observatory, London School of Economics and Political Science.

———. *The European Debt Crisis: The Greek Case*. Manchester: Manchester Univ. Press.

Sin, Nancy L., and Sonja Lyubomirsky. 2009. "Enhancing Well-Being and Alleviating Depressive Symptoms with Positive Psychology Interventions:

A Practice-Friendly Meta-Analysis." *Journal of Clinical Psychology* 65 (5): 467–87.

Sinek, Simon. 2009. *Start with Why: How Great Leaders Inspire Everyone to Take Action.* London: Penguin Books.

Smith, Anna Marie. 2015. "Subjectivity and Subjectivation." In *The Oxford Handbook of Feminist Theory,* edited by Lisa Disch and Mary Hawkesworth, 956–70. Oxford: Oxford Univ. Press.

Soja, Edward W. 1998. *Postmodern Geographies: The Reassertion of Space in Critical Social Theory.* 5th ed. London: Verso.

———. 1980. "The Socio-Spatial Dialectic." *Annals of the Association of American Geographers* 70 (2): 207–25.

Sotirakopoulos, Nikos, and George Sotiropoulos. 2013. "'Direct Democracy Now!': The Greek *Indignados* and the Present Cycle of Struggles." *Current Sociology* 61 (4): 443–56.

Sotiris, Panagiotis. 2018. "Disciplined and Punished." *Jacobin,* August 31, 2018. https://www.jacobinmag.com/2018/08/greece-syriza-tsipras-memoranda -austerity-odyssey.

Sotiropoulos, Dimitri A. 2004. "The EU's Impact on the Greek Welfare State: Europeanization on Paper?" *Journal of European Social Policy* 14 (3): 267–84.

Sotiropoulou, Irene. 2016. "Collective Viewing of Value(s) and the Struggle for What Is Valuable: The Case of Grassroots Initiatives." *World Review of Political Economy* 7 (1): 56–84.

Soudias, Dimitris. 2021a. "Neoliberalisation and the Social and Solidarity Economy in Greece." *Greece@LSE,* December 15, 2021. https://eprints.lse .ac.uk/112967/.

———. 2021b. "Subjects in Crisis: Paradoxes of Emancipation and Alter-Neoliberal Critique." *Sociological Review* 69 (5): 885–902.

———. 2020. "Griechenlands COVID-19-Krise und die Ökonomisierung von Sicherheit" [Greece's COVID-19 Crisis and the Economization of Security]. *Soziopolis: Gesellschaft beobachten.* https://www.ssoar.info/ssoar/handle /document/77033.

———. 2018. "On the Spatiality of Square Occupations: Lessons from Syntagma and Tahrir." In *Riots and Militant Occupations: Smashing a System, Building a World—A Critical Introduction,* edited by Alissa Starodub and Andrew Robinson, 75–95. Lanham, MD: Rowman & Littlefield.

———. 2015. "Policing January 25: Protest, Tactics, and Territorial Control in Egypt's 2011 Uprising." *Middle East Topics & Arguments* 4: 170–82.

———. 2014. *Negotiating Space: The Evolution of the Egyptian Streets, 2000–2011.* Cairo: American Univ. in Cairo Press.

Soudias, Dimitris, and Philipp Katsinas. 2022. "The Political Imaginary of Happiness in Greece." ENA Institute for Alternative Policies, April 2022. http://eprints.lse.ac.uk/114875/.

Souliotis, Nicos. 2013. "Athens and the Politics of the Sovereign Debt Crisis." In *Cities and Crisis: New Critical Urban Theory,* edited by Kuniko Fujita, 237–70. Thousand Oaks, CA: SAGE Publications.

Souliotis, Nicos, John Sayas, and Thomas Maloutas. 2014. "Megaprojects, Neoliberalization, and State Capacities: Assessing the Medium-Term Impact of the 2004 Olympic Games on Athenian Urban Policies." *Environment and Planning C: Government and Policy* 32: 731–45.

Spivak, Gayatri Chakravorty. 2012. *An Aesthetic Education in the Era of Globalization.* Cambridge, MA: Harvard Univ. Press.

Stathakis, Giorgos. 2001. "Oikonomikos fileleutherismos kai to egkcheirēma tou eksygchronismou" [Economic Liberalism and the Project of Modernization]. Paper presented at "Ideological Currents and Intellectual Trends in Today's Greece," Eighth Scientific Conference of the Sakis Karagiorga Foundation, Panteion Univ., Athens, Greece, March 28–31, 2001. http://pandemos.panteion.gr/index.php?op=record&type=0&q=%CE%A3%CF%84%CE%B1%CE%B8%CE%AC%CE%BA%CE%B7%CF%82&page=1&scope=0&lang=en&pid=iid:9338.

Stavrides, Stavros. 2016. *Common Space: The City as Commons.* London: Zed Books.

———. 2015. "Common Space as Threshold Space: Urban Commoning in Struggles to Re-Appropriate Public Space." *Footprint* 16: 9–19.

———. 2012. "Squares in Movement." *South Atlantic Quarterly* 111 (3): 585–96.

Stavrou, Achilleas. 2011. "Ē 'panō plateia' ē otan milane oi mazes 'oe, oe, oe, sēkōthēkame ap' ton kanape . . . ' [The "Upper Square" or When the Masses Speak: "Oe, Oe, Oe, They Got off the Couch . . ."] In *Dēmokratia under Construction: Apo tous dromous stis plateies* [Democracy under Construction: From the Streets to the Squares], edited by Christos Giovanopoulos and Dimitris Mitropoulos, 31–40. Athens: A/Synechia.

Steinmetz, George. 2005. "Positivism and Its Others in the Social Sciences." In *The Politics of Method in the Human Sciences: Positivism and Its Epistemological Others,* edited by George Steinmetz, 1–56. Durham, NC: Duke Univ. Press.

Stephenson, Niamh, and Dimitris Papadopoulos. 2006. *Analysing Everyday Experience: Social Research and Political Change*. London: Palgrave Macmillan.

Stonebridge, Lyndsey. 2016. "Inner Emigration: On the Run with Hannah Arendt and Anna Freud." In *Psychoanalysis in the Age of Totalitarianism*, edited by Matt Daniel Pick and Matt Ffytche, 42–55. Abingdon, UK: Routledge.

Straume, Ingerid S. 2011. "The Political Imaginary of Global Capitalism." In *Depoliticization: The Political Imaginary of Global Capitalism*, edited by Ingerid S. Straume and J. F. Humphrey, 27–50. Malmö, Sweden: NSU Press.

Streeck, Wolfgang. 2016. *How Will Capitalism End? Essays on a Failing System*. London: Verso.

Strübing, Jörg. 2008. *Grounded Theory*. 2nd ed. Wiesbaden, Germany: Verlag für Sozialwissenschaften.

Susen, Simon. 2014a. "Is There Such a Thing as a 'Pragmatic Sociology of Critique'? Reflections on Luc Boltanski's *On Critique*." In *The Spirit of Luc Boltanski: Essays on the "Pragmatic Sociology of Critique"*, edited by Simon Susen and Bryan S. Turner, 173–210. New York: Anthem Press.

———. 2014b. "Luc Boltanski: His Life and Work: An Overview." In *The Spirit of Luc Boltanski: Essays on the "Pragmatic Sociology of Critique"*, edited by Simon Susen and Bryan S. Turner, 3–28. New York: Anthem Press.

Susen, Simon, and Bryan S. Turner, eds. 2014. *The Spirit of Luc Boltanski: Essays on the "Pragmatic Sociology of Critique"*. New York: Anthem Press.

Tavory, Iddo, and Stefan Timmermans. 2014. *Abductive Analysis: Theorizing Qualitative Research*. Chicago: Univ. of Chicago Press.

Taylor, Blair. 2013. "From Alterglobalization to Occupy Wall Street. Neoanarchism and the New Spirit of the Left." *City* 17 (6): 729–47.

Theodossopoulos, Dimitrios. 2014. "The Ambivalence of Anti-Austerity Indignation in Greece: Resistance, Hegemony and Complicity." *History and Anthropology* 25 (4): 488–506.

Thompson, John B. 1982. "Ideology and the Social Imaginary: An Appraisal of Castoriadis and Lefort." *Theory and Society* 11 (5): 659–81.

Thrift, Nigel. 2008. *Non-Representational Theory: Space, Politics, Affect*. Abingdon, UK: Routledge.

Till, Chris. 2014. "Exercise as Labour: Quantified Self and the Transformation of Exercise into Labour." *Societies* 4: 446–62.

Trapeza Chronou Athēnas. 2018. "FAQ Trapeza Chronou" [FAQ Time Bank]. https://athens-time-exchange.herokuapp.com/ (site under maintenance or discontinued).

Traynor, Ian, and Smith, Helena. 2011. "Papandreou Survives Confidence Vote on Handling of Greece Debt Crisis." *Guardian*, June 21, 2011. https://www.theguardian.com/world/2011/jun/22/george-papandreou-wins-confidence-vote.

Trimikliniotis, Nicos, Dimitris Parsanoglou, and Vasilis S. Tsianos. 2015. *Mobile Commons, Migrant Digitalities and the Right to the City*. London: Palgrave Macmillan.

Trott, Carlie D. 2016. "Constructing Alternatives: Envisioning a Critical Psychology of Prefigurative Politics." *Journal of Social and Political Psychology* 4 (1): 266–85.

Trouillot, Michel-Rolph. 2003. *Global Transformations: Anthropology and the Modern World*. London: Palgrave Macmillan.

Tsakalotos, Euclid. 2008. "Modernization and Centre-Left Dilemmas in Greece: The Revenge of the Underdogs." *Hellenic Observatory Papers on Greece and Southeast Europe* 13.

Tsavdaroglou, Charalampos. 2017. "Stasis: The Catalyst for the Circulation of Common Space: Protest Camps in Athens, Istanbul and Idomeni." Heteropolitics International Workshop, Thessaloniki, Greece, September 13–15, 2017.

Tsianos, Vasilis S. 2016. "Metropolitan Stasis@Real Democracy@Post-Representative Hegemony: On the Sociology of 'Social Non-Movements' and Assemblies." In *Subjectivation in Political Theory and Contemporary Practices*, edited by Andreas Oberprantacher and Andrei Siclodi, 219–36. London: Palgrave Macmillan.

Tsimouris, Giorgos. 2014. "From Invisibility into the Centre of the Athenian Media Spectacle: Governmentality and Immigration in the Era of Crisis." In *Crisis Scapes: Athens and Beyond*, edited by Jaya Klara Brekke, Dimitris Dalakoglou, Christos Filippidis, and Antonis Vradis, 78–81. Athens: Synthesi.

Tsomou, Margarita. 2014a. "Das Versuchskaninchen baut am eigenen Labor . . . ! Zum Aufschwung solidarischer Ökonomien als Exoduspraktiken im Griechenland der Krise" [The Guinea Pig Builds Its Own Laboratory . . . ! On the Rise of Solidarity Economies as Exodus Practices in the Greece of the Crisis]. *kultuRRevolution* 66/67: 7–17.

———. 2014b. "Der besetzte Syntagma-Platz 2011: Körper und Performativität im politischen Alphabet der ›Empörten‹" [The Occupied Syntagma Square of 2011: Body and Performativity in the Political Alphabet of the "Indignants"]. In *Versammlung und Teilhabe. Urbane Öffentlichkeiten und performative Künste* [Assembly and Participation. Urban Publics and Performative

Arts], edited by Regula Valérie Burri, Kerstin Evert, Sibylle Peters, Esther Pilkington, and Gesa Ziemer, 113–41. Bielefeld, Germany: Transcript.

Turner, Viktor W. 2008. *The Ritual Process: Structure and Anti-Structure*. 2nd ed. New Brunswick, NJ: AldineTransaction.

———. 1986. "Dewey, Dilthey, and Drama: An Essay in the Anthropology of Experience." In *The Anthropology of Experience*, edited by Viktor W. Turner and Edward M. Bruner, 33–44. Urbana: Univ. of Illinois Press.

United Nations Development Programme. 2022. Greece: Human Development Indicators. https://hdr.undp.org/data-center/specific-country-data#/countries /GRC.

Vaiou, Dina. 2014. "Is the Crisis in Athens (Also) Gendered?: Facets of Access and (in)Visibility in Everyday Public Spaces." *City* 18 (4–5): 533–37.

van de Sande, Mathijs. 2013. "The Prefigurative Politics of Tahrir Square— An Alternative Perspective on the 2011 Revolutions." *Res Publica* 19 (3): 223–39.

van Gennep, Arnold. 2011. *The Rites of Passage*. 2nd ed. Chicago: Univ. of Chicago Press.

van Stekelenburg, Jacquelien, Bert Klandermans, and Wilco W. van Dijk. 2011. "Combining Motivations and Emotion: The Motivational Dynamics of Protest Participation." *Revista de Psicología Social* 26 (1): 91–104.

Varoufakis, Yanis. 2011. *The Global Minotaur: America, the True Origins of the Financial Crisis and the Future of the World Economy*. London: Zed Books.

Varvarousis, Angelos, and Giorgis Kallis. 2017. "Commoning against the Crisis." In *Another Economy Is Possible: Culture and Economy in a Time of Crisis*, edited by Manuel Castells, Sarah Banet-Weiser, Sviatlana Hlebik, Giorgos Kallis, Sarah Pink, Kirsten Seale, Lisa J. Servon, Lana Swartz, and Angelos Varvarousis, 128–59. Cambridge: Polity

Vasilaki, Rosa. 2019. "Law, Order, and Repression in Greece." *Jacobin*, December 30, 2019. https://jacobinmag.com/2019/12/exarcheia-greece-athens -squats-police-tsipras.

Vestergren, Sara, John Drury, and Eva Hammar Chiriac. 2017. "The Biographical Consequences of Protest and Activism: A Systematic Review and a New Typology." *Social Movement Studies* 16 (2): 203–21.

von Mises, Ludwig. 1998. *Human Action: A Treatise on Economics*. Auburn, AL: Ludwig von Mises Institute.

Wallace, James D. 2008. *Norms and Practices*. Ithaca, NY: Cornell Univ. Press.

Weber, Max. 1978. *Economy and Society*. Berkeley: Univ. of California Press.

West, Cornel. 2004. "Finding Hope in Dark Times." *Tikkun* 19 (4): 18–20.

Whittaker, David, and William A. Watts. 1971. "Personality Characteristics Associated with Activism and Disaffiliation in Today's College-Age Youth." *Journal of Counseling Psychology* 18 (3): 200–206.

William and Flora Hewlett Foundation. 2020. "Hewlett Foundation Announces New, Five-Year $50 Million Economy and Society Initiative to Support Growing Movement to Replace Neoliberalism." December 8, 2020. https://hewlett.org/newsroom/hewlett-foundation-announces-new-five-year-50-million-economy-and-society-initiative-to-support-growing-movement-to-replace-neoliberalism.

Williams, Raymond. 1965. *The Long Revolution*. 2nd ed. Harmondsworth, UK: Penguin Books.

Wilson, Japhy, and Erik Swyngedouw, eds. 2014. *The Post-Political and Its Discontents: Spaces of Depoliticisation, Spectres of Radical Politics*. Edinburgh: Edinburgh Univ. Press.

World Economic Forum. 2000. *The Global Competitiveness Report 2000*. Oxford: Oxford Univ. Press.

Wright, Erik Olin. 2010. *Envisioning Real Utopias*. London: Verso.

———. 1989. "The Comparative Project on Class Structure and Class Consciousness: An Overview." *Acta Sociologica* 32 (1): 3–22.

Yates, Luke. 2015. "Rethinking Prefiguration: Alternatives, Micropolitics and Goals in Social Movements." *Social Movement Studies* 14 (1): 1–21.

Ylinenpää, Håkan. 2009. "Entrepreneurship and Innovation Systems: Towards a Development of the ERIS/IRIS Concept." *European Planning Studies* 17 (8): 1153–70.

Youkhana, Eva. 2015. "A Conceptual Shift in Studies of Belonging and the Politics of Belonging." *Social Inclusion* 3 (4): 10–24.

Zafiropoulou, Maria, and Konstantinos Papachristopoulos. 2016. "Greek Civil Society's Online Alternative Networks as Emergent Resilience Strategies in Times of Crisis." *Social Communication* 2 (2): 6–19.

Zevnik, Andreja. 2014. "Maze of Resistance: Crowd, Space and the Politics of Resisting Subjectivity." *Globalizations* 12 (1): 101–15.

Žižek, Slavoj. 2010. "A Permanent Economic Emergency." *New Left Review* 64: 85–95.

Zolberg, Aristide R. 1972. "Moments of Madness." *Politics and Society* 2: 183–207.

Index

abductive reasoning, 29, 31, 243

affect, 101–2, 146–48, 196–97

affirmative sabotage, 243–44, 262

Aganaktismenoi, 12, 12n7

alternative economy initiatives, 213–15

alter-neoliberal critique, 28, 239–41, 256–57; and affirmative sabotage, 243–44; against economization, 242–46; and the nondenumerable, 246, 246n2; paradox of, 249; against positivism, 243; against productivity, 248–49; against psychologization, 246–47; and public pedagogies, 241–42; against quantification, 245–46; against utilitarianism, 244

alter-politics, 9–10, 118, 203

anarchist initiatives in Greece, 12, 126, 126n2, 171–72, 260–61

ANTARSYA, 174n9

anti-crisis, 81, 86–87, 114, 114n12, 259

anti-politics, 9, 18, 210–11

antiquity, 48–49, 184–85

Athens Polytechnic uprising, 158–59, 158n1, 184

austerity, 2, 46–67, 88, 257. See also neoliberalism

authoritarianism, 184–85

autonomy, 19, 106, 224, 263; from the state, 211, 236

Benjamin, Walter, 6n3, 146–47, 170

Bentham, Jeremy, 59n22, 156

Bookchin, Murray, 236

Bourdieu, Pierre, 7, 10, 15, 89, 93, 162

buycotting, 231

capitalist imaginary, 2, 7–9, 78–79, 221

Castoriadis, Cornelius, 6, 7, 125

City Plaza squat, 209–13, 209n3

classical antiquity, 48–49, 184–85

Clinton, Bill, 42

collectivization, 152–54, 172, 204. See also individualization

commonality of vulnerability, 144–45

commons. See space, and prefigurative commons

competition: and bank bailouts, 88; and neoliberalism, 52–53, 51n11, 53n13, 84–85; among wage earners, 63–65. See also national competitiveness

competitiveness. See national competitiveness

consumerism, 66–70, 68n32, 72, 205–6, 231–32

COVID-19 pandemic, 257–58, 259–60

creativity, 221–22

crisis, 80–81, 93, 107–8; of capitalist imaginary, 2, 7–8, 259–60; neoliberal management of, 87–88, 253;

300   Index

crisis (*cont.*) progressive signification of, 81, 89–90, 108, 116; regressive signification of, 81, 86–87, 111–12; spatial manifestations of, 90–91, 109. *See also* anti-crisis; Greek government-debt crisis

critique, 21–23; artistic, 224; in neoliberalism, 219–20; pragmatic sociology of, 22, 162, 200–201, 220–21. *See also* alter-neoliberal critique; demystification; Greek government-debt crisis; self-critique

cultural dualism, 48–49. *See also* modernization, and culturalism; self-orientalization

debt, 65–66, 65n28, 66n29

de Certeau, Michel, 169

democracy, 184–85, 186; direct, 125–26, 137–38, 180; and neoliberalism, 180–82; representative, 122, 179–84; and Zymōsē, 133–34. *See also* depoliticization; self–governance

demystification: of representative democracy, 179–84; of the state, 159–63, 178–79, 184–86, 193. *See also* critique

depoliticization: and modernization, 56, 72; in neoliberalism 53–55; of parliamentary politics, 182–83; of space, 98. *See also* subjectivity, apolitical

dialectics. *See* social dialectics

Diamandouros, Nikiforos, 49, 49n8, 50

economics, 42, 54–55, 55n17, 228

economization, 229–32, 242–46

emotions. *See* affect

entrepreneurialism, 224–29

epistemology: and modernization theory, 48; and neoliberalism, 35, 53–54, 223, 245–46; and pragmatism, 29, 243; and radical imagination, 10, 256; of the South, 243

European Commission, 5n2, 43, 43n5. *See also* First Economic Adjustment Programme for Greece

European Monetary Union, 41, 61

European Union, 42–44, 48, 61

ethics: egalitarian and antiauthoritarian, 10, 125, 156–57, 171; and neoliberalism, 69–70, 223, 251n1; and subjectivity, 10, 155, 202, 234, 238

ethnographic walks, 35, 166–67

experience, 20–21; paradox of, 21; poverty of, 6n3; and temporality, 30, 40; transformative, 20, 154–55, 212. *See also* subjectivity

feminization of care, 261

financial crisis. *See* crisis; Greek government-debt crisis

financial deregulation, 61n25, 62, 65–66

financial literacy, 65

First Economic Adjustment Programme for Greece, 5n2, 46–47

Foucault, Michel, 17–18, 23, 192, 200, 240, 242

Fukuyama, Francis, 7

gender, 132, 139, 227n15. *See also* intersectionality

general assembly of the Syntagma Square occupation. *See* Syntagma

Square occupation, general
assembly of
general strikes: of June 15, 2011, 141,
163–66; of June 28, 2011, 166–67
governmentality, 57–59; 57n21, 105
Greece 2.0 National Recovery and Resilience Plan, 258
Greek government-debt crisis, 46–47,
82–83, 88; left-wing critique of, 85;
neoliberal critique of, 83–85. *See also*
crisis
Grigoropoulos, Alexandros, 3n1

happiness: and consumerism, 70, 75;
political imaginary of, 259–60; and
positive psychology, 6, 247; in Syntagma Square occupation, 149
Hayek, Friedrich, 51n11, 52, 52n12,
56n20, 144, 236
history of Syntagma Square, 94–95,
96–97. *See also* Syntagma Square
occupation

individualization, 64, 71–72, 73–76,
73n40, 77. *See also* collectivization
intersectionality, 9, 13, 30, 99, 150, 247.
See also gender

Kirzner, Israel, 227–28

labor market deregulation, 62–65
leadership, 118, 138–39, 226
Lefebvre, Henri, 82, 99–100
liminality, 92, 108, 111, 187
livability of a common life, 189

logic of numbers, 42–43, 54–55, 259
loneliness, 74–75, 75nn42–43, 151–52

managerialism, 222–23, 234. *See also*
self-management
Marx, Karl, 169, 245
Marxism, 35, 157, 176, 243
measurement, 54, 245–46
Menoume Mazi, 260–61
Merkel, Angela, 82
metaphors, 91–92, 99, 103, 146–47
metaphysics, 53–54, 98, 246
methodology. *See* research approach
Mitsotakis, Kyriakos, 257–60
modernization: and consumerism,
66–70, 72; and culturalism, 45,
47–51, 68, 71–72, 77, 83; and depoliticization, 56, 72; and European
Union, 42–44, 48, 61; and financial
deregulation, 65–66; and governmentality, 57–58; and individualized
subjectivity, 72–76, 77; and labor
market deregulation, 62–64; and
modernization theory, 47–48; and
national competitiveness, 42; and
neoliberalism, 39, 41, 51; and New
Democracy; 42n3, 62; and PASOK,
37, 41, 42n2; and privatization
of state assets, 59–62; resistance
against, 45–46, 45n6; and the state,
39, 49–51

national competitiveness, 41–44, 43n5,
54–55, 54n15, 55n17, 57, 60
Nea Demokratia. *See* New Democracy
neighborhood initiatives, 195, 196,
216–17, 260–61

302   Index

neoliberalism, 8, 51n11, 52, 56–57; and authoritarianism, 185; and competition, 52–53; and consumerism, 69, 231–32; and democracy, 180–82; and depoliticization, 53–55, 182–83; and economization, 229–32; and entrepreneurialism, 224–29; and epistemology, 35, 53–54, 223, 245–46; and ethics, 69–70, 223, 251n1; and governmentality, 57–58; and leadership, 226; and loneliness, 74–75; and managerialism, 222–23, 234; and modernization, 39, 41, 51; and national competitiveness, 54–55; and psychologization, 154, 232–35; and quantification, 54, 245–46; reproduction of, 219, 224n12; role of critique in, 220–22; and self-help, 226, 235; and self-improvement, 234–35; spirit of, 51, 51n10; and the state, 39, 236–37; and subjectivity, 19, 68, 70–73; and uncertainty, 2, 53, 251–52

New Democracy, 42n3, 62, 209. *See also* Mitsotakis, Kyriakos; political parties

new public management, 56, 56n19

Olympic Games. *See* 2004 Summer Olympics

Omopsychia, 152–53

Orientalism. *See* cultural dualism; modernization, and culturalism

Otto of Greece (King), 94–95

Papademos, Lucas, 46

Papandreou, Andreas, 7, 37

Papandreou, Georgios, 46–47, 166

parliamentary democracy. *See* democracy, representative

PASOK, 37, 41, 42n2. *See also* modernization; political parties; Simitis, Costas

police repression, 105, 141–43, 145, 158–59; 163–72, 192–93. *See also* state; violence

political parties: ANTARSYA, 174n9; New Democracy, 42n3, 62, 209; PASOK, 37, 41, 42n2; role in Syntagma Square occupation; 2n6, 33–34, 121–22, 123–24, 172–75, 181; SYRIZA, 33–34, 173–74, 173n8, 181–82, 194–95, 255. *See also* democracy, representative

Polytechneion. *See* Athens Polytechnic uprising

positionality, 30

practice theory, 18, 117, 119, 130

pragmatism (philosophy), 18, 29–30

prefiguration, 14n, 118–19, 128–30, 128n4, 155, 206–7. *See also* radical imagination; spontaneity

privatization of state assets, 59–62

public order, 104

public pedagogies, 200, 212–13

psychologization, 154, 232–35, 246–47

quantification, 54, 245–46

radical imagination, 5–10, 118, 156; affectivities of, 119–20, 146–54; and belonging, 149–52; and capitalist imaginary, 9–10; and collectivization, 152–54, 155–56; and Communitas, 153; conditions of possibility of, 113–15; and epistemology, 10, 256;

limits of, 168, 174–78; and mutual respect, 130–31; and Omopsychia, 152–53; and self-confidence, 132; and self-governance, 134–39; and selflessness, 123–24, 181–82; and self-organization, 139–43; and solidarity, 143–46; and trust, 152; and unradical imagination, 9; and voicing one's opinion, 130–31; and Zymōsē, 133–34. See also prefiguration; spontaneity

Rancière, Jacques, 3, 92, 186, 187
research approach, 28–36, 94
risk, 65, 73n40, 227

Schumpeter, Joseph, 227, 227n15
self-critique, 231–32, 255
self-governance, 134–39
self-improvement, 230, 232, 234–35
selflessness, 123–24, 181–82
self-management, 232, 234–35
self-organization, 139–43
self-orientalization, 46n7, 71–72. See also cultural dualism; modernization, and culturalism
self-responsibility, 63, 65, 73, 226, 237
Simitis, Costas, 37–38, 55–56, 83–84
social and solidarity economy, 213–15, 215n7
social dialectics, 14–15, 91, 93, 207
social entrepreneurship, 228–29
solidarity, 229; and individualization 71–72, 75; and radical imagination, 143–44; and violence, 145–46, 166, 170, 176–77
solidarity movement in Greece, 199–200
space, 82, 92–93, 98–100; depoliticization of, 98; and place, 94–98; and practice, 100–101; and prefigurative

commons, 200, 207–15; and presence, 100–102; and stasis, 102–3; and territoriality, 103–5, 142–43, 164. See also Syntagma Square occupation, spatiality of
spontaneity, 125–27, 155
spontaneous orders, 236
Stability and Growth Pact, 61
stasis, 82, 102–3, 105
state: and authoritarianism, 158–59, 184–85; autonomy from, 211, 236; bypassing of, 216, 236; demystification of, 159–63, 178–79, 193; imagination of, 161–62, 236–37; and lack of service provision, 141, 236–37; limits of, 141, 162, 215–19; and modernization, 39, 49–51; and neoliberalism, 39, 236–37; and ordoliberalism, 52; paradox of, 161, 163; and representative democracy, 179–84; and repression, 192–93; sabotage of, 216–18; and self–organization, 140–41; study of, 161n3; and territoriality, 104–5, 162. See also police repression; violence
state of exception, 114, 169, 180, 185, 252. See also anti-crisis
subjectivity, 15–20; apolitical, 32–33, 132, 187–89, 191–92; and catharsis, 201–2; emancipatory, 201–7; entrepreneurial, 224–28; ethical, 10, 155, 202, 234, 238; and governmentality, 58–59; liberal, 19, 52–53, 188; and liminality, 187; and modernization, 72–77; neoliberal, 19, 68, 70–73; paradoxical, 239–40, 255; political, 4, 18, 16, 92, 178–79, 186–93, 190n18; and practice theory, 18–19, 117; prefigurative, 118; psychologized, 232–35; transformation of, 198–99

304   Index

SWOT analysis, 228–29
Syntagma Square occupation, 4–5,
    11–15; changing norms within,
    106–8; cleaning of, 141–43, 165;
    dance and music in, 165, 177, 177n11;
    general assembly of, 134–35, 163,
    180; and happiness, 149; and leader-
    ship, 118, 138–39; lower square of,
    14–15, 112–13; lyra player in, 164–66,
    164n4; and openness, 134, 190;
    perceived ownership of, 103, 105,
    142–43; police repression of, 105,
    141–43, 145, 158–59; 163–72; precur-
    sor norms of, 117–18, 120–29; role
    of political parties in, 12n6, 33–34,
    121–22, 123–24, 172–75, 174n9, 181;
    social control in, 105–6; solidarity
    in, 143–46; spatiality of, 82, 92–93;
    upper square of, 13, 109–12, 110n6,
    111n8, 112n9, 161; working groups
    of, 13–14, 139–40. *See also* history of
    Syntagma Square; space
SYRIZA, 33–34, 173–74, 173n8, 181–82,
    194–95, 255. *See also* political parties

tactics, 164, 168–69
tear gas, 142, 145, 166; as bonding,
    176–77
temporality. *See* experience, and
    temporality
territoriality, 103–5, 142–43, 164
Thatcher, Margaret, 58

think tanks in Greece, 261–62
3 September 1843 Revolution, 94–95
time banks, 14, 137–37, 214–15
trust, 151
Tsipras, Alexis, 257
2008 Greek riots, 3n1
2004 Summer Olympics, 7, 44–45

uncertainty: and entrepreneurial-
    ism, 225, 227; and the future, 2–3,
    78–80; and managerialism, 222;
    and neoliberalism, 53, 251–52; and
    privatization and deregulation,
    53, 60–63; and self-responsibility,
    59–60, 63, 87
undercommons, 248
unthought-of, the, 25, 108
utilitarianism, 222, 244–45

violence: and law, 170–71; and nonvio-
    lence, 120–121, 165, 168–72, 169n6,
    175–76; and solidarity, 145–46, 166,
    170, 176–77

waking up, 91–92, 107
Weber, Max, 49, 51n10, 56, 129
Williams, Raymond, 241–42

Zymōsē, 133–34

Dimitris Soudias is a postdoctoral researcher at the Research Centre for the Study of Democratic Cultures and Politics (DemCP), University of Groningen. His current research builds on political sociology and cultural economy approaches to study such issues as creativity, happiness, social innovation, and entrepreneurship in neoliberalism. Prior to joining the University of Groningen, Dimitris held research positions and fellowships at the London School of Economics, the University of Amsterdam, Philipps-Universität Marburg, and Freie Universität Berlin. He is the author of *Negotiating Space: The Evolution of the Egyptian Street, 2000–2011* (American University in Cairo Press, 2014).

Printed in the USA
CPSIA information can be obtained
at www.ICGtesting.com
LVHW041926061023
760214LV00003B/91